USSR

e Story of Soviet Ru

y WALTER DURANTY

colossal myths about Russia
'ntil recently the world
', have been total casualt
'of events.

' new Russia stand'
'' mighty giar

USSR

The Story of
SOVIET RUSSIA

By
WALTER DURANTY, 1884-
Author of "I Write as I Please"

J. B. LIPPINCOTT COMPANY
PHILADELPHIA   NEW YORK

Under Government regulations for saving metal and paper during the war, the size and bulk of this book have been reduced below the customary peacetime standards. Only the format has been affected. The text is complete and unabridged.

to

MELCHIOR

who once took out a mote from mine eye.

PERMISSION TO USE excerpts from the author's earlier publications has been courteously granted by the following:

The Viking Press, Inc. ("Duranty Reports Russia," 1934)
Simon & Schuster, Inc. ("I Write As I Please," 1935)
Esquire, Inc. ("Stalin; Dealer in Destiny," Coronet Magazine, June, 1943)

Contents

Chapter 1

"THE OCCASION PRODUCES THE MAN"

The first thing to know and understand and remember about Russia is that it is utterly different from the Western world, and that our standards of comparison cannot be applied to it. This is equally true about the former Tsarist Russia and the modern U. S. S. R.—Union of Socialist Soviet Republics, in which the word Russia has no place—because the whole process of Russian national life and political development was not like that of the West. Therefore, I repeat, no comparison is possible.

This sounds like a sweeping statement, but it is not based upon the somewhat hasty premise that Russia has been fifteen or more percent Asiatic in blood, and perhaps often fifty percent Asiatic in mentality. Especially as regards contempt for death, which might be stated as contempt for life. Asia's misfortune—or its strength—has been that life is sometimes so little worth living that it can easily be relinquished.

An interesting point about the Slavic race, which today occupies Russia, Poland, Czechoslovakia, Bulgaria and Yugoslavia, is that the word "Slav" does not mean or imply, as some Westerners have fondly thought, anything to do with slaves. The word means "glorious"—"Slava Bogu" (glory to God). Which indicates immediately that the Slavic nations have no inferiority complex. In fact, I should say, the opposite. The Slavs don't wail at walls, nor ever attempt, like the Germans, to tell you how great they are. They say, on the contrary, "We are a backward people, dark ignorant masses of people who don't know this nor know that, although we are eager to learn." In their hearts they think, "We are Slavs, and that means glorious. We are the heirs of the future, although much of our past is dim." A superiority complex.

The determining factor in Russian history has been the flatness of the Russian land. All European Russia, from the Ural Mountains to the Polish border in the West, from Leningrad, formerly St. Petersburg, to the Caucasus in the South, is flat. Nowhere crags or mountains to provide strongholds and points of defense. Geography more than climate determines the fate of nations. Western Europe evolved into the feudal system because robber barons and chiefs were able to take and fortify high points of ground, around which, thanks to their protection, grew communities of artisans and traders. These strong points and these robber barons gave protection also to farmers, or peasants, in the neighborhood. In Russia no such strong points existed, and no such protection was possible. Therefore no such communities of traders and artisans and of the surrounding farmers were created.

In Western Europe those communities came ultimately to represent the light of democracy in the darkness of the middle ages. During the centuries of struggle between kings and barons these communities played, as we say, "both ends against the middle," and acquired, now from king and now from barons, the rights which Americans today regard as their natural heritage. In Russia there was none of that, and from the earliest days Russian history has been conditioned by flatness and the absence of strong defensive barriers against invasion. No mountain ranges to defend, no crags on which to build strong fortresses, no chance for feudal barons and the communities around them which wrested from them the rights of our Western democracy.

The land of Russia was open to attack, and was attacked by the Mongol-Tartar hordes, and enemies from west and north. It was an open land, exposed and undefended, and was therefore forced, in self-defense, to submit itself to one strong ruler, because the small local defense strongholds were lacking. Thus one might say that Russia was doomed to autocracy from the outset. The country stood or fell in accordance with the strength of its central authority; there were no possibilities of local, or feudal, defense.

The early history of Russia falls exactly into this pattern, a fight for a strong central protective power against outer enemies. One of its early leaders was pre-Romanof Ivan, surnamed The Terrible, who took the first steps toward the unification of Russia. After his death there were invasions of enemies, since always the flat Russian plain lay open to attack. But the seed which Ivan sowed bore fruit, and his successors continued to strive for national independence. Slowly but with invincible persistence they broke the attempts at foreign domination, until there came Peter (Romanof) the Great, who had a new and different vision. Peter was not content to fight the invading Swedes and finally to destroy the army of the hitherto invincible Charles XII at Poltava in the Ukraine; he was the first to dream of a Russia which might call upon the West for aid in the development of its natural wealth and resources.

Both Tsars, Ivan and Peter, had to fight and did fight against their own nobles. But the latter had no strong points to hold against the central power, no tough burghers to assist them with arms and money—in return for fresh privilege and greater freedom. So Ivan overcame the nobles and created a strong Russia under one central authority. After Ivan Russia once more grew disunited and weak, until Peter Romanof completed Ivan's work. His internal struggle was less against the nobles, who as a class had never fully recovered from Ivan's blows, than against a semi-noble semi-warrior caste called the Streltsi, a sort of Pretorian Guard or power behind the throne. Peter crushed the Streltsi as Ivan had crushed the nobles, and by doing so implanted upon his country the absolute authority of the centre over its vast circumference. Henceforth the Kremlin was the supreme and focal point, and the Tsar was Tsar of All the Russias, sole lord and master of all the Russians. To put it bluntly, there were no free men in Russia, as we consider free men. The Tsar was lord of all, the high justice and the low, and in his sight the great noble or the bishop was no more important than the peasant or the worker. He could and did tear down the mighty from their seats and exalt the humble and weak. He could marry a village girl and make her Empress of Russia, or exile a Prince of the Church, as he pleased.

Thus as a result primarily of geography, there was established the Tsarist Autocracy which endured until the fall of Nicholas II. Naturally there grew around it offshoots, its instruments and mechanism, its military and managerial system, generals and governors and a great host of bureaucrats. Their leaders, drawn from the former nobility which had submitted to the Tsar, or joined to its daughters by marriage, were the landlords of Russia, holding huge estates by royal grant, as did the relatives of the Imperial family. There was a relatively small trading class and a larger body of artisans working individually or in groups, who could hardly be described as Labor in the Western sense of the word. They were craftsmen, but until the latter years of the nineteenth century Russia was an agricultural country with little organized industry of its own. (As late as 1896, for instance, there were less than four million factory workers in a total population of a hundred and forty million. Even by 1917, when the Revolution occurred, there were only ten million industrial workers in the whole country.) Finally, there was the immense peasant population, millions of men and women who worked the land by the sweat of their brows with the most primitive instruments and methods. Mentally and physically they were debased almost to the level of animals, and until less than a hundred years ago they were sold like animals with the land on which they dwelt.

Greek philosophers were willing to admit, or at least to discuss, the principle that a benevolent despotism was the best form of government. A further condition is necessary: that the despotism must be strong. The strength of the Tsarist autocracy was proved by the fact that it lasted, as I have said, from Ivan the Terrible to Nicholas II, despite foreign wars that were often disastrous and its own internal dissensions or "palace coups." Some Tsars were more "liberal" than others, but theirs was not the liberalism of democracy as we conceive it, and was devoted chiefly to bolstering the power and position of the Emperor. It is significant that Alexander Mikhailovich, the second Romanof, called upon his fellow-rulers in Europe to undertake a holy war against Cromwell and the English Regicides, and that the great Empress Catherine refused to recognize the government of the American Revolution. Liberal ideas and foreign travel were discouraged for all save a chosen few of the ruling class, and the Imperial authority consistently utilized the great influence of the Orthodox Church to maintain the masses in the "state in which it had pleased God to place them," that is, in abysmal ignorance and subservience.

Nevertheless, the effects of foreign wars, notably the conflicts with Frederick the Great and Napoleon, contributed to break down the aloofness of Russia which was one of the "secret weapons" of Tsarist autocracy. A similar effect was produced, more slowly but no less surely, by the Russian desire, first expressed by Peter, to obtain Western aid in the development of the country's vast natural resources. It seems as though the Russians have always wished, even in modern times, to remain apart and exclusive and yet simultaneously to share in and benefit by the progress of the West. As Russian industry gradually developed, in the second half of the nineteenth century, with the influx of foreign capital and the spread of education which it required, the nation became restive and began to feel that the rigid system of autocracy was like an iron band around a growing tree. The unrest, at first confined to the educated classes, began to permeate the new industrial proletariat, until throughout the country there was a sense of impending events, as when an ice-bound river heaves and groans in the springtime. At the outset the movement was one of discontent rather than of revolt, and comparatively limited in scope. It might easily have been canalized or curbed by wise and resolute measures, but unfortunately for Tsardom, the Emperor Nicholas II was a man of weak and vacillating character who not only blew alternately hot and cold but made the fatal error of allowing his country to be drawn into two losing wars.

The question has often been asked why a Marxist revolution should have occurred in Russia, the most backward and agricultural of white nations, whereas Marx himself predicted that it would come first in an advanced industrial state. My answer is that the Russian Revolution was only *apparently*, or I should better say *accidentally*, a Marxist revolution. To be quite accurate, it was Marxist because Lenin who rode and to some extent directed its wave was himself a Marxist, and by force of his will and genius was able to guide it along Marxist channels. In reality, however, it was the revolt of an enslaved mass against the intolerable burden of a corrupt and weakened rule, a revolt more national than Marxist, similar, in fact, to the French Revolution of 1789. This is a point of cardinal importance which cannot be stressed too strongly, because it has determined the course of Soviet history. Later I shall explain why Lenin became a Marxist, but for the moment I digress to review briefly the Marxist doctrine.

Marx had argued that Capitalism, by which he meant the exploitation of men by Money, would ultimately produce a small minority of "bosses," the moneyed group, and a great majority of their hire-lings, the proletariat. One fine day, said Marx, the latter would find they had "nothing to lose but their chains" and would forcibly seize everything, banks, factories, railroads, mines and the rest, from the hands of the privileged few. Marx expected this to occur in one of the highly industrialized countries of Europe, like Britain or Ger-many. He did not foresee an additional exploitation, that of colonial or semi-colonial slaves. This was the use by the capitalist rulers of Western Europe of colored labor in the Congo, the Dutch and British East Indies and China to produce raw materials, rubber, tin, palm oil, foodstuffs, and a hundred other commodities which could be sold with such profit that the lot of the Western workers could be maintained above the Revolution level. Indirectly they too were profiting from the underpayment of their fellow proletarians in the East. This was pointed out by the German Communist, Rosa Luxem-burg, whose views upon the "Theory of Colonial Slaves as a Hin-drance to Social Revolution in Europe" were later adopted by Lenin. Marx also forgot something else. His book, "Das Kapital," has been described as the Old Testament of the Bolshevik faith. It is a remark-able treatise on modern economics, but it has the defect that Karl Marx, a German Jew who emigrated to England, underestimated the compelling importance of nationalism, meaning love of country, in the world. Nationalism is the strongest of the imponderable forces which move mankind, stronger than religion, even than hunger or love; it is the strongest force of all. Men and women will die for their country, for its flag and what that means to them, more readily than for anything else.

No one can deny that Jews have the strongest racial conscious-ness of any people, or that it has been reinforced for more than two thousand years by a strong religious consciousness. Nevertheless, Jewish revolutionaries, from Marx to Trotsky, have been inclined to underestimate the love-of-land-or-country force which impels men and women to fight against a foreign invader. Thus it seems that Marx was wrong on two counts. His "proletarian masses of Western Europe" were kept sweet by the crumbs of colonial profits which fell from their masters' tables, and, secondly, were drugged into eager obedience by the potent opium of nationalism.

On the other hand, Marx was correct in his definition of the basic principles which should lead, and will always lead, to social revolution. He said that when the great majority of a nation was unhappy and downtrodden, when it felt that too few were getting too much at the expense of too many, it would rise and sweep away this privileged minority. Lenin went further than Marx. Informed by his experience of the abortive revolutionary movement in Russia which followed the disastrous war with Japan in 1904-05, he developed what might almost be called a "Blueprint for Revolution." He said that not only was there required widespread popular dissatisfaction, but the other conditions were also necessary: that the ruling class should have lost confidence in itself as well as losing the confidence of those it ruled; and last but not least, that the army and police force which were its instruments of rule should have been so broken by defeat in battle as to be of little value. In the war against Japan of 1904-05, the Russian Army was beaten and the Tsarist power correspondingly diminished. Beaten, I said, not broken, with the consequence that the revolutionary movement in 1905-06 which followed the war was crushed—if only by a narrow margin—by armed forces which still remained loyal to the Emperor. Lenin took that lesson to heart, and therefore added his fourth of the conditions requisite for social revolution. I repeat them now again:

1. That the great majority of the people is thoroughly dissatisfied and finds its life intolerable;
2. That it has lost confidence in and respect for its rulers;
3. That the rulers have lost confidence in themselves.

And then Lenin's fourth condition, that the ruler's strongest weapon, the army and the police force, has been broken. There you have it in a nutshell.

These conditions did occur in 1917. This time the army was thoroughly beaten, not partially, as by Japan twelve years before. The ill-fed, mentally starved, exploited Russian masses, eighty percent of the population, now felt obscurely that their rulers had somehow let them down, had sent their sons to slaughter and *not given them enough in return*. That is a dominant phrase, the not giving enough in return. So long as the feudal lords of Europe gave protection to the communities around them, the *droit de seigneur*, the taxes and other highhanded proceedings, were accepted not always willingly, but without revolt. When, however, the need for protection vanished, the communities began to grumble and ask why they should give the girls to their lord's enjoyment, or pay money into his pocket. So then the Russian people felt unkind towards the Tsar, because they felt he had failed them, had been unworthy of their trust. They no longer revered him dumbly, but began to ask loudly, why should he be set above them, to send their sons to death, *and what did he give in return?* It was not a sufficient answer to say, as the Orthodox Church of Russia did say, that the Tsar was appointed by God. Because then came a second question: What about God Himself?

Lenin's fourth condition, the defeat of the army in war, was patent for all to see; and his third condition also, the lack of confidence by the rulers in themselves, was no less true. In this connection I was told a story which reveals and explains many things. I don't need to give the narrator's name, but as a junior officer of an élite regiment in St. Petersburg, he was on guard one night in 1916 in the Tsar's personal apartment. The Emperor had known my friend when he was a member of the *corps des pages,* the nursery of future generals and governors in the Tsarist State. The Autocrat of All the Russias got up from his desk at midnight and came over to my friend, who was standing near the door. He said kindly, "I hope you are not tired, at least not so tired as I am. I am very tired, with all this weight on my shoulders, because between you and me I am only a little grey man, and very tired tonight."

That was the tocsin of doom, when the highest imperial ruler can speak thus of himself, as only "a little grey man." So Catherine would not have spoken, nor Peter nor Ivan the Terrible. So, however, spoke Nicholas II, and paid for it with his life.

It is wrong to say, or believe, and Lenin never said it, that he "made" the Russian Revolution. You don't make a revolution: it occurs. All you can do is take advantage of circumstances, and perhaps, if you are nimble, fortunate, courageous and astute, you can jump to the tiller of a drifting ship and direct it along the course which you have planned beforehand. That was what Lenin did. He did not so much "seize" power in Russia as pick up from the gutter the sceptre which had passed from the nerveless hands of Tsar Nicholas to the well-meaning but equally feeble hands of Kerensky. Lenin's hands were neither nerveless nor feeble. He took the sceptre and held it and used it to mold his country in a new way along untrodden paths. Of the men who have lived on earth, Lenin was one of the greatest. During his years of exile he thought and planned and wrote. Literally, as I said, he prepared a "blueprint for revolution," coldly considering the errors he and his associates had committed in 1905-06, and comparing them with the French Revolution, which was a true social revolution, although later diverted, after the death of Marat and Robespierre, and with that of Oliver Cromwell in England, which was not wholly a social revolution but nevertheless did mean a real shift of power. Lenin took and analyzed all of this, to make his careful blueprint.

I never shall forget the speech of his widow, Krupskaya, made to the All-Union Soviet Congress on the day after Lenin died. When she told how it came about that Lenin adopted Marx as his master and guide through life, she said: "My husband was young and only seventeen when the Tsarist police took his older brother, whom he adored, and hanged him, because he had received a letter from a college friend who was involved in the assassination of Tsar Alexander II. The elder brother of Vladimir Ilyich (Lenin) had no share or part in the killing of the Tsar. The letter from his friend was a letter from a friend, completely devoid of any conspirative intention. But on account of that letter the brother of Lenin my husband was hanged by the Tsarist police, and that brutal, unjustified act released a bolt of lightning to shatter the Tsarist throne. From that day onwards Lenin set himself to destroy a society in which such things were possible. He sought long for a thread to guide him through the labyrinth of politics, and finally reached the conclusion that Marx held this guiding thread, that Marx was right in saying that Capitalism, the use of money by men to exploit their fellow-men, was the worst of human evils and had to be destroyed."

Krupskaya was a strong, outstanding woman. Heavy and plain, physically unattractive, she had devoted her whole life to Lenin and his cause. She spoke with a deep voice like a man's, and her words rang true as she told the Congress in its hour of mourning why Lenin had done what he did and what it meant to him. She touched no personal note. She told us the simple facts, slowly and impressively in her deep man's voice.

It is a strange and paradoxical thing that the Bolsheviks, who had one of the greatest individual leaders of all time, profess to decry the importance of individual leadership. They maintain that the

Occasion produces the Man, and refuse completely to accept Carlyle's theory of Hero-worship, that the leader can direct or even create circumstances. Lenin said, with justice, that circumstances cannot be created, but his life proved that a leader can direct.

In war even more than in peace—and what is social revolution but an explosion of civil war?—the skill and determination of a leader are perhaps the most important single factor. Lenin had the advantage of knowing exactly what he wanted and how he proposed to achieve it. His years of exile had been devoted to the most careful study and preparation, to fit himself and his followers for the moment when conditions and circumstances should be ripe for revolution, so that then they could grasp the opportunity and take control of affairs. When I said that Lenin did not "make" the Revolution in Russia, I meant it therefore in the sense that he did not make the circumstances or conditions which led to it, but from his arrival at Petrograd in the beginning of April to his actual seizure of power on November seventh he was following a path he had chosen beforehand. Because he knew that his task and that of his party was first of all to judge which of the forces involved was the most important, and secondly to be so prepared that when the situation presented itself they would be masters of the situation. In Russia, therefore, Lenin aimed chiefly at the industrial workers as being the vanguard and most socially conscious element of the proletariat. He did so for three good reasons. Firstly, because the industrial workers were still almost part of the villages; they represented the most active and intelligent section of the peasantry, rather than being an urban mass. Secondly, they were easy for Bolshevik orators to reach in the cities and towns, either by word of mouth or by newspapers which most of them could read. Their peasant brethren, on the other hand, were mostly unable to read, and in those days could not be reached by radio. Thirdly, they could be mobilized through their labor unions to anti-capitalist and even revolutionary action, by strikes ostensibly for higher wages to meet the increased cost of living, and by the more subtle Marxist doctrine that Capital did not provide an opportunity for Labor, as it always had maintained, but was simply a parasite on Labor's body and should therefore be destroyed.

Chapter 2

RASPUTIN, KERENSKY, LENIN

IN THE SPRING of 1917 two events occurred in the space of less than four weeks, which determined the fate of Russia: the abdication of the Tsar, Nicholas II, in the second week of March, and the return of Lenin from exile in the first week of April.

In signing the act of abdication, Nicholas, that weak, vacillating, tired little grey man, proved himself strong as Samson to pull down the whole edifice of society whose principal pillar he was. For several months he had been commander-in-chief of the army, as well as Autocrat of All the Russias, and it was at his own headquarters at Mogilef, on the west front, that he resigned his throne. Exactly why he did so has never been clearly understood. His own position and that of his armies were hazardous indeed, but neither was utterly desperate. At the risk of over-simplification, I shall try to explain it as follows. The truth of the matter is that he was induced to abdicate by a person or persons close to him, perhaps of his own family, who feared that he would make a separate peace with Germany. The reason for this fear was their knowledge that the Empress Alexandra, a German-born princess of Hesse, had become convinced that the only hope of saving the throne for her husband and son lay in peace at any price. Of course the Empress was right; the war had never been popular in Russia, and by the beginning of 1917 its strain had become intolerable. On paper Russia's manpower was inexhaustible, but ten million killed—perhaps the figure was higher—would have been a frightful price to pay for victory, and instead they had died in vain since most of Poland and part of the fertile Ukraine were

21

already occupied by the enemy. Most of the Russian dead were peasants, the ignorant amorphous mass which formed over eighty percent of the population, but with them had been slaughtered their landlords, the officers of the Guards from general to lieutenant, who were really the backbone of the Tsarist regime. The villages were weary of war; they lacked hands to till the fields, and even the richest agricultural areas were menaced by starvation. Transport had broken down, and the towns and cities were hungry although the urban workers had benefited somewhat by increased wages. The trading class had also profited by the war, but now the shortage of consumer's goods, and of food itself, had begun to threaten them too.

In any case, the second week of March, 1917, brought an outbreak of strikes, presumably of economic origin although there may have been other more subtle reasons, in Petrograd. The Tsar sent from Headquarters peremptory instructions to suppress the strikes by force. The armed police force of the capital was curiously supine. It was fully competent to handle riots, but it was not employed. Why it was not employed is unknown, but one may guess that there were powerful influences in Petrograd, both Russian and foreign, which had decided to get rid of the Tsar and his German Empress because they believed that she would persuade him to make a separate peace with the enemy. When the Tsar learned that small effort was being made to check the "riots," he sent orders, as I said, to use troops against the rioters. This apparently was attempted, perhaps genuinely, perhaps perfunctorily. At any rate, the troops refused to fire on the rioters, and almost overnight there was a sort of new regime in Petrograd—I choose my words deliberately—which aimed at substituting a semi-parliamentary authority for the autocracy of the Tsar. Everything was so confused and chaotic that the truth is hard to find, but there seems to be a kernel of fact in the whole medley, that some people had decided that the war must go on, and that therefore Nicholas and Alexandra must go out. A tentative "government," which never ventured to call itself more than a Provisional Government, was formed in Petrograd, and two of its representatives, Guchkov and Shulgin, were sent to Headquarters to tell the Tsar more or less bluntly that he would have to abdicate. If he had been a man of stronger character he would have dismissed them or simply had them shot, but I suspect that there were others in his immediate entourage to support the deputies' demand. In fact, it was a cooked-up job, and the tired little lonely man lacked courage to resist it, or skill to perceive its consequences. Someone whispered in his ear and another put pen in his hand . . . and he signed his own death warrant . . . and theirs. At first the Tsar wished to abdicate in favor of his son, and later of his uncle, the Grand-Duke Michael; but already the swift current of events was sweeping the regime to destruction. From that day onwards the story of Russia reads like a Greek tragedy, the fatal causes which led to an inevitable end. The Tsar Nicholas was caught in a net of circumstances, like Oedipus and Louis XVI of France. Resolute action might have saved him, but he could neither resolve nor act. There is reason to believe that the garrison of Petrograd was still loyal to its Emperor, although the loyalty of its commanders is less certain. Stories were current at the time that the Tsar wished to move troops from Headquarters to the capital, and that "railroad workers" blocked the move or persuaded the troops to disobey. There may have been some truth in this, but it is more probable that transportation was already so disorganized that the movement of two or three divisions was next to impossible.

In attempting to explain the tragic end of Tsardom, one cannot ignore the fantastic relationship of the Empress Alexandra and the Siberian monk Rasputin. The basic facts of the story are sufficiently well known to be told quite briefly. The ruling family of Hesse suffered from haemophilia, the "bleeding sickness," which only afflicts males but is transmitted by females. In such cases blood refuses to coagulate, and even a trifling scratch may cause death. Should victims survive to manhood, they die young from internal bleeding. Alexandra's son, the late-born heir, in a family of daughters, to the Imperial throne, was a haemophiliac. His mother, a deeply religious woman, must have prayed despairingly that the curse should be lifted from her son. And prayed in vain, until one day her friend Countess Virubova told her of the monk Rasputin.

It has been stated that the life of the little Tsarevich was saved three times by Rasputin—and so his mother believed. The first time she saw it happen was in the Imperial Palace at Livadia, in the Crimea, which wasn't a palace at all, but a pleasant country home set in gardens of flowers and beauty. If I remember rightly, the child, then four or five, knocked his knee on the edge of a fish-pond, and it bled and went on bleeding. Doctors were in attendance, but what could the doctors do? Then—this is hard to accept, but this is how it happened—the tall, dark, dirty, sweaty, bearded monk from Siberia, with his deep, hypnotic eyes, came to her and said, "Daughter be not afraid, your son will not die but live." He laid his hand on the child, and blood ceased to flow from the knee. That was the first time.

Rasputin was a rascal, but even the Bolsheviks at their most bitter never suggested that the relationship between this licentious and hyper-sexed reprobate and the Tsarina was anything save that of a woman who loved her son, and a man who for some reason had power to stem the flow of blood which could drain the child's life away. George Borrow, I think in "Lavengro," has a story about some gypsy who had power to check haemorrhage in animals. At any rate, Rasputin did it three times for the son of Alexandra, Empress of Russia. I forget the second time, although it served to cement his hold upon her mind. The third time was deep in the heart of the storm, when the clouds over Russia were dark with a burden of lightning and thunder, and the Tsar had assumed command of his troops in a final desperate attempt to avert the coming doom. The boy was staying with his father at Headquarters, and developed a large boil in his armpit which grew worse and worse, with high and higher fever. They knew it should be lanced, but to haemophiliacs the wound of a knife is death. The Tsarina was at Tsarkoe-Selo, near Petrograd, five hundred miles away, getting messages every half-hour about the state of the child, each message worse than the last, until she understood that he was fated to die, and something worse than that, to die far away from her, when she couldn't see him or touch him or hold his head in her arms, to ease, if might be, his passing.

Again Rasputin came to her and said, "Daughter, do not lose faith." It was late at night, and the Empress did not see him until six o'clock the next morning. He was spent and exhausted, and he said, "Daughter, all night I have striven with God, as once the Prophet Jacob strove with Him, for the life of your son. I strove, and I prevailed. God told me, 'The child will live,' but He told me something else, that your life and the life of your son and your husband and your daughters is tied and enwrapped with mine, that so long as I live, you too will live and flourish, but when I die you will not long survive me."

I was told this amazing story, almost Byzantine in its combination of credulity and legend, by a woman in Moscow in 1921, who declared that she learnt it from her sister, formerly a servant at the Imperial Court. I have tried vainly to check its authenticity, and all I can say is that it seems to correspond to the whole fantastic episode of Rasputin. The story continues that an hour later the Tsarina received a message saying that to the astonishment of the surgeons and doctors at Headquarters, the young prince's boil had subsided and his fever had gone down, and he was out of danger. Perhaps that will help to explain why this German woman, born Princess Alexandra of Hesse, had such reverence for the dirty licentious Siberian monk who called himself Rasputin.

Rasputin was always in need of money to gratify his vices. He undoubtedly was connected with war profiteers and contractors, for whom he obtained lucrative orders by his influence over the Empress; and there is also reason to believe that he had treasonable relations with what would nowadays be called the German "Fifth Column" in Russia. Even more than the Allied blockade, the war on two fronts was breaking Germany's heart; but if peace could be made with Russia there was still a chance of victory in the West. It is more than probable that the German Fifth Columnists paid Rasputin to direct the Empress towards a peace which she herself desired in order to save her husband, whom she controlled, and her son, whom she adored. The war-to-the-end party in Petrograd was aware of this, and struck swiftly. Rasputin was lured into the trap of his own lust and killed by Prince Felix Yussupof, with the aid, or at least complicity, of Dimitri Pavlovich Romanof, the Tsar's cousin. As often in such cases, the motives were somewhat mixed; but one of the reasons was that they knew Rasputin's influence over the Tsarina, and that he was urging her to make peace at any price with Germany.

Deprived of his support, a prey to despair and superstition that verged on mania, the Empress lost courage and will, as her letters published later lamentably reveal. In a sense Rasputin had been her backbone as well as her guide, as she had been for the Tsar. The death of her "Friend" left her powerless to uphold the feeble hands of her husband, who without her fell easy victim to his own weariness and those who advised him that abdication was better than struggle. Neither he nor they were aware that Russian society depended upon the person and authority of the Emperor, and that without him the whole edifice would collapse. The plan, if plan there was, to put Grand-Duke Michael on the throne, died stillborn, and the Tsarist regime was immediately replaced by what looked like a liberal republic, headed by men of good will, Prince Lvov, Professor Miliukov, General Rodzianko, and other honored citizens who were not only loyal to their French and British allies but had long striven to lead Russia along the unfamiliar path of Western Democracy. They were loyal and well-meaning, but politically inexperienced and, alas, quite incapable of understanding, much less defeating, the maelstrom of forces released by the crash of Tsardom. They did not understand what was happening or might happen, but one man understood, a small, sandy-haired, stocky, professorial-looking exile named Vladimir Ilyich Ulianof, self-named Lenin. The Germans had two strings to their bow. Their plan for separate peace with Russia through Rasputin and the Tsarina had failed. Lenin, its alternative, succeeded.

Future historians may well reckon April 3, 1917, the day on which Lenin returned to Russia after ten years of exile, as a date comparable in importance to the Hegira of Mohammed. At the time, to the world at large and even to the Russians, Lenin's return would have scarcely been noticed save for the fact that he and his friends had been allowed by the German Government to travel from Switzerland across Germany to the Russian border in a sealed train, although Germany and Russia were still at war and these men were Russian nationals. The Germans allowed him thus to travel because they hoped and believed that he would carry a virus—to use the jargon of the period—infecting with fatal gangrene the wounded Titan of the North. For this purpose they gave Lenin safe conduct and, it is said, furnished him with money.

I once asked Trotsky if it was true that Lenin came to Petrograd with a fund of German gold.

He looked at me enigmatically and replied, "Whether it's true or not, of one thing you can be sure, that the gold was not employed for any but Lenin's purposes."

As it happened, Lenin's purpose and that of the Germans did for the moment coincide. Having failed to make a separate peace through the agency of Rasputin and the Empress, the Germans evidently hoped that Lenin and his associates would hasten the process of Russian disintegration until the country was unable to go on fighting. They knew that he had consistently opposed the war as a monstrous example of capitalist greed and folly, and were confident that the Bolsheviks would strike at the root of national patriotism which they had always denounced as one of the capitalist devices by which the masses were tricked into obedience. For his part I believe that Lenin foresaw that a great social upheaval, a real revolution rather than the transfer of power from one section of the ruling class to another, was possible if not probable in Russia, and hoped, as I said earlier, to direct and control it. At any rate, from the moment of his arrival in Petrograd, where he was given a triumphal reception at the Finland Railway Station, he never ceased to attack the whole structure of bourgeois society and to demand its replacement by a system of Marxist collectivism. His speech that day ended with the words, "Long live the Socialist Revolution," and on the following day he issued what are known as his "April theses," which declared that the first stage of the Revolution had now been completed by the downfall of Tsardom, and that the task ahead was to carry out the second stage, which would give power to the people instead of to the bourgeoisie. He advocated nationalization of all land and confiscation of landed estates, the creation of a single national bank, and the establishment of a soviet republic rather than of a parliamentary regime. Finally he issued the slogan "No support for the Provisional Government," which had been formed after the Tsar's abdication by the more liberal members of the Duma.

If proof were needed that the person and position of the Emperor was the core and foundation of Russian society, and that his removal would throw the whole vast machine out of gear, it was amply forthcoming. Almost immediately after the collapse of the Tsar's single authority it became apparent that there were in reality two authorities in Russia: the Committee of the Duma and the Executive Committee of the Soviet[1] of Workers and Peasants. The former

1 The word "soviet" means "council," and the chief difference between it and a parliamentary assembly lay in the fact that soviet members were chosen by a public show of hands from the group they represented, but were liable to suspension and replacement at any time if the said group changed its collective mind or felt that the men it had chosen no longer expressed its will.

was mainly composed of men of wealth and standing although reputedly liberal in their views, like Rodzianko, a big landowner, Professor Miliukov, chief of the Constitutional Democrats, and Prince Lvov, who had been mentioned as a possible Prime Minister before the fall of the Tsar. The Soviet at that time was controlled by the Social-Revolutionary and Menshevik[2] parties. The Social-Revolutionaries had always been strongest amongst the peasants, who formed the rank and file of the Army, whereas the Mensheviks represented the petit-bourgeois urban elements of the country, small producers and traders, artisans, the "white-collar proletariat" and the more prosperous workers. The Bolsheviks[2] at first had only a small minority in the Executive Committee, although as months passed their power and numbers rapidly increased.

The Workers' and Soldiers' Councils had taken an active part in fomenting the strikes and disorders which led to the abolition of Tsardom, and in preventing attempts made to suppress them by force. Thus the railway workers are said to have blocked an attempted troop movement upon Petrograd from the army zone, and later did prevent the escape of the Imperial Family. On the other hand, there was a link between the Duma and the Soviet in the shape of the Socialist deputies of the former—men like the Social-Revolutionary Kerensky—who were also members of the Soviet Executive Committee. Chiefly through their efforts an initial compromise was reached between the two authorities after the fall of the Tsar and a Provisional Government was formed, headed by Prince Lvov, Rodzianko, Miliukov and other prominent liberals, in which the Soviet held no seats, although it agreed to support the Government. In return the Government issued a program which met the approval of the Soviet. Nevertheless the seeds of conflict between the two

2 "Menshevik" means "minority," and "Bolshevik" "majority." These terms were first applied in 1902 to the two sections of the Social Democratic Party which split upon a question of policy. Both sections called themselves Marxian Socialists, but the majority (Bolsheviks) headed by Lenin advocated violent *Revolution*, while the minority (Mensheviks) hoped to achieve Socialism by a gradual and more orderly process of popular education and *Evolution*. In 1917 Lenin renamed his majority section *Communist* Party, in memory of the Communist Manifesto of Karl Marx, and of the first (Communist) International which Marx had founded. The official title of Lenin's party henceforth was VKP (b), from the initial letters of the Russian words *V*sosoyousny *K*ommunisteechisky *P*artei (*bolshevik*), or in English, All-Union Communist Party (majority). The words "Bolshevik" and "Communist" later became synonymous.

bodies remained and grew mightily in the months which followed.

It is difficult to describe adequately the state of confusion which existed throughout Russia. Contemporary writers have compared it to a spring thaw on a great Siberian river, when its smooth surface becomes overnight a crashing medley of ice floes. The comparison is apt because the floes continue to churn and clash thunderously for days or even weeks, but are moved irresistibly in a common direction. So the current of national disintegration bore Russia ever more swiftly towards complete revolution.

Although the provinces for the most part accepted the abolition of Tsardom and pledged allegiance to the Provisional Government, a thousand different groups were claiming or seizing local power. Freedom of Speech, denied for centuries, was acting like potent wine throughout the length and breadth of the country. Everyone talked at once, without coherence or plan. Newspapers sprang up like mushrooms, shouting for war or shrieking for peace, demanding immediate elections and new laws, higher wages and lower prices, and above all more food. Meanwhile the peasants, in sporadic and spontaneous but universal action, began to satisfy their age-old hunger for land and to repay centuries of serfdom, hunger and oppression. They did not wait or care for laws to nationalize land or confiscate the property of landlords. If the owners resisted they were killed and their homes were burned. If they accepted tamely the seizure and distribution of their estates, livestock, produce and equipment, they were often unmolested or allowed to escape with their personal possessions and valuables. As the news of this great plunder-boom reached the Front, peasant soldiers deserted by tens of thousands, eager to share the booty, shooting or overpowering any who tried to stop them. Except on the main lines, transport was disorganized, and even they were choked by hordes of fugitives or soldiers trying to return home, who hung like a swarm of bees on the sides and roofs of the cars. Soon the whole country, Front and Rear alike, was in a state of chaos.

In all this fantasy and confusion there was one man able to see and read the signs of the times, who knew exactly what he wanted. In the first days after his arrival in Petrograd Lenin seems to have regarded the Soviet of Workers and Soldiers little more favorably than the Provisional Government. He exposed the petit-bourgeois character of Menshevik and Social-Revolutionary ideology, which did not aim at a proletarian or genuinely socialist (i. e. Marxist) revolution, but was willing to compromise with the "bosses" and passively follow their lead. It was on this very point, the question of compromise, and a gradual evolution towards Socialism, as opposed to the theory of a swift, violent revolution, advocated by Marx and Lenin, that the Bolsheviks and Mensheviks had split many years before. Before long, however, Lenin perceived that the alliance between the Provisional Government and the Soviet was more apparent than real, that they were in fact two powers, or at least a dual power, with aims already diverse, which might easily be conflicting. He promptly decided to work upon this duality and exploit its possibilities of conflict by "direct action" in the lower councils of workers, soldiers and peasants everywhere, which he hoped would ultimately win for the Bolsheviks control of the Soviet Central Executive Committee.

Lenin therefore called the Bolsheviks to a Conference attended by one hundred and fifty-one delegates who represented upwards of a hundred thousand members from all parts of Russia. This seemed but a drop in the country's vast sea of population, but the Bolsheviks had the advantage of cool-headed experienced leaders and of lower ranks which had been disciplined and tried by years of "underground" work in circumstances of the greatest difficulty, danger and suppression.

In a long report to the Conference, Lenin explained with characteristic lucidity and authority the nature of the task confronting the Bolsheviks, and the problems they had to solve. Their main aim, he said, was to bring about the "second stage" of the revolution, which would put power in the hands of the true proletariat, the manual workers, soldiers and poor peasants. For this it was necessary to wrest the support of the Councils of Peasants, Workers and Soldiers from the Mensheviks and Social-Revolutionaries, the "lackeys of the bourgeoisie." Except, he said, for a few generals, landlords and capitalists, and their lackeys and foreign allies, the country was weary of war. The Party must therefore put forward the slogans of "Peace," "Land for the Peasants," and last but not least, "All Power to the Soviets." In some degree this was a change from Lenin's earlier views and tactics, and may have startled some of his followers. But Lenin never shrank from change when he thought the occasion required it, and always could refute any charge of opportunism with the pitiless logic of facts. The Conference adopted his slogans unanimously, and in six months rose through them to victory.

Lenin's reasoning was justified, because the first open rift between the Provisional Government and the Soviet occurred on the question of peace or war. Ever since the abdication of the Tsar, Russia's allies, France and Britain, had been trying to obtain a promise that the Provisional Government would not make a separate peace. The Foreign Minister, Miliukov, was induced to send a note to the Allies stating that his government intended to observe the obligations it had undertaken and continue the war until victory was attained. This became known to the populace of Petrograd on the day after Labor Day, May 1st. Immediately demonstrations of protest followed, and on May 3rd and 4th tens of thousands of workers paraded the streets of the capital with banners, "Down with the War," "All Power to the Soviets," "Publish the Secret Treaties." In the face of this storm Miliukov and Guchkov, the War Minister, were forced to resign, but through the efforts of Kerensky and Tseretelli, a former Menshevik member of the Duma who had been banished to Siberia by the Tsar but returned to become a popular member of the Soviet, a clash between the "dual powers" was averted and a coalition government was formed. Five minor seats in the Cabinet were given to Soviet representatives, one of which, Post and Telegraphs, was taken by Tseretelli. Kerensky was moved from the Ministry of Justice to the War Ministry, a promotion which later had significant effects. Finally, Tereshchenko, former Minister of Finance, replaced Miliukov as Minister of Foreign Affairs.

Ostensibly the Soviet had gained a notable success by the admission of its representatives to the government; actually it, or rather they, had been "taken into camp." Because it was not long before Kerensky in particular had become a champion of loyalty to the Allies and the continuance of the war to final victory. The reason for this conversion was a new and vital factor in international affairs, which strangely enough appears to have escaped the notice of Soviet historians; indeed it is not even mentioned in the official history of the Bolshevik Party when it describes events of this period. I refer to the entry of the United States into the World War. Already in Petrograd there were hundreds of French and British diplomats, officers and agents, civil and military, official and unofficial, patriotically determined to keep Russia in the war at all costs, irrespective

of past and future suffering and bloodshed, provided only that the
Germans would still have to fight on two fronts. With few exceptions these foreigners seem to have been utterly bewildered by the
mad hurly-burly and foaming cross-currents of Russian life. Their
memoirs and news dispatches show that they were aware they were
sitting on a volcano, but unable to gauge the forces which might
produce an eruption. In the midst of their doubt and discouragement, America's entry was more than a tonic or a hope; it was a
rejuvenation and a certainty of final victory. In addition, their
numbers and influence were greatly increased by union with their
American colleagues in the Russian capital. They were inspired not
only by new confidence but by a terrifically impressive talking-
point, the inexhaustible wealth, resources and manpower of the
United States. Here, I feel certain, is the answer to a riddle which
has puzzled so many students of Russian affairs at this period—why
did Kerensky resolve to continue the war and even to attempt at
midsummer the forlorn hope of an offensive against the Germans?
By that time, it is worth noting, there had been a further reorganization of the Provisional Government. The three constitutional ministers had resigned and had been replaced by Socialists. Kerensky, as
War Minister, had almost the powers of a dictator. His enemies have
said that he yielded weakly to Allied pressure, his friends that he
was loyal to his word. Surely it is simpler to recognize that he and
his colleagues, and one might say four-fifths of the educated people
in Russia, were so hypnotized by the power and prestige of the
United States that they thought a miracle could be worked. Unfortunately, the peasants and the peasant soldiers and most of the urban
workers were not educated. They knew little of America and cared
less, and if any of them were told about America's entry and what
it meant, they probably thought it was another trick to fool them
into further misery and slaughter. For them the war was over.

The Bolsheviks, to be sure, were well aware of this and every
other difference between the educated minority and the illiterate
masses. Their party was leaping forward in influence and numbers,
especially amongst the urban workers, in provincial towns as well
as in Petrograd and the other cities. They did not yet attempt seriously to challenge the power of the Social-Revolutionaries in the
villages, but were content to work upon the peasants through the
soldiers, amongst whom their speakers and recruiting agents were

ever more active and successful. As a result, the number of Bolshevik delegates in factory and military soviets everywhere grew steadily at the expense of rival Socialist parties, although the latter still held majorities in the higher Soviet organizations. Thus at the first All-Russian Congress of Soviets, which met in Petrograd on June 16th, the Bolsheviks had less than fifteen percent of the delegates. True, their rivals were divided and uncertain, while the Bolsheviks were compact and resolute, but their discipline did not compensate for numerical inferiority. It did, however, count immensely at a mass demonstration held on July 1st under the auspices of the Petrograd Soviet at the graves of the "victims of the Revolution." Here, as at similar demonstrations in Moscow and other cities, the Bolsheviks "stole the show." Their banners and slogans were brighter and more daring, their orators louder and more convincing, their cohorts more solid and organized. Rival speakers were shouted down and their banners trampled. New adherents flocked in thousands to the Bolshevik cause, and Lenin and his comrades hailed the day as a triumph. But that same night the All-Union Congress of Soviets in a closing vote decided by a large majority to support the war policy of the Kerensky government. Although the Congress did not know it, Kerensky's policy was already being put to the ultimate test of battle at that very hour. The Russians attacked in Galicia on a dangerously wide front, and took the Austrians by surprise. The Austrian line was broken and many prisoners and guns were captured. Then the enemy rallied, and as German divisions came into action the Russians were driven back in headlong disaster. Their officers died bravely, but no sacrifice could avail to spur men on who had no heart for fighting, nor even the weapons and munitions with which to fight. In a brief two-weeks' campaign the enemy occupied all Galicia and swept forward unchecked into the Western Ukraine. As a combat force the Russian Army had ceased to exist.

When the news of disaster became known in Petrograd on July 15th, the reaction was tremendous. For forty-eight hours half a million workers surged through the streets of the capital and round the headquarters of the Petrograd Soviet and the All-Russian Central Executive Committee of Soviets, demanding immediate peace. For some reason, probably because Lenin did not think that the time was ripe, the Bolsheviks seem to have played a small part in this affair, and certainly were not its leaders. Nevertheless, when the movement was bloodily suppressed on the third and fourth days by "trusty" troops which Kerensky had summoned to the capital, the Bolsheviks were the first to suffer. A warrant was issued for Lenin's arrest, but he escaped. Most of the other prominent Bolshevik leaders were thrown into prison, the "Pravda" and other Bolshevik newspapers were suppressed, and orders were given for the Red Guard to be disarmed. It is a moot point whether Kerensky showed fatal weakness, as his critics have charged, in not shooting the arrested "Reds" and any other Bolsheviks he could catch, or whether he spared their lives from motives of humanity or policy. At any rate, his failure to "act vigorously" seems to have disgusted the upper bourgeoisie, which had been much encouraged by the suppression of the July revolt. The commander-in-chief, General Kornilov, put himself at the head of what was called for the first time the Counter-Revolutionary Movement, and demanded the abolition of all the Soviets, high and low, and the execution of "Red traitors." At this point Kerensky became alarmed by the fear of a military dictatorship. At first he had appeared to make common cause with the reactionaries, but now he hung in mid-air, like Mohammed's coffin, between the forces of Right and Left. Disregarding his protest, Kornilov early in September sent an army corps to attack the capital under the command of General Krymov. The unhappy Kerensky appealed to the "Left" for aid, and the Bolsheviks responded. The Red Guard was rearmed, trenches were dug round the city, with barbed wire entanglements, thousands of Red sailors arrived from the fortress-port of Kronstadt, and last but not least, railroad workers were instructed once more to bar passage to the troop trains. Then a new factor intervened; Bolshevik spellbinders went out boldly to meet the oncoming soldiers and exhort them not to attack their "comrades and brothers." The appeal, and the measures of self-protection, were effective; the military coup fizzled out like a damp squib and Krymov died by his own hand. Kornilov and his chief subordinate, General Denikin, who later led one of the counter-revolutionary armies in the Civil War, were arrested. But again Kerensky's clemency, or vacillation, played him false. He speedily released them and thus alienated whatever popular sympathy he had regained. Thenceforward the whilom dictator was no more than a cork bobbing about on the rising tide of revolution. Because by mid-September, the date of Kornilov's defeat, the Bolsheviks had at last acquired a majority in the Petrograd Soviet. Less than a week later the Moscow Soviet also endorsed the Bolshevik program of hundred percent revolution and complete break with "counter-revolutionary bourgeois parties and their socialist lackeys." Amongst the latter a split occurred, and two new groups, the "Left" Social-Revolutionaries and "Left" Mensheviks, were formed, both pledged to support the Bolsheviks. The Left Mensheviks were neither numerous nor important, but the Left Social-Revolutionaries were a valuable accession to Bolshevik strength. It was evident that the second All-Union Congress of Soviets, which was scheduled to open on November 7th, would have a Bolshevik majority, which was already the case in the Central Executive Committee of the Soviets and in almost all the urban soviets of the provinces.

Lenin saw that the moment was approaching when the Bolsheviks must make their effort to control the forces of disruption. The process of social decay had reached a climax; further delay might plunge the country into a state of hopeless anarchy. On October 20th he returned to Petrograd and said boldly that the time had come for the Bolsheviks to seize power, which, he declared, was possible since they now controlled the Workers' and Peasants' Soviets in the principal cities and towns. Many of his followers were hesitant, and some of them even attempted to oppose him, for which they paid dearly in later years. There was, however, a hard core of resolute men who had been toughened by years of underground work in Russia and already looked with contempt, which also later bore fruit, upon the doubters, who, they considered, had been softened by Western exile. On October 23rd the Central Committee of the Party decided to strike without delay. Trusted leaders were dispatched to the chief provincial and military centers to prepare their comrades for decisive action.

A wave of uneasy anticipation swept over the country, and all men knew that the final crisis was at hand. Kerensky made feverish efforts to meet the coming storm, but his oratory had lost its power. The time for words was past. Nevertheless it is said that he provoked the actual outbreak by sending, on November 6th, armored cars to seize the Bolsheviks' central printing plant. Be that as it may, Lenin struck that night. His Red Guards had been pouring into the city all day, and the next morning they surrounded the Winter Palace, occupied the post and telegraph offices, the railroad stations, the ministries and the state bank. Kerensky and the Provisional Government took refuge in the Winter Palace, issuing futile proclamations and vowing to fight to the death. A salvo from the Revolutionary cruiser "Aurora," which had steamed up the river from Kronstadt, speedily ended this farce, although it did little damage, and the Palace was stormed almost without bloodshed. When the second All-Russian Congress of Soviets opened that night at the Bolshevik Headquarters in the Smolny Institute, the issue was already settled. Kerensky escaped and as before attempted to summon troops to his aid. Again he found a military commander, the Cossack General Krasnov, willing to assist him; but this time the troops themselves refused to move a step. Kerensky made good his escape, but Krasnov was arrested. In Moscow there was more of a struggle and some bloody fighting, which ended when an artillery regiment, encamped on what is now the Moscow Airport, shelled the Kremlin and forced it to surrender. Similar scenes occurred in other cities, but by mid-November the Bolsheviks were masters of Russia.

Chapter 3

"NOR ANY CHART TO GUIDE THEM"

LENIN DID NOT waste a moment in exploiting his victory. In an all-night session on November 7-8, the All-Union Soviet Congress proclaimed the supreme power of the State to be the Council of People's Commissars, with Lenin as Premier and Trotsky as Commissar of Foreign Affairs. Trotsky, born Lev Davidovich Bronstein, was the son of a prosperous Jewish farmer near Kherson, in the Southern Ukraine. He received a good education at a middle-class school in Odessa, and took an active part in the abortive revolutionary movement of 1905 in St. Petersburg, where he was chairman of the Workers' Soviet. When the Revolutionary Party split into two parts, Bolsheviks (majority) and Mensheviks (minority), Trotsky followed an independent line, characteristically, but more than once tried to reconcile the Mensheviks with the majority and to urge them to a more vigorous policy. The outbreak of the War found him in France, from which he was expelled at the end of 1916. He reached New York in mid-January, 1917, where he stayed for ten weeks, writing and lecturing. At the end of March he left the United States for Russia, but was arrested in Halifax and detained for a month, then released, to arrive in Petrograd at the beginning of May. Although nominally still independent, he rapidly swung towards the Bolsheviks, and was prominent in the July uprising, which failed. By the time of the October Revolution (November 7th, new style) Trotsky had thrown in his lot with the Bolsheviks and was elected a member of the Politburo of the Communist Party, as well as Commissar of Foreign Affairs, but he

37

always retained the right to think and speak for himself and to raise criticisms which often brought him into conflict with his fellow-commissars, most of whom were members of the Bolshevik Central Committee.

The first act of the new government was to decree that all land belonged to those who worked it, without rent or other payment. This was more than a sop to the peasants, and confirmed the allegiance of the Left Social-Revolutionaries, who were the most influential agrarian party. Simultaneously measures were taken to secure supplies of food for the capital and other cities. The next day Trotsky was instructed to send a wireless invitation to all belligerents to declare an armistice without delay. The Allied governments protested indignantly, and their representatives in Russia made overtures to the commander-in-chief, General Bukhonin, in the hope that he would act against the new government. Lenin promptly put Krylenko, a member of the Bolshevik Central Committee, in the place of Bukhonin, who shortly afterwards was torn to pieces by mutineers. The Bukhonin episode did much to confirm the Allied belief that Lenin was an agent of the German Government, a view which soon communicated itself to the new American Ambassador, Mr. Francis, who at first had taken a less hostile attitude.

The German government promptly accepted the armistice proposal, and after brief negotiations within the German lines, a truce was signed on December 5th. The Germans made no territorial or other demands, and even agreed not to transfer troops to the Western Front from the East, but the ink was scarcely dry on the document before this promise was broken. The Allied High Command soon learned about these transfers, which it felt to be only the beginning of a wholesale troop movement from east to west. The Allies must have known that Lenin was powerless to prevent it, but their hatred of the Bolsheviks was redoubled.

The third act of the new government was a reward for the workers. On November 11th a universal eight-hour day was decreed, and subsequent measures were enacted to put control of industry in the hands of the factory soviets.

The Bolsheviks were masters of Russia, but they had heavy handicaps at home and abroad. The country was a wilderness of disorder, disease and hunger, its richest provinces in hostile hands, its transport system disrupted, its reserves of livestock, grain and vegetables, even of seed grain, all but exhausted. Neither Lenin nor his followers had any experience of government, nor any chart to guide them along the untried paths they had pledged themselves to follow. They had won power as the champions of the masses to establish for the first time in history a Marxist proletarian state, but Marx himself had planned his new order for a highly industrialized and class-conscious community rather than a backward agricultural country like Russia, whose eighty percent of peasants were little more politically alert than slaves enfranchised overnight. Finally, Marx had declared that his brand of socialism was impossible in a single state, although it is probably true that when he used the word "state" in this context, he was thinking of countries like England, France or Germany, rather than a vast entity sprawling over two continents, like Russia.

Abroad, the Bolshevik position could hardly have been worse, and it is no exaggeration to say that Allied leaders regarded the Bolsheviks with loathing and dismay. The reason for this hostility was not only the instinctive repugnance of a capitalist and class society towards the "Red" regime, but the profound conviction that Lenin had been a German tool from the outset, and that he was determined to "betray" the Western Powers by concluding a separate peace. When later he did so, Allied fury knew no bounds. All the weapons and devices of their powerful propaganda services were put in action against the Bolsheviks. They had nationalized women, violated the sanctity of the Home, involved in common destruction the temples of God and the money-changers—no charge true or false was too extravagant for Allied hatred to employ and Allied panic to disseminate. Since the days of Attila and his Huns, no leader had been so execrated as Lenin, no people so vilified as the Russians.

Lenin at first paid little heed to these thunder clouds in the West. For one thing, he was working night and day to set the tottering Russian house on a more stable foundation and bring some order out of its chaos. Secondly, he appears to have honestly believed that events in Europe would sooner or later follow a course parallel to Russia's, that the war's stalemate, slaughter and exhaustion were bound to end in social revolution, when the masses at last realized the callous trickery through which they had been led to sacrifice by their capitalist masters. Indeed, Lenin subsequently justified the "surrender" Peace of Brest-Litovsk by the statement that it was not only a vitally needed breathing-space for the young Soviet Republic but that it would soon be nullified by the liberated German masses. In this connection one is forced to conclude that Lenin made one of the rare political errors of his career: he disregarded, or seriously underestimated, the weight and speed of American intervention in Europe. Instead of stalemate and exhaustion, sudden victory crowned the Allied standards in the autumn of 1918. Instead of social revolution throughout Europe, the victors were able to suppress revolutionary outbreaks in the vanquished countries, and even to press their campaign against the "Red menace" within the Russian borders. Looking backwards, it seems that both sides had good cause for their respective attitudes. Lenin had no firsthand knowledge of America, and was therefore perhaps too ready to accept the initial German view that so rich, peaceful and remote a country would never play a preponderant part in the European War and swing the balance so effectively in favor of the Allies. Moreover, as things turned out, Lenin's forecast of events in Europe was not wholly wrong. Marxist governments actually held power for a time in Bavaria and Hungary, and "Red" uprisings in Berlin and other German cities in the winter of 1918-19 were only suppressed with heavy loss of lives and property. The Allies in return blamed their defeats in the spring and early summer of 1918 upon the Bolsheviks, whose withdrawal from the war had allowed the Germans to transfer a million men from the Eastern Front to the West. They felt that victory had come in the nick of time to save them from dreaded "Red virus" which had already permeated much of Central Europe. From their hate and anxiety was bred the "Bolshevik bogey" whose invisible presence did much to vitiate the post-war settlement of Europe and was to prove, two decades later, one of the most valuable trumps in Hitler's hand.

Regardless of Allied enmity and its future consequences, Lenin opened formal peace negotiations with Germany on December 22, 1917. The task proved less easy than the Bolsheviks had hoped. The Germans were now aware of Russian impotence, and their appetite grew with eating. To the Soviet proposal of an equal peace without annexations or indemnities, with self-determination of peoples by plebiscites or national elections, the Germans replied by a demand for the "liberation from Russia" of Poland, Finland and the Baltic States and independence of the Ukraine. Trotsky thereupon declared that the war was at an end, but broke off negotiations with a refusal to sign such a "peace of annexation." Nearly twenty years later, when Trotsky had been proclaimed "an enemy of the people," his equivocal attitude at Brest-Litovsk was bitterly denounced by the official History of the Communist Party, as follows: "Although Lenin and Stalin, in the name of the Central Committee of the Party, had insisted that peace be signed, Trotsky, who was chairman of the Soviet delegation at Brest-Litovsk, treacherously violated the direct instructions of the Bolshevik Party. He announced that the Soviet Republic refused to conclude peace on the terms proposed by Germany. At the same time he informed the Germans that the Soviet Republic would not fight and would continue to demobilize the army. This was monstrous. The German imperialists could have desired nothing more from this traitor to the interests of the Soviet country. The German government broke the armistice and assumed the offensive. The remnants of our old army crumbled and scattered before the onslaught of the German troops. The Germans advanced swiftly, seizing enormous territory and threatening Petrograd."

This post-factum verdict is highly prejudiced, but it is true that the Germans promptly occupied Pskov and Narva, on the Russo-Estonian border, brushing aside feeble Russian opposition. The road to Petrograd lay open before them, but Lenin was not able to put through his peace policy without a savage struggle in the Central Committee of the Communist Party. The Russian people are never so stubborn as when their position appears desperate, and there was a moment when many of Lenin's associates reproached him with cowardice or worse. He spoke strongly for peace at any price, not only because he knew that resistance was impossible, but because he believed that European revolution was not far distant. The issue hung in the balance, and the Committee decided to remove the capital from Petrograd to Moscow. This was clearly a move to continue the war, and was adopted through the influence of Bukharin, one of Lenin's closest friends, who argued that peace on the German terms was a betrayal of the Revolution and spoke wildly about arming every worker and using the peasants as guerrillas. He was supported by the Left Social-Revolutionaries, whose opposition to the German terms was so determined that when Lenin finally carried his point they actually broke with the Bolsheviks. Trotsky's attitude was equivocal. He propounded the formula "Neither peace nor war," but did not explain what this meant in practical terms. His attitude served only to embitter the discussion, whose memory remained to become a nail in many a coffin.

Lenin stuck to his guns, but was forced to threaten resignation before the Committee was willing to agree with him. Once that agreement was obtained, by a narrow majority, Lenin took swift action. Chicherin, a former diplomat and noble who had become a revolutionary exile and after a brief imprisonment in England had returned to Russia to join the Bolsheviks, was appointed Foreign Commissar in Trotsky's place and instructed to resume negotiations with Germany immediately. Meanwhile, however, the decision to evacuate Petrograd, should the worst befall, was being carried into effect. Chicherin met the triumphant Germans on February 28th, and three days later accepted their terms in full and further agreed to recognize a treaty signed earlier between them and the allegedly independent government of the Ukraine. The Russians abandoned Poland and the Baltic States and promised to pay a huge indemnity in cash and raw materials. The Finnish question was settled out of hand by a German invading army under General von der Goltz, who smashed Red resistance with fire and sword.

After a brief debate full of tears and anguish, the (seventh) Congress of the Communist Party ratified the Treaty of Brest-Litovsk by an overwhelming majority, and its example was followed by the Congress of Soviets. The German General Staff thus gained a momentous success. It now had at its disposal the rich grain fields of the Ukraine, the oil of the Caucasus, and huge supplies of copper, iron and other needed materials which the Russians were pledged to deliver. Last but not least, Ludendorff, freed from the burden of war on two fronts, was able to launch—a few days after the treaty was signed—an all-out bid for victory in France. But Lenin had won his breathing-space. Henceforth too, Moscow instead of Petrograd was back in its old place as capital of Russia. The change, although made unwillingly, was not without significance, because to the great majority of the Russian people, "Mother Moscow" was the ancient center of their national life, whereas the new capital which Peter had built was something alien and artificial. The "return" to Moscow was like a withdrawal of the Russian people into its own shell and symbolized its determination to be master of its own house, without regard for foreigners.

The Bolshevik Revolution was accompanied by a certain amount of looting and acts of violence against the possessing classes. In all such moments of confusion the rats—criminals of the underworld— come out of their holes; it did not add to Bolshevik prestige abroad that many of them wore Red armbands or rosettes and posed as "commissars confiscating bourgeois property."

There was at once a spontaneous rush from the poorer quarters of the cities and towns to secure lodging in the houses of the wealthy. This too was chalked up against the Bolshevik account. On the other hand, the Red Guards did their best to suppress looting and disorder, and there was a famous episode in Petrograd, where mobs had invaded the wine cellars, when bottles were broken by thousands and casks broached so that fire-hoses could pump the contents into the river and canals. At the outset, indeed, Lenin seems to have wished, or at least been willing, to co-operate with the bourgeoisie in the urgent tasks of starting his administrative machine and of buttressing the shattered structure of Russia's national life. His overtures were generally cold-shouldered. Thus the personnel of the Foreign Office walked out in a body when Trotsky invited their collaboration. It was the same with other departments of state, with the banks and financiers and big manu- facturers, although the judiciary and the legal profession as a whole proved for a time more amenable, as did the junior employees of the posts and telegraphs. Many scientists, including the famous physi- ologist Pavlov, continued to work unperturbed, and their example was largely followed by the theatrical profession, by musicians and members of the ballet corps. The attitude of the bourgeoisie, soon developed into a regular boycott, can be ascribed to the stubborn streak in the Russian character, which led them, even at the expense of their own interests, to let the Bolsheviks "stew in their own juice." There was, too, their conviction, widely shared abroad, that the Bolshevik regime could not last long. Lenin himself surprised an English friend of mine by saying gleefully one cold January morning, "Well, we have now held power longer than the Paris Commune," as if that was cause for satisfaction. The persistence of belief in the instability of the Bolshevik regime did much to hamper a later settlement between the Soviet Union and the Western Powers.

Lenin met bourgeois passive resistance, which he bluntly described as sabotage, head-on. When the banks and financiers held aloof, he decreed nationalization of the banks. He created a Supreme Economic Council to manage the large factories, which were also nationalized, and to handle big business. Actually it was not until May, 1918, that any one industry was fully nationalized, when a sugar monopoly was decreed under the management of the Supreme Economic Council. In June similar monopolies were announced, mainly for purposes of internal revenue, on tobacco, matches, spices, tea and coffee. The important oil industry was nationalized at the same time, and at the end of the month a decree was issued to seize all industrial and commercial enterprises with a capital of a million roubles or upwards, as state property henceforth. Many commentators have regarded these measures as the first steps towards the era of "Militant Communism," which began in the late summer of 1918 and lasted for three years. In my opinion they were acts of self-protection, adopted unwillingly or at least prematurely, to prevent "sabotage" from stopping the wheels of industry and trade. It goes without saying that they tended to envenom relations between the Bolsheviks and capitalists in Russia and the West.

A series of decrees which brought great odium upon the Bolsheviks were those which abolished privileges hitherto enjoyed by the Orthodox Church and confiscated its immense holdings of real estate and other property, with the exception of sacred vessels, jewelled icons and vestments, whose value was imposing. The original confiscation of Church land, which was later followed by an order to close and seize monasteries and convents, was part of the first Bolshevik pledge that land henceforth should belong only to those who worked it. The order against the monasteries and convents, which had flourished in Holy Russia and given useful service in education and care for the sick and needy despite charges of corruption and misconduct, did not come into effect until later, when Lenin saw that he would have to fight all "bourgeois" opposition. It was, however, not universally applied at first, and the Bolsheviks seem to have been reluctant to force issues with the Church, which had a strong hold upon the peasant masses.

At the outset they contented themselves with "disestablishing" the Orthodox Church and proclaiming the equality of all religions in Russia and universal religious freedom. "Henceforth," they said, "churches and priests of all faiths become a charge upon their congregations instead of being supported by state grants or accumulated wealth. A Jewish, Roman Catholic, or Protestant congregation has as much right to have its priests and place of worship anywhere in Russia as the Orthodox faith, whose privileges now cease."

The effect was immediate. With a few exceptions the whole strength of the Orthodox faith was thrown in the counter-revolutionary balance, and everywhere at home and abroad its sharpest weapons—notably anti-Semitism, which was responsible for the revival of the forged "Protocols of Zion," and "pogroms" by "White" forces that claimed thousands of Jewish victims in the Ukraine from Kiev to Odessa—were directed against the "godless Bolshevik usurpers." The victory over the White generals undoubtedly was accompanied by vengeance upon the Church that aided them, and in the minds of the victors the bitterness remained.

The Bolsheviks had three reasons for hostility towards the Church, two of which were obvious but the third more subtle. First, they regarded it as one of the principal pillars of the Tsarist regime, to which it was bound by ties that were centuries old. It was also owner of vast wealth, and therefore by interest and tradition opposed to the Bolsheviks and their system. Second, religion itself advocated the exact antithesis of Bolshevik teaching. The Bolsheviks wished to stir up the masses, to spur them to revolt, to make them think for themselves and to capitalize their discontent. Religion, they thought, was, as Marx put it, "opium for the people," to keep them satisfied "in that state of life in which it pleased God to place them" here on earth, so that their submission and obedience would later win them a place in Heaven, as the parable of Lazarus and Dives suggests. But it was precisely this apathetic acceptance of misery and oppression that the Bolsheviks were most anxious to destroy, so that on these two counts they and the Church were immediately locked in conflict.

Finally, Bolshevism itself had many of the aspects of a new fanatical religion, which, like all new religions, was a foe to earlier faiths. It accepted no supernatural deity, no life beyond the grave, but it was compact of dogma and doctrine, its followers were zealots for a Cause above themselves, and to complete the parallel, it even had books of Authority and Power, the works of Marx and Lenin, whose "texts" were cited as affirmatively by orthodox Bolsheviks as those of the Bible and Koran by Christians and Mohammedans.

The Church had naturally been antagonized by the seizure of its property, by the avowed atheism of the Bolsheviks, and by the fact that many of its representatives, great and small, had perished in the first storm of the revolutionary struggle. It was, too, conservative by tradition, although it contained powerful elements which had long been advocating reform in regard both to a more liberal system of government and within the Church itself. In the months immediately following the Revolution it did not attempt to challenge Bolshevik authority, but the village priests in particular shared the anti-Bolshevik sentiment which had been growing under the influence of the Left Social-Revolutionaries. The latter, as related earlier, broke with the Bolsheviks over the Brest-Litovsk treaty, on patriotic grounds. There were, however, other reasons for the breach between the countryside and the Bolsheviks. First of all, the cities and towns had to be fed, but they were unable to provide goods for the peasants in return for their produce. The peasants declined to accept paper money, which they found worthless, and this led to a system of unpopular food requisitions. The Bolsheviks seem to have done their utmost to supply the peasants with goods, but the shortages in the cities were already so great that little could be done. They also tried to institute a rationing system of food and commodities in the urban centers, but "speculation" and black markets were so rife that in March, 1918, Lenin founded the Extraordinary Commission (Che-ka). Its chief function was at first to combat speculation, but growing clouds in town and country alike dictated its use as an instrument against counter-revolution, which soon became its principal task and remained so when its name was later changed to OGPU, or Gay-pay-oo, and later still to NKVD (Department of the Interior). A rose by any name . . . remains a rose.

A secondary but serious peasant grievance arose from Bolshevik unwillingness to give any documentary titles to land. The peasants argued that Lenin had promised them land free from mortgage or rent. Why, then, they asked, did he not give each man a stamped paper to confirm his ownership? Village resentment grew steadily, and by the spring of 1918 the Bolsheviks could not fail to perceive that grave trouble was impending. The resentment of the former bourgeoisie was implacable. Their agents and political parties, the Cadets, Mensheviks, and Right Social-Revolutionaries, were ever more active and daring. Generals and other army leaders in the provinces, especially the Cossack region of the North Caucasus, had recovered from the shock of revolution and were openly recruiting battalions of officers and "trusty" troops. The peasants sullenly nursed their grievances, which were fanned by the Left Social-Revolutionaries. Worse still, there was discontent amongst the urban workers. Like the Children of Israel after the Exodus, they grumbled that they had been led into a wilderness. Even the Red Guard in Petrograd and Moscow showed signs of disaffection. In all of this no doubt there was an element of inevitable reaction from the extravagant hopes which had attended the hour of victory. The Bolsheviks were learning that it was far easier to destroy than to construct, and were greatly hampered not only by the lack of trained administrators but of technicians, from directors of banks, factories or stores down to engineers and bookkeepers.

The first evidence of trouble, however, came from an extraneous cause. During Russia's last year of war a free Czechoslovak corps, some fifty thousand strong, had been formed to fight side by side with the Russians against the Austrian oppressors of their fatherland. They were technically war prisoners, but actually had moved over to join the Russians whenever possible, to escape from the hated Austrians. After the Bolshevik Revolution the Allies suggested that this corps be moved across Siberia to Vladivostok, whence the Allies would transport them to the Western Front. The Bolsheviks agreed on condition that the Czechs allowed themselves to be disarmed. Artillery and tanks were indeed surrendered, but the Czechs retained machine-guns and rifles, and by the middle of April their trains were strung across the Trans-Siberian Railroad from Kazan on the Volga to the outskirts of Vladivostok. At this point, by accident or design, reports became prevalent in Western Europe that the Bolsheviks were rearming Austro-German prisoners and sending them back westwards to fight against the Allies. As a matter of fact, this report was carefully investigated by an Allied military mission from Moscow and found to be baseless; the Russians were simply repatriating unarmed Austro-German prisoners in accordance with the Treaty of Brest-Litovsk. The rumor, however, reached the Czech trains, where it caused such fury and commotion that when one of their detachments met a trainload of Austro-German prisoners somewhere in Siberia about the middle of May, there was a bloody scuffle. Red soldiers tried to intervene and were shot down by the Czechs. Lenin at once demanded that the Czechs give up their arms. They not only refused but successfully resisted Red attempts to disarm them by force. By June they were virtually at war with the Bolsheviks throughout Siberia, and at the end of the month their Vladivostok forces upset the Bolshevik regime there and replaced it by a pro-Ally "Liberal" government. The smouldering discontent of the peasants and other elements of the population then burst into open flame, and Siberia changed almost overnight from Red to White. By the end of July the tail of the Czech column had become its head, and was moving westwards towards the Urals with the slogan "Free Russia from Red Tyranny."

As might be expected, the various Czechoslovak contingents formed rallying points for the anti-Bolshevik movement in the Siberian towns where their trains were halted. Tens of thousands of formerly privileged classes had managed to escape to Siberia, including officials, functionaries and officers of the Tsarist Army. With Czech support they hastened to set up local governments, although as yet there was no central authority. Meanwhile regiments of ex-officers and "loyal" soldiers were created to join the Czechs as they moved westwards. Early in July one such force approached the Ural city of Ekaterinburg (later Sverdlovsk) where the Tsar with the Empress and their children and half a dozen members of the household had been living for some weeks, comfortably enough in a large house, but none the less prisoners. Perhaps it had been Lenin's intention to allow the Imperial Family to leave Russia via Vladivostok, and there is reason to believe that his representative in Ekaterinburg tried to protect them against local vengeance. But the workers of Ekaterinburg could not forget the punitive expeditions of General Rennenkampf carried out in the Urals by the Tsar's orders after the abortive revolution of 1905-06. Seventy thousand men and women are alleged to have perished in this bloody repression, whose iron entered deep into the Ural soul. When news came that the "Whites" were advancing from the West, the local soviet held a hasty meeting which decided to execute "Nicholas the Murderer"—that was the phrase they used—and all those with him, the sentence to be carried out immediately. Shortly after midnight the Imperial party was told to "prepare for a long journey." The Tsar apparently had no inkling of the fate in store, for he merely grumbled about waking up the children in the middle of the night. The victims were led downstairs to a ground-floor basement where they were immediately shot to death, probably with machine-guns, as the walls and floor were pitted with bullet-holes when the Whites captured the city a few weeks later. The bodies were taken to the neighboring woods and burned so completely that no vestige remained, although a large emerald, supposed to have been sewn by the Tsarina into her clothing, is said to have been found in the middle of the burnt patch. At that it is possible that only the clothing was burned and that the bodies were weighted and thrown into one of the many surrounding lakes. All accounts of the killing, which took place on the night of July 18, 1918, written then or later, agree that every one of the victims was riddled with bullets and that none of them could possibly have escaped. This wanton deed sent a thrill of horror through the Western world and did much to strengthen the hand of Soviet Russia's enemies.

Lenin had no delusions about the approaching crisis and made no attempt to palliate ominous symptoms by wishful thinking. To the outer world the Bolshevik leaders appeared as a resolute bloc prepared to use any means, however harsh, expend every effort, however desperate, to hold what they had won. The official history of the Communist Party, written many years later with the partial purpose of exposing Trotsky's insincerity and the criminal weakness, or worse, of his followers, stresses divisions and doubts in the Bolshevik Central Committee, but no sign of this was apparent in the early months of 1918 as Lenin mobilized his forces to defend the Revolution. Decree after decree was issued to counteract passive resistance and centralize the state's resources under Bolshevik control. The powers of the Extraordinary Commission (Che-ka) created in December of the previous year were widely extended, and its ruthless chief, Felix Djerjinsky, was given unlimited scope and powers against all forms of counter-revolution. On April 2nd conscription was reintroduced, and the Red Guard was replaced by a real Red Army, to whose crimson flag recruits flocked by tens of thousands. Munition plants which had been in process of conversion for peacetime production swung back again to war work. Communists everywhere, who now numbered over a quarter of a million, were galvanized into feverish activity and warned that their lives must be held of no account in the coming trial by fire.

The first blow was struck by the Social-Revolutionaries, whose two wings, Left and Right, had made common cause against the hated Bolsheviks under the leadership of Kerensky's former War Minister, the veteran conspirator and arch-plotter, Boris Savinkov. By his orders the residence of the German Ambassador in Moscow, Count Mirbach, was bombed on July 6th and Mirbach was shot to death. Savinkov's purpose was clearly to provoke a rupture with Germany, but the Germans then were staking everything upon their final offensive in France—launched on July 15th and shattered by Foch's counter-blow four days later—and contented themselves with a sharp protest and a demand for punishment, which the Bolsheviks were only too eager to grant. Thus foiled, but undiscouraged, Savinkov made a surprise seizure, with a comparatively small force, of the town of Yaroslavl, one hundred and eighty miles north of Moscow on the railroad to Archangel through Vologda, due east of Petrograd. It is worth recalling that when the Soviet Government fled from Petrograd to Moscow, at the time of the Brest-Litovsk negotiations, the ambassadors of Britain, France and the United States had withdrawn with their staffs to Vologda. It is impossible to say how far the Allies were implicated in Savinkov's revolt, although the Bolsheviks have always declared that Allied officers and other agents conducted or prepared the wrecking of freight trains carrying copper, scrap iron, grain and oil to Germany under the Treaty of Brest-Litovsk. Savinkov hoped to make Yaroslavl a center of insurrection, and doubtless counted on the Czechoslovaks to divert the Kremlin's attention. But their vanguard was still east of the Ural Mountains, and the young Red Army struck so swift and hard from Petrograd and Moscow that the rebel stronghold was conquered in less than two weeks. Savinkov left his followers to die and escaped in disguise to Poland. The Social-Revolutionaries then resorted to their old and favorite weapon, personal assassination.

In Tsarist days the question of individual assassination had been a matter of more than academic discussion between the Bolsheviks and other revolutionary groups. It was practised consistently by the Social-Revolutionaries and the anarchists, but the Bolsheviks had always condemned it, not from humanitarian motives but as ineffective and likely to provoke costly reprisals. Lenin also made it clear that he preferred mass action to individual action, and thought that time and energy were better spent in mass education and preparation for action than in isolated terrorist blows. The Social-Revolutionaries, however, thought differently, and on the night of August 30, 1918, an S-R. girl named Fanny (or Dora) Kaplan seriously wounded Lenin as he was leaving a factory meeting in Moscow. The next day Uritsky, head of the Petrograd Che-ka, was shot dead by another S-R. assassin. These two acts unleashed the celebrated "Red Terror," which for once required no exaggeration by the Soviet's enemies abroad. Five hundred of the most prominent "bourgeois" Russians that the Che-ka could lay hands upon were immediately killed in Moscow and Petrograd, not, it was frankly admitted, on account of any complicity in the assassination campaign, but simply as a warning and example, to strike terror in the hearts of the regime's opponents. One of the leading Chekists, Latsis, wrote a monograph defending, or rather explaining, the Terror, which he said was designed to save greater bloodshed later by shedding some blood now. Latsis wrote in substance, "We shall frighten you into submission; innocent or guilty, you will never know when or where the blow may fall upon you." To heighten the effect, Che-ka arrests were invariably carried out in the dead of night, and often the families of victims were left in total ignorance of their fate.

Lenin's condition was critical for several weeks, and the surgeons then found it impossible to extract a bullet which had lodged near the upper part of his spine. This may well have shortened his life.

The beginning of the Terror, provoked as it was by the Social-Revolutionaries, may be said to have marked also the outbreak of the Civil War and foreign intervention, and the introduction of the "Militant Communism" era which lasted for three years. In actual fact the time-coincidence was not exact; the Terror began at the end of August, whereas the Czechs, soon joined by anti-Bolshevik Russians, opened hostilities in June. The first foreign "invasion" was made by the British at Murmansk in July, ostensibly to prevent large supplies of war material which had accumulated there from

being shipped to the Germans as part of the Brest-Litovsk "tribute."
Three weeks later several members of the British, French and
American embassies moved suddenly from Vologda to Archangel,
where a British armed contingent two thousand strong disembarked
on August 2nd, abolished the local soviet and set up a "Provisional
Government of the North." This force was subsequently reinforced
by British and American troops to the number of 25,000 men and
20,000 White Russian soldiers. About the same time British and
French troops landed at Vladivostok, followed by a Japanese division on August 12th (later increased to 70,000 men) and two
American regiments from the Philippines on the 15th and 16th.
In this case the pretext for invasion was to protect the Czechoslovaks.

The advent of Militant Communism was gradual rather than fixed
upon any definite date. Nevertheless, it was closely connected with
the Civil War and Intervention, against which it and the Terror were
used as means of retaliation and self-defense.

Chapter 4

THE HOSTILE CIRCLE

THE TWO-AND-A-HALF YEARS from the spring of 1918 to the autumn of 1920 had a vital effect upon the future of Soviet Russia and its relations with the rest of the world. One might almost say that the "character" of the new regime and its citizens was formed and hardened in the fire of civil war and by the long fight against hunger, disease, hardship, and at times defeat. At the outset the Civil War caught the Bolsheviks ill-prepared, with depleted resources of munitions and supplies and half-trained troops which were often led by former Tsarist officers of doubtful loyalty. Attempts to insure the Army against this weakness by attaching Bolshevik commissars, without military experience, to every unit, produced a confusion of powers which often did more harm than good. At first sight it seemed that the "Whites" held most of the trumps. They occupied Siberia and most of the Caucasus provinces up to Rostov-on-Don, and had strong jumping-off places in the North and West. From their foreign supporters they received armed assistance—an Anglo-Japanese victory over the Red forces on the Ussuri River won back the Maritime Provinces of Siberia—and great quantities of war equipment and supplies, foodstuffs and money.

On the other hand Bolshevik territory formed the solid center of a hostile circle. They were united, single of purpose, and ready for any sacrifice of their energies and lives; whereas the Whites and their foreign advisers were constantly at loggerheads, with leaders, both military and political, who often cared for nothing but the promotion of their personal interests.

In those years of struggle and tribulation the Bolsheviks were driven to three fundamental conclusions by which their policies were determined. First, that the rulers of the capitalist countries of the West were their implacable enemies, never to be trusted, least of all when they spoke fair-sounding words. Second, that the only sections of the Russian people upon whom they could entirely rely were the poor peasants and manual workers, with of course the soldiers drawn from both groups; the upper bourgeoisie, the former nobles, landlords, businessmen, industrialists, functionaries, ex-officers, the higher clergy and the rich peasants (kulaks) were bitterly hostile, while the middle peasants, small functionaries, petty businessmen, artisans and white-collar employees were not to be relied upon. Speaking generally, they would try always to side with the strongest and owe allegiance to the winner. In this conclusion allowance was made for exceptions, and it was recognized that the support of the "indeterminate middle," the small urban bourgeoisie and the middle peasants, was a prize worth fighting for and an almost necessary condition for success. [As will be seen later, this factor came prominently to the fore in Lenin's decision to introduce his New Economic Policy (NEP) in 1921, and in Stalin's campaign to collectivize agriculture in the years 1929 to 1933.] The third conclusion reached by the Bolsheviks was that Militant Communism as such, that is, an untried series of extremely radical measures which had rather been forced upon them than willingly adopted save by a handful of Marxian fanatics, was not yet a practical working system. The home and the family, religion and the Church, property and a diversified wage scale acording to merit and capacity, were ancient human institutions hallowed by centuries of usage, dearer to men's hearts than sexual laxity and marital freedom, than atheism, however philosophic, and than a complete pooling of ownership and a single flat rate of wages for everyone.

By way of corollary or accompaniment to these main conclusions, there were some secondary points for the Bolsheviks to consider. Thus foreign intervention revealed, to an extent which surprised many of the internationally-minded Bolshevik leaders, the strength of nationalism in the heart of the average Russian and the stubborn determination to defend every foot of *his* land against an alien invader. The Civil War taught the lesson that complete equality between officers and men, at least in time of action, was impossible. Here, too, there must be a distinction of rank in accordance with merit and capacity. Many of the Bolsheviks began to see, however dimly and reluctantly, that distinctions and gradations of rank were inevitable and necessary in any organized regime, especially if its system was highly centralized. They saw, too, that the abhorred class distinctions and class barriers were a natural rather than artificial growth, that "class" was simply the perpetuation of rank from one generation to another, and that if they wished to avoid the creation of a new "ruling class" they must be careful to prevent the transmission of rank and honor from father to son. The son might have an initial advantage due to his father's fame, but he must not inherit advancement, must earn it for himself. Finally it became apparent that though men would fight and die for a cause, there was something within them which called for recognition by their fellows; in short, that medals and decorations were not only the due reward of heroism but its outward symbol for others to emulate. Thus Napoleon, who knew soldiers, instituted the Legion of Honor.

It goes without saying that many of the factors I have mentioned had no immediate influence on Bolshevik thought or policy, but they were straws to show how future winds might blow. And something more than that, they were in a sense the yardstick to gauge two divergent schools of thought amongst the Bolshevik leaders. As stated earlier, the Bolsheviks presented to the outer world a solid front in which no crevices of disunion or faction were apparent. But the official history of the Communist Party records that despite Lenin's irresistible logic and firm hand upon the reins there were elements of discord among his followers. In the first place there was rivalry and jealousy between two groups, the so-called "Western exiles"—men like Trotsky, Radek, Kamenev and Zinoviev—who had spent most of the past ten years under the free skies of Switzerland, France or England, and the others—Stalin, Molotov, Voroshilov— who had continued to work "underground" in Russia during the period of repression at daily imminent risk of their liberty and life, spied upon, arrested, imprisoned, sent to Siberia, but somehow managing always to escape and resume their desperate struggle. In the truest sense of the phrase they had "borne the labor in the heat of the day," and could not but feel envy of the "Westerners" who not only had lived in ease and safety but had enjoyed close contact and companionship with Lenin himself. Such was Lenin's ascendancy that no one thought or suggested that he too was a Westerner. Lenin was a man apart, above and immune to any personal criticism. This, however, did not mitigate the divergence between his followers, which soon was extended from a personal to an ideological plane. The men who had stayed in Russia to be tried and toughened by persecution were more realistic and suspicious and less inclined to compromise. They regarded the Westerners, particularly Kamenev and Zinoviev, as impractical, softies and theorists. There was a further divergence, that speaking generally the Westerners laid greater stress upon the international aspects of Bolshevism and the possibility of World Revolution than did their rivals, who were primarily concerned with the Revolution in Russia and the prospect of building a successful Socialist state. During Lenin's lifetime the doctrine of internationalism held pride of place, and the smoldering dispute between the two groups never burst into open flame; but it was later to prove one of the causes of a disastrous and internecine struggle.

The Bolsheviks made up in energy and zeal what they lacked in military and administrative experience. In the early summer of 1918 the Czechs were beaten between the Urals and the Volga and retreated to the shelter of the mountains. Later in the year a strong Red Front was formed against the British and Americans in the North to bar any attempt on their part to join the counter-revolutionary forces in Siberia. In the autumn Stalin and Voroshilov conducted a brilliant defense of the key Volga city of Tsaritsin (now Stalingrad) against a White army which had advanced from the Don region with the aim of joining the Whites from Siberia and making a single front from the Urals to the Black Sea. [In the course of the Tsaritsin battle Stalin found it necessary to dismiss as untrustworthy former Tsarist officers appointed by Trotsky. The latter sent a cable of indignant protest, which is still preserved in the archives of the War Commissariat with a pencilled note across it in Stalin's writing, "Pay no attention." In his autobiography, "My Life," Trotsky mentions that there were at one time 30,000 ex-Tsarist officers in the Red Army, and stresses the sharp conflict of views between him and Stalin during this period. He also admits that he was constantly appealing to Lenin for support against Stalin and Voroshilov.] By the end of November the Bolshevik position was improved, although on the eighteenth of that month the chief "White" leader, Admiral Kolchak, had managed to unify Siberia by establishing at Omsk a pompously termed "All-Russian Government" with himself as dictator.

Winter brought a temporary breathing-space, which the Bolsheviks used to train their new troops, increase the production of arms and munitions, improve transport, and as far as possible accumulate supplies for a renewal of the struggle which Lenin believed was inevitable now that the Allied hands were freed by the defeat of Germany. He had not lost confidence in final victory, but foresaw that the fight would be long and bloody and inflict almost intolerable hardships upon the exhausted country. He accordingly instructed Chicherin, as Commissar of Foreign Affairs, to approach the Allies with a view to a peaceful settlement. Chicherin addressed a note to that effect to the American State Department on January 12th. Somewhat to his surprise, it is said, Lenin learnt that the American, British, French and Italian plenipotentiaries in Paris had considered favorably, on January 16th, a plan for Russian settlement suggested by Lloyd-George. The upshot was President Wilson's proposal that members of all Russian groups, including the Bolsheviks, should meet to negotiate peace on the island of Prinkipo, in the Bosporus. The Russian monarchist émigrés, however, and the "governments" of Admiral Kolchak and other White generals, refused to agree, and the matter was dropped for a time. Lloyd-George, with the support of Colonel House, then President Wilson's closest adviser, did not abandon hope of a settlement, and early in March a representative of the State Department, William Christian Bullitt, was sent to Russia with a project approved by the American and British delegations to the Peace Conference. Bullitt was met in Petrograd by Chicherin and Vice-Commissar of Foreign Affairs Litvinov, who had recently returned to Russia from an unsuccessful attempt to get himself accepted as Soviet Ambassador in London. They were at first somewhat skeptical, but finally decided that Bullitt's mission was important, and accompanied him to Moscow to talk with Lenin. After two days' discussion the Bolsheviks agreed to accept the Allied terms, which were (1) that all the various governments in the former territory of the Tsars, including the Bolsheviks, should retain and have jurisdiction over the area they now occupied; (2) that all foreign forces should be evacuated from Russian soil; (3) that all the different governments would demobilize their armies and grant amnesties to political prisoners; (4) that all of them should agree to recognize Russian debts, whether contracted by the Tsar or by the Provisional Government. Bullitt returned to Paris triumphant at the beginning of April and was warmly congratulated by Lloyd-George and Colonel House; but to their dismay President Wilson proved an unexpected obstacle. According to one story, he was annoyed that Bullitt had breakfasted with Lloyd-George before reporting to him. Alternatively it has been suggested that the President had lost confidence in Colonel House, with whom he was on the verge of a rupture. At any rate he refused to see Bullitt or take any further interest in the matter. Another factor which may have influenced him was a sudden rapid advance by Kolchak's forces, which occupied Kazan, on the Volga, before the end of March and once more planned to effect a junction with the White armies of General Denikin striking northward towards Moscow from the Donets region. It seemed probable—the French were especially confident—that the Russian problem would be solved by a White victory, and the American President probably decided that Kolchak would not accept the Bullitt conditions.

As it turned out, the Allies were once more the victims of their wishful thinking. Far from collapsing, the Red Army routed Kolchak and chased him back beyond the Urals. They checked Denikin, and an attempted diversion by Anglo-Russian forces in the North met disaster when the Russian rank and file mutinied, killed their Russian and British officers, set their heads on bayonets and marched over to join the Reds with all their arms and equipment. But a Bolshevik attempt to cut Denikin off from his base by an advance upon Rostov and the Cossack country further south was defeated, and in the month of September Denikin moved again northward to capture Orel, only two hundred miles south of Moscow, and to threaten Tula, the chief Bolshevik arsenal. Simultaneously another White general, Yudenich, stormed at Petrograd from the Estonian border with a force of 25,000 men led by British tanks and equipped with British artillery and machine-guns.

This double danger was alarming, and Trotsky goes so far as to say in his memoirs that Lenin for a moment contemplated abandoning Petrograd without a struggle. Of this there is no independent evidence, but there is little doubt that there was a moment of near-panic as Yudenich's scouts pushed forward to within sight of the former capital. On October 17th the Reds rallied and drove the enemy back across the Estonian border, where most of them died miserably of typhus in the next three months. Representatives of the American Red Cross who visited the White Russian camp at Narva declared that conditions there were appalling and estimated that of fourteen thousand men, eleven thousand perished in the course of a few weeks. Before the end of October Denikin was badly beaten near Orel, and his army literally fell to pieces. By December he had retreated to the port of Novorossisk on the Black Sea, from which he made good his escape to Constantinople with his staff, leaving the rest of his army to its fate. In Siberia Kolchak was driven from his capital, Omsk, in November, and resigned command a month later. In January he took refuge with the Czechs near Irkutsk, who handed him over to the Bolsheviks in return for a safe-conduct eastwards for their trains. Kolchak was put on trial before a military tribunal, condemned to death as a traitor and shot on February 7th. That marked the end of the Civil War, although the Crimea and a narrow bridgehead on the mainland and most of Transcaucasia were still occupied by anti-Bolshevik forces. Allied troops remained at Odessa, Archangel, Murmansk, and in the Maritime Provinces of Siberia, for some time longer, then gave it up as a bad job and went home. The Japanese, however, and their Russian puppets were not yet prepared to relinquish their hold upon Vladivostok and the coast up to Khabarovsk.

There were five reasons why the Soviet Government defeated intervention and won the Civil War:

1. Apathy of foreign intervention forces and their lack of coordination;
2. Corruption and political ineptitude of the White leaders;
3. Growth of military efficiency in the Red Army and its leaders;
4. Bolshevik ability to win over the middle peasants and small bourgeoisie;
5. Revolutionary outbreaks in European countries.

1. Apathy of foreign intervention.

Except for the Japanese, who invaded the Maritime Provinces of Siberia with such set purpose that they retained Vladivostok until virtually forced out in 1922 by the Washington Naval Conference, foreign intervention was only half-heartedly directed against the Bolsheviks, especially in the case of the Americans. General Graves, who commanded the American contingent in Siberia, made no secret of the fact that his main object was to keep an eye upon the Japanese. He maintained an impartial attitude towards the various Russian factions, and more than once his men defended the local population from notorious freebooters like the Cossack General Semyonof, who were operating with Japanese connivance. The American troops in the North made no bones about saying they were at war against Germany, not Russia. When Germany collapsed they staged a near-mutiny to the tune of "Home toot sweet," and were speedily withdrawn. The British northern contingents were mainly composed of volunteers, with specially high rates of pay; but they and their fellows in the Anglo-French military and naval units were physically and morally depleted by four long years of war. They took no active part in fighting the Reds, and were content to support their White allies. In the North the latter left them flat to join the Reds with arms and equipment, while in the French fleet at Odessa a serious mutiny occurred which led to the French evacuation of that important city.

Throughout the whole intervention period there was a deplorable absence of coordination and simultaneous action between the various anti-Bolshevik forces. Politically-minded French and British generals ran hither and yon with fantastic schemes of uniting the most disparate and mutually hostile races, parties, politicians, troops and soldiers in a sort of Christmas pudding to destroy the Bolsheviks; but in the whole two years from 1918 to 1920 the only joint action achieved by the foreign invaders or their Russian protégés was the widely separated attacks of Denikin and Yudenich in October, 1919, which ended in total failure.

2. Corruption and ineptitude of the Whites.

The two principal White leaders, Admiral Kolchak and General Denikin, were honest men and brave, competent soldiers, but neither had any political experience or acumen, and both were surrounded by greedy and unscrupulous subordinates intent upon feathering their own nests. The leaders were further bewildered by their French and British advisers, who generally pulled with vigor in opposite directions.

In the summer of 1919 the Bolsheviks intercepted a series of letters from an officer on Denikin's staff to an old friend on the staff of Kolchak. The writers said bitterly: "Colonel R"—Denikin's Chief of Staff, afterwards shot in a Nice hotel by one of his former subordinates—"is our evil genius. The General . . . trusts him implicitly and is completely under his influence . . . Unless he is removed our cause is ruined." He went on to say that ammunition, rifles and machine-guns, even tanks and artillery, were sold almost openly to infamous middlemen, by whom they were actually resold to the Reds. That soldiers at the Front were ill-fed and threadbare, without boots or greatcoats, while civilians at the Rear wore army coats and boots and were gorged with army rations. He concluded by begging his friend to persuade Kolchak, "who has the reputation of being a firm and honorable leader," to send as supreme commander a commission empowered to investigate these abuses and punish those responsible.

Unfortunately, conditions in Siberia were little better. American and British officers in Vladivostok have told how they saw freight cars of shells and military supplies destined for Omsk deliberately unloaded to make room for cases of champagne and brandy, boxes of French perfume, soap, silk stockings and lingerie and similar non-essential luxuries. As one of my friends put it bluntly, "The cities and towns under Kolchak's jurisdiction were a shocking combination of brothel and black market."

Worse, however, than corruption, or at least more useful to the Bolsheviks, were the attempts of the Whites to set the political clock back. Their advancing armies were accompanied by a host of former landlords, industrialists and businessmen burning to recover their former property. Kolchak and Denikin might issue liberal decrees to settle or postpone the vexed question of ownership, but in practice former landlords simply seized land, equipment and animals which they said had been "stolen" from them, and found plenty of officers and soldiers ready to shoot any peasants who resisted. The kulaks (rich peasants) and middle peasants had generally secured more of such spoils than their poorer brethren. These were the groups which had turned against the Bolsheviks and welcomed the Counter-Revolution, to which they now became the bitterest of foes. The same thing occurred in factories and business enterprises, usually accompanied by violence and shooting, in addition to the customary "execution" of alleged Communists and "Red agitators" who had been unable to escape. The peasants were further embittered by requisitions of food and livestock on a scale which the Bolsheviks had never equalled. Many of the White officers and their civilian friends spoke openly of the day when a Tsar would be restored and the rebellious masses "put back into their proper place."

3. Growth of Red Army efficiency.

Revolutions naturally release great stores of pent-up energy and bring to the fore men of humble origin but great capacity. This held good for the Red Army as for Napoleon's Marshals, and as the Civil War continued the Red commanders gained vastly in stature and experience. In that harsh school incompetence was rapidly eliminated, merit no less rapidly rewarded. The rank and file learned to trust, obey and follow the men who led them, and officers and soldiers together became a disciplined fighting force instead of a green if enthusiastic rabble. This process was hastened as the months passed by the substitution of young Red officers who had won their spurs for ex-Tsarist commanders of dubious loyalty.

4. Bolshevik "conquest" of the middle peasants and small bourgeoisie.

The attitude of the Bolsheviks towards the middle peasants and the numerous small handcraft workers in town and country was a subject of keen discussion in the Party's Central Committee at this time. Then, as often happened afterwards, the Bolsheviks wavered between the two phrases, "He that is not with us is against us" and "He that is not against us is on our side." During the Civil War the issue was decided for Lenin by the Whites, whose reactionary methods set all the peasants—eighty percent of the population—against them. He had frequently stressed the importance of the middle peasants as a link with the handcraft workers and the more energetic elements of the rank and file white-collar employees and the Army. Thus he wrote at this period: "Learn to come to an agreement with the middle peasant without renouncing the struggle against the kulak, and always relying firmly on the poor peasant." The program adopted by the eighth Congress of the Party, which met in March, 1919, contained the sentence: "We must undertake the gradual and systematic enlistment of the middle peasant in the work of Socialist construction." The middle peasants did not share in the minds of their fellow-villagers the unpopularity of the kulaks (the word means "fist") who squeezed the poor and landless peasants in a grasp of debt. The rapid collapse of Kolchak and Denikin was greatly aided by guerrilla activities behind their front lines, in which middle peasants and artisans took a vigorous part.

5. Revolutionary outbreaks in Europe.

A series of revolutionary movements in East-Central Europe—Berlin, Bavaria, Hungary and Latvia—tended to distract the attention of Allied leaders in Paris. They were due rather to war-exhaustion and despair than to Bolshevik propaganda, but were undoubtedly inspired by and sympathetic to the Bolshevik cause. Thus even in England the Labour Party, which was not Communistically inclined, conducted a successful campaign for "Hands off Russia" among the stevedores and dockworkers to prevent the loading of munitions and supplies for White or intervention forces.

It was partly with the idea of organizing and utilizing this foreign sympathy that Lenin formed the Third (Communist) International (Comintern) in March, 1919, although he had other more serious motives. The Bolsheviks had long believed that the Second International was Socialist in name alone, and that its members were enslaved by a spirit of compromise and cooperation with the ruling bourgeoisie, whose governments their leaders entered and whose lackeys they became. Lenin therefore had resolved to reconstruct the obsolete First International of Marx and Engels on a new and more permanent basis. The time, moreover, seemed ripe for Moscow to take the lead of the Communist parties that were springing up and gaining ground—actually gaining power in Hungary and Bavaria—in all directions, and Lenin may have still believed, however wishfully, in the possibility of international revolution. The first Congress of the new body voted the formation of an Executive Committee known as IKKI, with permanent headquarters in Moscow, presided over by Zinoviev, who was a member of Lenin's

"Politburo," as the small inner ruling junta of the Bolshevik Central Committee was called.

Whatever were the hopes with which the Comintern was launched, it probably did more harm than help to the Soviet State. At best it never had much more than a nuisance value, and its services in spreading Bolshevik doctrines abroad and in acquiring useful information about other countries were largely nullified by the harmful effect of charges of espionage and unwarranted interference. The very existence of the Comintern and its Moscow IKKI was an eyesore and challenge to capitalist governments, and undoubtedly delayed their recognition of the Soviet Union and consistently hampered the establishment of friendly relations.

Chapter 5

A TEMPORARY RETREAT

THE EXECUTION OF Kolchak marked the beginning of another short breathing-space for the Soviet Union. Accordingly the Ninth Congress of the Party, which now numbered over 600,000 members, devoted most of its attention to economic problems, especially industry and transportation, when it met in March, 1920. A State Planning Commission (Gosplan) had recently been formed, and the Congress approved a ten years' program for electrification, in connection with the development of the metallurgic industry. This was the first of the long-range "plans" which later became the central feature of Soviet economy. Shortly before the Congress convened, the Council of Workers' and Peasants' Defense had been transformed into the Council of Labor and Defense (STO) which was designed to act as a sort of General Staff for industry on the centralized basis of Militant Communism.

There was crying need for improvement in all directions. Agricultural production was only half of the pre-war total, and industry had fallen far lower than that, with the result that many workers and white-collar employees were forced into the semi-illegal life of "bagmen," as traffickers in food and other commodities were termed. The matter was complicated by the prospect of demobilizing a part at least of the Red Army, which had swollen to nearly five million. Trotsky conceived the idea of forming Labor armies, that is of Labor conscription, to use demobilized soldiers and bagmen under semi-military discipline, for the reconstruction of agriculture and industry. The measure was exceedingly unpopular with the workers, especially the labor unions, but Trotsky carried it through the Central Committee. It had the further ill effect of arousing the suspicion and enmity of the Poles, who professed to regard it as a device to avoid real demobilization and to prepare an attack upon them. (In the previous January France, England and Italy had raised the blockade against Russia with the tacit but mutual understanding that the Red Army would be reduced to a peacetime level.) The Soviet Government had offered peace to Poland in January, 1920, on terms similar to those accepted by Finland and Estonia, of no annexations or indemnities. Whether the Poles were genuinely alarmed by the Labor army, or whether their appetite was whetted by belief in Soviet weakness, by receipt of quantities of war material from France and by a food loan of $50,000,000 from the United States, is immaterial, because at the end of March they countered the Russian peace offer with a demand for the Polish frontier of 1772, a big payment in cash, and the occupation of the Russian town of Smolensk as a guarantee. When the Bolsheviks indignantly declined, Poland prepared openly for war and seized Kiev at the beginning of May, with much of the surrounding Ukrainian territory as well as a wide belt of Russian soil further north. Simultaneously the White General Wrangel, who still held the Crimea, extended his "bridgehead" on the mainland towards the Donets industrial region with the evident aim of joining hands with the Poles. The Bolsheviks appear to have been taken somewhat by surprise, but they soon rallied, retook Kiev in June and advanced along the whole front. The Polish retreat became a rout, and the Red Army swept on to the gates of Warsaw. In addition to the threat to the capital, powerful Red forces had advanced still further westwards on a line parallel to the German border; but the Left Wing of the Red Army had delayed before Lwow and Cracow instead of swinging northwards to complete a converging movement upon Warsaw. The agitation in Europe was profound. Though the Red outbreaks in Hungary, Bavaria, Saxony and Austria had been scotched, revolutionary sentiment was still strong and widespread. The French and British governments dreaded the possible effects of a sovietized Poland, which would in fact make Russia Germany's next-door neighbor.

Lenin was fully aware of the same possibility, and he is said to have insisted upon the drive against Warsaw when some of his military advisers were advocating a more cautious policy. After much hesitation the French Government decided that the transfer of troops through Germany might do more harm than good owing to unsettled conditions there, but they did send Foch's Chief of Staff, General Weygand, with a score of officers.

The French Mission reached Warsaw to find a train standing in the railroad station ready to evacuate the Polish Government, which had yielded to panic, although the Polish Commander-in-Chief, Marshal Pilsudski, was anxious to go on fighting. Weygand's arrival brought reassurance, and after a hurried council of war the Marshal and the General undertook a maneuver worthy of Foch himself. Like Foch at the first Battle of the Marne, they denuded their flanks of troops and made a strong attack in the center, southeast of Warsaw. By good fortune or design they found a gap in the Bolshevik lines and were able to outflank the Red center and left wing almost without striking a blow. The Reds retreated as rapidly as they had advanced, and most of their right wing sought safety by crossing the border into Germany, where they were disarmed and interned. Both armies were too exhausted for further combat, and the Polish forces halted when they had driven the enemy beyond their former frontiers. An armistice was signed in Riga on October 11th, and in the following March a peace treaty gave Poland some minor additions of territory in White Russia and the Ukraine.

Undismayed—or spurred—by their setback in Poland, the Bolsheviks struck at Wrangel, the last of the White Generals, who had been checked on the banks of the Donets River before he could join the Poles. Forced back into the Crimea, the Whites made a stand on the strongly fortified Isthmus of Perekop which linked the "island" to the mainland. By a daring march across the ice of an unusually early winter, the Bolsheviks turned the Perekop defenses and overpowered the Whites in a short but bloody battle. Immediately Wrangel's rear crumbled, like that of Denikin and Kolchak. With Franco-British aid he managed to evacuate a considerable part of his forces and civilian sympathizers to Constantinople; but the Bolsheviks were masters of the whole island by the end of November.

Thus ended the Civil War and Intervention, in complete victory for the Bolsheviks, but it had been won at a fearful cost. The harvest of 1920 was less than half the pre-war average—it actually fell to a little more than one-third in the following year—and at the end of 1920 it was estimated that industrial production was barely one-seventh of the pre-war total. The output of pig-iron in particular, which is the basis of modern industry, had dropped to little more than 100,000 tons, 2.4 percent of the pre-war figure. The production of coal was at an equally catastrophic level through flooding and neglect of mines, while the oil fields were still in the hands of anti-Bolshevik governments, although the latter were evicted without much trouble in 1921. There was an acute shortage everywhere of manufactured goods, as well as such necessities as bread and meat, fats, clothing, kerosene, soap and matches and medicine. Epidemics raged almost unchecked, and the death rate for the year is said to have reached the figure of eighty-five per thousand. Transportation was shot to pieces, with three-quarters of its locomotives and two-thirds of the freight cars destroyed or unfit for service.

To make matters worse, upwards of three million Russians had fled or been driven from their country. They included nobles, landlords, generals, bankers and industrialists, but the great majority of them were less prominent members of the former bourgeoisie, professional and business men, engineers and technicians—in short, the higher and better educated strata of the white-collar bourgeois class, managers and experts who received ample salaries and were the chief driving force in the economic life of the nation. Their defection increased the Bolsheviks' difficulties tenfold. It was a case of the blind leading the blind, or of a whole nation trying to pull itself up by its own bootstraps; the Bolsheviks had discipline, determination and energy, but they did not know how or where to begin.

It has pleased Soviet historians to blame the troubles of this period upon four years of imperialist war and three years of interventionist war; that is, to say naïvely that it was all the fault of native or foreign capitalists. There is some truth in this assertion, but one cannot overlook the stagnation and resentment caused by Militant Communism. As matters stood at the beginning of 1921, a preponderant majority of the Russian people were individualists, peasants, petty traders and homecraft workers. Except for soldiers and untrained functionaries, the remainder were industrial and white-collar workers now threatened with unemployment because there was no one to run or restart their factories, mines, mills and other enterprises.

Militant Communism's principle of a single wage level for all was killing initiative and incentive. Its rigid prohibition of private trade was bewildering and abhorrent to peasants and workers alike, and signs were not wanting that the relaxation of marital ties and the campaign against the Church were unwelcome to large sections of the proletarian masses. The Bolsheviks seemed for once to have lost touch with popular sentiment, and to have disregarded popular discontent in their preoccupation with plans for future policy and development. In March they were rudely awakened by a mutiny in the fortress of Kronstadt, which had been considered the cradle of the Revolution. Simultaneously the peasants of the central province of Tambov spontaneously but unanimously refused any longer to hand over their grain and other food products in return for worthless currency or empty promises. Troops sent to enforce obedience made common cause with the peasants, and the whole province flamed into disaffection which threatened to spread to neighboring areas.

The Bolsheviks have since claimed that both these revolts were prompted by counter-revolutionary agents, but in reality they were the first eruptions of long-pent grievances. There was, however, this difference between them: the Kronstadt rebels belonged to the armed forces and only indirectly expressed the dissatisfaction of the workers and peasants from whose ranks they were recruited, whereas Tambov was a direct protest against conditions which had become intolerable. Lenin therefore struck first and savagely at Kronstadt. The citadel was stormed with heavy cost of life, and the ringleaders were shot without pity. In Tambov, on the contrary, he used conciliation. Quantities of salt, kerosene, soap and cheap cotton cloth were rushed into the heart of the recalcitrant area and bartered for foodstuffs in the open, "free" markets. "Disaffection" promptly subsided, but its lesson was not lost upon Lenin, who probably had been less wedded to Militant Communism than some of his fanatical associates. At any rate he lost no time in putting before the Tenth Party Congress, which opened in March, a sweeping program of economic reforms. Its first plank was the replacement of the requisition system by a unified food tax, averaging about twelve percent of the peasant's production, to be paid in kind, grain, meat, vegetables, eggs or milk, as proved most convenient. The rest of his produce would remain at the peasant's disposal, for sale or barter or his own consumption. This was an urgent matter, and after approval by the Congress was established by decree. The second plank went further and marked not only the abandonment of Militant Communism but a distinct regression, as Lenin admitted, to non-socialist methods. Known as the New Economic Policy (NEP), it allowed "free" trade in shops and markets of cities, towns and villages by groups and individuals, middlemen and producers, without hindrance or restriction. Secondly, groups and individuals were henceforth permitted to engage in industrial and business enterprises, with the right to hire and fire labor and make what profits they could, subject of course to the trade union regulations and to state and municipal taxes.

After some discussion this, too, was approved by the Congress, but NEP was not legally established until the ninth of August, although free trade and small industrial production existed in practice all through the summer.

Although Lenin insisted that this startling change was only a temporary retreat, it was regarded abroad and by many Bolsheviks at home as a sign that the Socialist experiment had failed in the Soviet Union. Actually it was no more than an expedient to set rolling the idle wheels of industry and commerce, but it aroused keen opposition in the Party Congress, which by this time represented nearly 750,000 members. To some degree this was a foretaste of the prolonged and more bitter conflict which raged within the Party after Lenin's death, since in both cases a fanatical and vociferous body of Marxist diehards declared that practical measures of strictly national interest were heretical backsliding from the doctrines of Marxian-Socialist internationalism. There was also sharp divergence amongst the delegates to the Congress about the powers and functions of labor unions in the Soviet State. Feelings ran so high and differences of opinion were so violent on both these important questions that Lenin was led to make an impassioned plea for Party Unity, which he described as the cardinal and all-essential factor for this and every subsequent Congress to remember and preserve. In this connection it is interesting to note that the Congress ratified Lenin's appointment a few weeks earlier of Stalin as General Secretary of the Party. This was a key position of authority and influence, and it is most significant that Lenin awarded it to Stalin, leader of the "underground" laborers in Russia's vineyards during the pre-war period of repression, rather than to the more spectacular Trotsky or any of the Marxian purists among the "Western" exiles.

The Tenth Congress further authorized the Central Committee, as supreme permanent organism of the Party, to apply appropriate penalties to all Communists—including members of the Committee itself—guilty of violating party discipline, and especially of creating intra-party factions. Furthermore, the Central Committee was empowered to conduct a party-wide "purge" or test of members with a view to the reinforcement and maintenance of unity. The purge procedure had been instituted earlier to cope with the somewhat indiscriminate admission of new members to the Party during the Civil War, and in the year 1920 more than twenty thousand "undesirables" had been placed on probation or expelled. The touchstone by which Communists were tested was threefold, faith, works and conduct—a further instance of the parallel with religion— that is, knowledge of and belief in Marxist doctrine, obedience to party rules and instructions and performance of party duties, and personal behavior so scrupulously correct as to bring no slur upon the party name. At different periods exceptional stress was laid upon one or other of these three points, but serious dereliction in any of them was enough to warrant expulsion or a period of probation.

Intra-party controversy about NEP and the labor unions grew so fierce in the summer of 1921 that the charge of "factionism" (i. e. breaches of party discipline) was the chief criterion of the Purge (the Russian word is *chistka*, literally "cleansing") that year. The mechanism of the Purge was as follows: Every party member from high to low was called before the members of his cell, or unit, to answer the questions of a Board of Examiners appointed by the Central Committee. Other fellow-workers, friends or relatives, including non-Communists, might be present, to whom the Communist being examined could appeal for support and corroboration of his or her statements. The examiners also appealed to the "audience" to confirm or deny complaints and generally to elucidate each case. The 1921 Purge was so severe that the party membership was reduced from 732,000 (at the time of the Tenth Congress in March, 1921) to 532,000 at the Eleventh Congress in March, 1922. The Purge did not stop there; the efflorescence or "Saturnalia period" of NEP brought a host of new charges of "conduct unbefitting a Communist" against party members who yielded to the snares of Mammon and his fleshpots. Thus the Twelfth Party Congress, in April, 1922, represented a membership of only 386,000—scarcely more than half the 1921 figure.

Although the NEP decree was not actually signed until August 9, 1921, the intervening months after the Party Congress in March were spent in constructing and in some cases putting into action the machinery of transition. The most radical change involved was the reorganization of all national economy on a straight money basis. During the period of War Communism the financial tools of capitalism had been allowed to rust. Private banks, checks and securities had disappeared, and money had depreciated as more and more of the national budget was covered by inflation. By 1920 it was estimated that eighty-five percent of budget expenses was furnished by the emission of bank notes; the remainder was raised by requisition of food and commodities. For a time money not only lost value through inflation, but seemed almost to be passing from common use, as wages and salaries were "paid" in tickets which entitled the holder to a fixed portion of food and goods. Everyone lived rent-free, and there was no charge for travel on railroads, streetcars or other public means of transport. NEP quickly altered all that. Henceforth all State enterprises were ordered to issue a regular balance-sheet showing profits or losses. Cash wages were substituted for the ticket system, house-committees which acted as renting agents were authorized to charge rent on a graduated scale to correspond with the earnings and social position of the tenant (professional men and persons engaged in private business paid higher rates than workers or State employees) and were expected to maintain the premises under their charge in proper repair. Railroads and streetcars were permitted to charge fares for passengers and freight.

In these and other respects, such as the subsequent institution of a nationwide bank system, currency reform, and the formation of industrial and commercial "Trusts" financed by the new banks, NEP was, as its Communist critics declared, a reversion to capitalist methods. It was recognized as such by the Western nations, whose latent hostility was now dominated by the wish to do business with the Bolsheviks. In the spring of 1921 Great Britain signed a trade agreement with the Soviet which carried with it *de facto* recognition; similar agreements followed with Germany, Norway, Austria and Italy. Some Bolsheviks tried to explain NEP by the ambiguous phrase, "Socialist-Capitalism," but neither they nor foreigners seem to have realized that NEP was two things in one: first, a *temporary* expedient to hasten and facilitate national reconstruction; second, a reversion from the experimental, unpopular and unsuccessful system of Militant Communism to the tried and practical *methods* (not principles) of capitalism. NEP therefore was the first important step on a long road leading from the extreme Left towards the Center, and from the ideals of Internationalism and Communism to realities of patriotic self-sufficiency and self-defense, and of an economic system which might be described as State Capitalism, a term no more paradoxical than the Bolsheviks' own Socialist-Capitalism.

The part played by NEP in smoothing Russia's return to a more normal and balanced economy at home, and to the renewal of relations with the outer world, was enhanced by an event over which the Bolsheviks had no control. I refer to the Great Drought of the summer of 1921, when no rain fell upon Russia's richest grain fields along the Volga, in the North Caucasus and the Ukraine, from early May until the end of August. By midsummer it was apparent that the worst crop failure in Russian history was inevitable; for hundreds of miles the autumn and spring-sown grain barely covered the sun-cracked fields with a growth of foot-high withered stalks, brown and tenuous as hay. The specter of famine loomed imminent over forty million people whose last handfuls of grain had been used for seed, and who could expect small help from the rest of Russia, where other millions could hardly escape the same fate. Everywhere supplies were exhausted, and even the army reserves were dangerously low. By the middle of July over a million peasants had fled from their parched fields to urban railheads and the centers of Volga River transport, where they huddled in refugee camps rife with epidemics and the diseases of malnutrition. The magnitude of the impending catastrophe broke down the stubborn will and pride of the Bolsheviks. They allowed the internationally famous writer, Maxim Gorky, to appeal for aid to Herbert Hoover, chairman of the American Relief Administration (ARA) which had fed millions of starving children in Belgium and German-occupied France during the War and in Central and Eastern Europe afterwards. Hoover agreed to help, and his representative, Walter

Lyman Brown, quickly worked out a plan of action with Litvinov in Riga. It was first arranged that only children should be fed, but adults were soon included when it became evident that children could not be kept alive while their parents were allowed to die. The ARA had been supported by charitable contributions, but Russian need was so great that Congress allocated grain from government-owned stocks. At the peak of its activity the ARA was feeding eleven million Russians, children and adults. Other charitable bodies in Europe and America fed some three million more, and the Soviet Government took care of the rest. Altogether it was estimated that relief was extended to more than twenty-five million individuals. Deaths from starvation were held down below a million, but the toll of disease can hardly be computed. Perhaps altogether three million lives were lost, only a fraction of what might have been the most tragic death-roll in Russian history.

The crop failure silenced the last of NEP's Bolshevik opponents, who saw that even their most cherished principles must be sacrificed in order to avert complete disaster. Foreign aid to the stricken provinces had a yet more important effect. On one side it tended to destroy in the minds of Russians the intense hostility towards foreigners which had been provoked by years of Intervention. On the other, it conveyed, through foreign relief workers and the newspaper correspondents who accompanied them, a message to their countries that Russians were human beings instead of murderous fiends, that circumstances and centuries of ignorance and oppression were more to blame for the Revolution and its excesses than the Bolsheviks, and that the nation as a whole wanted nothing but to live and work in peace, and, if might be, to improve its sorry lot. Foreign relief thus helped to pave the way for better relations between the Soviet Union and the rest of the world, and its medical and sanitary departments gave the Russians a good start in the fight against epidemic diseases.

Chapter 6

GODS AND DEVILS

NEP WAS A strange and colorful panorama which opened timidly in 1921, flourished brightly in 1922 and 1923, and dolorously declined in 1924 and 1925. In the early autumn of 1921 business and industry were moribund in Moscow and the cities and towns of Russia. The skies of Moscow, Petrograd and the towns along the Volga were unmarred by factory smoke, and almost the only stores open in the Soviet capital were those selling musical instruments, obsolete scientific apparatus, secondhand books, apples and vegetables, and hairdresser-barber establishments—little oases of activity in long rows of shuttered or boarded-up window-fronts. Gradually the stores became more numerous, as former businessmen crept like cautious mice from their holes with commodities of all kinds that had been safely hidden for years. Moscow burst into a frenzy of cleaning, painting and repairing; streets were repaved, water and gas mains relaid, the rubble of burnt houses removed or neatly piled. By Christmas business was brisk throughout the city, and unemployment greatly diminished as factories large and small, state-owned, private or co-operative, were reopened. By universal consent Moscow had not had such a Christmas since 1913; it was like the old Roman Saturnalia festival held in the last week of December, when for three days servants and slaves were free to revel in their masters' houses. So, too, the "NEPmen," as the new private traders were called, made merry and lived high while their Bolshevik masters were glumly preoccupied with the Purge, which involved suspension of one Party member in every three. Amongst

75

other innovations the Moscow Soviet licensed gambling casinos for roulette and baccarat—to provide funds for repair of public utilities, streets and buildings—where one might see twenty-five thousand dollars in Russian and foreign gold coin, foreign bank notes, and piles of million-rouble Soviet notes (then worth about twenty dollars) staked on a single card. Luxurious private carriages drawn by well-bred trotters began to appear on the streets, and new-rich NEPmen gave ten-course banquets with foreign vintage wines in reopened de luxe restaurants at fifty or a hundred dollars a head. It was indeed a Saturnalia, while it lasted, and a fortunate few not only made good money but managed by hook or crook to escape with it abroad.

For a year or more it seemed as though the Bolsheviks were content to let the reins fall on the back of the Russian horse, but NEP and the Volga famine combined had the somewhat unexpected effect of reviving the dormant struggle between them and the Orthodox Church. It might be more correct to say that the famine was a pretext which the Bolsheviks used against the Church because they feared that it would profit by NEP's admitted retreat from Militant Communism. They may, too, have seen that conditions inside the Church lent themselves to an attack.

As pointed out in an earlier chapter, the Bolsheviks and the Church were clearly on opposite sides, but somehow there had never been a real showdown between them. During the Civil War the issue had so long wavered between defeat and victory that the Bolsheviks were doubtless reluctant to take violent action against the Church lest that throw an imponderable force into the balance against them, while the Church leaders in Moscow, Petrograd and other urban centers in Bolshevik hands did not dare to oppose them openly. The result was a sort of stalemate or armed truce.

The Orthodox Church of Russia had not been unaffected by the fall of Tsarism. Its first act after the abdication of Nicholas II was to elect its leading Bishop, the Metropolitan Tikhon, to the office of Patriarch, which had been abolished by Peter the Great more than two hundred years before. The Patriarch was supreme head of the Russian Church only, and had not the same authority over the other Orthodox Churches of the world as the Pope of Rome over Roman Catholicism, although to Russian churchmen his position was hardly less important and symbolic than that of the Pope to Roman Catholics. Church leaders had thus hastened to re-establish the Patriarchate because they hoped that it would help to check the growing demand for Church reform. The clergy of Russia was divided into two categories, the "White" and the "Black." The Black clergy were trained in monasteries and seminaries and took the same vows of celibacy and renunciation of worldly things as Roman Catholic priests. They formed the ruling hierarchy of the Orthodox Church, whereas the White, or lower clergy, took no such vows—indeed were required to marry—and were the village priests or clerical rank-and-file throughout Russia. For many years before the collapse of the Empire there had been a reform movement to abolish the distinction between White and Black, which virtually restricted the former from high Church office, and to simplify Church ritual by holding services in modern Russian instead of the ancient Slavonic, which few laymen could understand. At first sight the restoration of the Patriarchate was a victory for the ritualists and reactionaries in the Church, but the reform movement continued to gain strength.

The introduction of NEP in August, 1921, undoubtedly gave fresh confidence to the Church, and the traditional ceremony of "Blessing the Waters" was held that winter on the ice of the Moscow River by Patriarch Tikhon with great pomp and dignity and without molestation by the authorities. But only a few weeks later an important churchman, Archbishop Yevdokim of Nijni Novgorod, on the Volga, issued an appeal to all true believers to give their possessions to aid the victims of the Volga famine. "Even Church wealth should also be sacrificed," said the Archbishop, "for in this hour of terrible need he who giveth to the poor lendeth to the Lord." He quoted the New Testament to support his appeal, and referred pointedly to the example of Patriarchs in medieval days who sacrificed Church wealth to aid the country against Tartar or Polish invaders.

Archbishop Yevdokim was known to be one of the chief Reformers in the higher ranks of the clergy. With his supporters, Bishops Antonin of Moscow, Tikhon (not the Patriarch) of Kiev, and Peter, the Metropolitan of Siberia, he had criticized Patriarch Tikhon and the Metropolitans Agafangel of Yaroslavl and Benjamin of Petrograd as ultra-conservative. It is impossible to say whether he was acting in good faith as a Christian or was an ambitious self-seeking prelate, although contemporary evidence favors the former view. Churches and religious communities in the famine-affected areas had already assigned their treasures of jewels and precious vessels for relief, and there had been many public demands that their example should be followed by the Church establishments of Moscow, Kiev and Petrograd, whose treasure reputedly was enormous.

At any rate, the Bolsheviks hastened to use this apple of discord thrown into the Church's midst. On February 11, 1922, *Izvestia*, mouthpiece of the Soviet Government, announced that the authorities had empowered the Minister of Justice to seize without delay the wealth of *all* religious bodies and sects. The Patriarch and his associates must have regarded Yevdokim's action and the Government's decision as parts of the same piece. Far from acceding willingly to his appeal, they recommended a policy of passive resistance to the seizure of Church treasure. Armed clashes occurred in several cities, including Petrograd and Moscow, with the result that Metropolitan Benjamin and other Church leaders were arrested and the Patriarch Tikhon was placed under "domiciliary arrest" in the Donskoy monastery near Moscow.

The Bolsheviks pressed the advantage given them by the sincerity, credulity or ambition—whatever one cares to call it—of the Reformers. With official approval and support—about this no doubt is possible—the Reform movement was embodied in a new schismatic organization called "The Living Church," which not only demanded democratization of the Church hierarchy, the removal of distinctions between Black and White clergy, and the holding of services in modern Russian, but claimed that henceforth the supreme authority of the Church should be vested in an annual congress elected by all believers. As the critics of the Living Church were quick to point out, this was nothing short of a Church soviet on the usual Bolshevik lines. Archbishop Yevdokim seems to have been startled by the course events were taking, which speaks well for his initial sincerity. Henceforth he receded into the background and the principal place in the Living Church was taken by a priest named Vedensky, formerly a popular preacher in a fashionable Petrograd church, and a more enigmatic figure named Krasnitsky, known as "The Red Priest" because of his reported affiliations with Bolshevik

circles and his public attempts to reconcile Christian doctrine with
Bolshevism.

In August, 1922, the Living Church held its first congress in
Community Hostel No. 3 of the Moscow Soviet—the address is significant—and passed resolutions abolishing the monasteries and the
Black clergy, approving the Soviet Revolution and its government,
and demanding other measures of reform. The Reform leaders
claimed that they had received from Patriarch Tikhon authorization to hold the congress in the name of the Church. Tikhon, however, was under arrest and his supporters declared that he had not
given this authorization or that it had been extracted from him
under pressure. As I stated earlier, Tikhon had not actually opposed
the requisition of Church treasure, but was said to have issued a
circular instructing his subordinates to avoid it, and he and they
were therefore held responsible for such resistance as was offered.
Bishop Benjamin and several priests in Petrograd and Moscow were
tried and condemned to death. During their trial the prosecution
professed to have established the complicity of Patriarch Tikhon,
and it was announced that he too would be tried later on a capital
charge. Thus the Living Church seemed firmly in the saddle. Its
opponents, the Patriarch and the other Conservative leaders, were
imprisoned or cowed, and it basked in the approval of the authorities, but its success was more apparent than real. It was reckoned
at the time that perhaps seventy percent of the Russian churches
paid temporary lip-service to Living Church authority and approved the Reform movement in principle, but that not more than
ten percent were sincere in their allegiance. The vast majority, even
of the temporizers, felt in their hearts that the Living Church had
made an evil compromise with the Mammon of Unrighteousness.

Nevertheless, the priests in Moscow and elsewhere were executed,
and Metropolitan Benjamin of Petrograd shared their fate, and the
Patriarch and his other chief supporter, Metropolitan Agafangel,
remained in prison without any sign of protest or even disapproval
from Russian churchmen. The Bolsheviks may well have thought
that they had divided in order to rule, that the split within the
Church which they had fostered had fatally weakened their
sole remaining adversary on Russian soil. In January, 1923, on the
anniversary of the Russian Church Christmas, a blasphemous anti-

religious demonstration was staged by the Communist Youth Organization in the Red Square of Moscow, which ended with the burning of parody-images representing the "gods and devils of religion" and sacred icons, banners and texts. Even this roused no word of protest or evidence of opposition.

Two months later there was held in Moscow the public trial of a score of Roman Catholic priests of Polish origin, on charges of high treason. The basis of the charge was similar to that on which Russian Orthodox clergymen had earlier been condemned, of organizing obstruction to the Government and its decrees; but there was the additional accusation that some of the accused had engaged in treasonable activities during the Polish War of 1920. A further point involved was the ancient European quarrel as to whether Roman Catholic priests in any country might invoke the authority of Rome against that country's laws.

The trial began with violent denunciations and assertions by the prosecutor, which the defendants met with dignified denials. The evidence produced against them was not such as to have warranted their condemnation by a Western tribunal, but Article 58 of the Soviet Penal Code, the "blanket" law against treason, is so generalized and far-reaching that no one in Moscow was greatly surprised when the accused were found guilty and condemned to death. It was generally expected that the sentences would be commuted to imprisonment and that all the accused would shortly be exchanged for Red political prisoners in Polish hands, as had happened in other cases. There is reason to believe that the Soviet Government contemplated this easy and face-saving solution, but the ground was cut under its feet by a thunder of protest against the verdict and demands for immediate release of all the accused, which came not only from Rome but from all over the world. The Bolsheviks accordingly found themselves in the position of being forced to yield to foreign pressure, a point on which they were inordinately sensitive. They were willing, they declared, to spare all the defendants who had opted for Polish citizenship, but Monsignor Butchkevich, who had retained Russian nationality, was, they said, guilty of a heinous crime for which he must pay the penalty. Monsignor Butchkevich was executed on March 31st.

From a political standpoint this execution was one of the greatest errors ever made by the Soviet Government. Churches of all creeds and denominations throughout the world united in condemning the brutal and unjustified murder, as it was universally termed. Foreign Commissar Chicherin himself is said to have cried despairingly that this single act had ruined three years of patient diplomacy and efforts at rapprochement with the West. The furore thus caused was not without its effect upon the fate of Patriarch Tikhon and upon the Church controversy in Russia. The Patriarch's trial had been set for the beginning of April but was suddenly postponed until the 17th, two days after the opening of the Communist Party Congress. It was generally believed that Party delegates from all over Russia would thus have an opportunity to discuss the Patriarch's case and bring information about it from the communities they represented. The Living Church council met on May 3rd, and one of its first acts was publicly to expel from the Church, which it claimed to represent in toto, the Patriarch Tikhon as a traitor unworthy of his high office, and to announce that henceforth he would be known by his family name of Andrey Belavin. Two days later Vedensky, now regarded as the principal Reformist leader, was consecrated archbishop in a makeshift chapel which had formerly been the theatre of the Third Communist Hostel of Moscow. The three metropolitan bishops, Antonin of Moscow, Peter of Siberia, and Tikhon of Kiev, robed in full canonicals, performed the ceremony of consecration, impressive despite its tawdry surroundings. Then Vedensky made a powerful speech pledging the support of the Living Church to the Soviet Government, which led the Comparty mouthpiece, *Pravda*, to comment sourly: "Christians may bless Communism—well and good— but that doesn't mean that Communism blesses Christianity."

Vedensky's speech was indeed the swan song of the Living Church. The Patriarch Tikhon was not brought to trial but released on signature of a document admitting his "errors" and promising good conduct for the future. He promptly began a vigorous attack upon the Living Church, which found to its dismay that it could no longer count upon official support. It had served the purpose of the Bolsheviks, but they had no more reason to see a strong Living Church than a strong Conservative Church. They had used the former to undermine the latter, and were now content to see the process reversed. The Living Church, which had never been strong in the rural districts despite its own assertions, soon lost ground in the cities also. Whatever the need for reform and however great the sincerity of its leaders, the Living Church was fatally "tarred with a red brush," in the opinion of Russian churchmen. Its influence dwindled, although the intra-Church controversy continued to weaken the Church as a body. The dispute about Black and White clergy became insignificant with the total abolition of the monasteries, of which the most famous, like that of Kiev, became state museums. Services were held in Slavonic, even in churches which had temporarily joined the Living Church and adopted the use of Russian. Patriarch Tikhon successfully challenged the authority of the Living Church council, but was unable to secure complete ascendancy for himself and the Holy Synod. After his death a few years later no new Patriarch was reappointed, and Church affairs were directed by a governing body whose functions and formation represented a compromise between the Synod and the Council of the Living Church.

The worst effects of what had seemed for a time a deadly schism were thus averted, but there is no doubt that the Church had lost greatly in prestige and influence. The Reform movement, which might in happier circumstances have done much to vivify and modernize the Church, had been discredited and damaged almost beyond repair, while the old conservative element had seen its framework shattered and its leaders browbeaten and diminished. The real victor in the struggle had been the Soviet Government, which had amply achieved its prime object of disrupting and impoverishing, physically and spiritually, its last organized opponent in Russia. But the fruits of this internal triumph had been turned to ashes by the disastrous effects abroad of the execution of Monsignor Butchkevich.

Looking backward on the events I have just described, it cannot be said that either the Church or the Bolsheviks emerged with any great credit. The conservative Church leaders had shown themselves reactionary and indifferent or blind to the realities of a changed world; the Reformers had fallen prey to opportunism and intrigue and had unworthily "bowed the knee to Baal"; the Bolsheviks had overreached themselves by excess of cynicism and harshness. At all events official pressure upon the Orthodox Church grew less in succeeding years, or rather was exercised in a less overt and brutal manner. Anti-religious publications continued to appear, but

there were no more arbitrary closings of churches or public demonstrations against believers. The Bolsheviks pursued the more subtle
method of inducing rural and urban communities to vote that their
churches should be changed into motion picture houses, clubs,
theatres or concert halls, for which funds and other facilities were
provided in sharp contrast to heavy taxation for upkeep and insur-
ance imposed upon church congregations. Thus the number of
churches throughout the country grew steadily less. On more than
one occasion, however, the authorities found it necessary to conduct
campaigns against the Methodists, Lutherans and other non-Ortho-
dox denominations, whose influence and even numbers increased,
partly through the weakness and divisions of the Orthodox Church,
with which they were now on terms of full legal equality, partly
because their methods and ritual were simpler and more suited to
popular needs.

Several years later the First Five-Year Plan (1928-1933) and the
"class war" in the villages to "collectivize" Russian agriculture
brought a sharp renewal of conflict between the Soviet Government
and the Church. Most of the rural clergy were related by blood to
the richer peasants, whose side they naturally espoused in what
proved a bitter and often bloody struggle. Even so, it was these
individual "kulak-priests," as the Bolsheviks termed them, who were
the object of their attacks rather than the Orthodox Church as such,
or its upper hierarchy. But it was not without significance that
during this period the Moscow authorities decided to demolish two
of the most venerated religious edifices in the city, on the pretext
of "improvement and modernization." One was the gigantic cathedral of *Kristos Spaseetel*, built in the nineteenth century to commemorate the defeat of Napoleon, whose huge golden dome was
by far the most notable landmark to anyone approaching Moscow
by land or air. The other was the tiny chapel, six feet by six, of the
Iberian Virgin, at the Iversky Gate of Moscow's Red Square. This
was the most famous shrine in Russia, and its icon depicting the
Virgin and the Child had been an object of veneration for centuries. It was a lovely little chapel set against the central pillars of
an ancient bridge-like structure known as the "Boyar House," which
did somewhat obstruct the entrance to the Red Square. In this
shrine Ivan the Terrible begged pardon from Heaven after the
murder of his son, and Alexander I knelt in prayer while Napoleon's

cannon were thundering beyond the Moscow River. Here, six months later, he gave thanks to the Virgin for victory, and here in 1914 Nicholas II sought aid for Holy Russia in the war with Germany. It was here, too, in the side wall above the Boyar house-bridge, that the Bolsheviks had placed a sandstone block engraved in red letters: "Religion is the opium of the people."

One hot summer morning in 1929, a wooden fence was hastily erected around the shrine, and in five short hours it was entirely demolished. It was announced at the time that the icon would be placed in one of the few Orthodox churches left open in Moscow, not more than a score of the hundreds which had formerly existed; but actually it was kept in the Kremlin vaults.

The towering cathedral was reduced to rubble in an instant by an immense charge of explosive. It had been closed for services for some time, because it was already known that the site was destined for the projected "House of the Soviets," to be built on an even more grandiose scale and surmounted by a colossal statue of Lenin taller than the Statue of Liberty. The explosion rocked Moscow, but the extraordinary thing was that neither the demolition of the shrine nor the destruction of the cathedral caused any excitement or even attracted a crowd. I myself watched the Iberian shrine being torn down. There was one policeman on duty, who said no more than "Keep moving there" to small groups of curious passers-by. On neither occasion was there any report of prayers being said in any churches or other signs of regret and sorrow, much less protest. The cathedral was in fact an ugly modern building, but the little shrine was beautiful and, one might have thought, unutterably dear to the hearts of the Russian people. Its unlamented destruction seemed final proof of the Church's impotence and defeat. Yet no one familiar with Russia, countryside and cities alike, could fail to know that despite pressure and persecution the spirit of belief and religion had not vanished from Russia and was still present amongst the young as well as older people. The number of churches was less, but they were always crowded and priests and congregations alike showed a reverence and devotion that perhaps was all the stronger because of the trials by which the Church was afflicted.

Chapter 7

THE NEW REPUBLIC

DESPITE ITS FROTHY extravagance and numerous abuses—afterwards paid for dearly by thousands of thoughtless citizens who had danced for a time too gayly in the sun—NEP did perform real service. In urban reconstruction the tax on the gambling hells produced the equivalent of $5,000,000, which tended to stifle criticism, as repairs were urgently needed. NEP further helped to restart the wheels of trade and small industrial production, and most important of all, to stimulate the rural food supply. The peasants now could get tools, utensils and cheap clothing, of which they had been deprived for years, in return for their crops and produce. The harvest of 1921 (in cereals, vegetables and fruit) had been little more than a third of the pre-war average. In 1922 it nearly doubled, with abundance of eggs and poultry, and in 1923 the total crop was not much lower than pre-war.

Catherine the Great once said that a single good harvest could atone for ten years of shortage or misrule. The (relatively) bumper crops of 1922 and 1923 justified her words as far as the food supply, health and well-being of the Russian people were concerned. But they led, in the autumn of the latter year, to a serious economic crisis owing to the disproportion between prices of food and goods. Trotsky adroitly named it the "scissors" crisis, because the price graphs of food and goods showed the latter steadily rising as the former fell, like scissors-blades opened wide. "Unless," he said, "we can close the scissors, the country faces economic ruin and the political consequences of conflict of interests between town and country." In terms of figures the price of farm products was less than two-thirds of the pre-war level, while the price of goods was four-fifths higher than pre-war, as state trusts and co-operatives, now required to keep books and show a profit, blithely raised rates to meet an insatiable demand for manufactured goods, and their example was avidly followed by private producers and artisans. The crisis grew so acute that the peasants hoarded their produce and refused to buy goods from the cities, which threatened industrial stagnation. In alarm the government ordered goods to be sold at cost or even below it, which relieved the crisis, although the paper profits of the trusts were swept away.

The "scissors" crisis focused the attention of the Soviet Government upon the continuous depreciation of currency which was one of the causes of the crisis and a perpetual element of weakness in the nation's economic life. Prior to the introduction of NEP, more than three-fifths of the budget had been met by currency emission, but the New Policy expressly enjoined that henceforth budgets must be balanced as far as possible from revenue. This was accomplished in the course of two years by the establishment in May, 1923, of a "single agricultural tax" payable by the peasants in cash instead of kind, and by the development of other taxation in the form of excise duties and income, property and inheritance taxes, until the peasant furnished only a small part of the national revenue, most of which now came from the urban population. The remainder was provided by the profits of state industry and business, and by internal loans. In the autumn of 1921 the State Bank was given sole authority to issue bank notes, as well as to serve as a central fount of credit for the newly-formed Agricultural and Industrial Banks, which had branches in all the principal centers of the country. A year later the State Bank began to issue a new form of bank note, whose unit was the *chervonetz*, with a gold value of ten pre-war roubles ($5.146). The chervonetz notes were originally issued in denominations of one, three, five, ten, twenty-five and a hundred, and were secured by the bank's gold reserve of not less than twenty-five percent of the total emission. For a time they circulated side by side with *sovznaki* (earlier "Soviet notes") whose depreciation had reached astronomical figures. It had actually become the practice to lop off three or more noughts from the sovznaki at the end of each year, so that the million-rouble notes of 1923 represented a million million roubles in terms of 1921. To prevent the operation of the celebrated Gresham Law, that good currency is chased out of circulation by bad currency, the ratio between the stable gold-backed chervonetz notes and the vertiginously falling sovznaki was officially announced from day to day, which caused much confusion and dispute and greatly hampered business. By March, 1924, the State Bank held enough gold for the emission of sovznaki to be discontinued, and in May they were completely withdrawn from circulation on an exchange ratio of twenty million roubles for one chervonetz. Allowing for the above-mentioned removal of noughts, the true conversion rate of the original Soviet rouble would have been about fifty million million roubles for one American dollar. These figures sound incredible, but currency inflation in Germany and Austria reached equally ridiculous heights. By midsummer, 1924, Soviet currency was wholly reformed on a gold basis in the form of chervonetz notes with small treasury bills—one, three and five roubles—and silver and copper coins to make change. These bills and coin had no gold backing of their own, but their emission was strictly controlled and their value maintained by enforced legal parity with the chervonetz issue.

The currency reform not only eased internal economic difficulties but served to encourage the confidence of foreign businessmen in Russia's financial stability. One of the clauses of the New Economic Policy provided for the granting to foreign capitalists of "concessions" for mining and other industrial and commercial operations on Soviet territory. Some such agreements were negotiated, although fewer and less successful than had been hoped; but they helped to attract foreign interest to the Soviet market. The arrival of foreign Commercial Missions in the spring and summer of 1921 brought a renewal of foreign trade, which was at first exclusively handled by the Foreign Trade Monopoly Commissariat, but later this was supplemented by the *Centrosoyous* (Central Union of Co-operatives) which did a large export business in foodstuffs and was instrumental in obtaining long-term credits in England and Germany.

Russia was in urgent need of machines and machine-tools, medicines, chemicals, scientific instruments, and in the famine year of 1921, foodstuffs. Its imports that year therefore greatly exceeded exports, in terms of pre-war gold roubles 208 millions' worth of imports against 20 millions' worth of exports.

In 1922 the figures were: imports 270 millions, exports 81 millions.
In 1923 (the second good harvest year): imports 144 millions,
exports 206 millions.
In 1924: imports 234 millions, exports 369 millions.

If this were a fairy-tale it might be said that the good fairies who met at the cradle of the infant Soviet Republic wished it courage, clearsightedness, perseverance, determination and unbounded energy. But the wicked fairy added the curse that it would always be misunderstood and traduced. It is hard for any country to know another thoroughly, and, to be sure, Soviet Russia from the outset did much to discourage alien investigation. Nevertheless, there is no parallel in history to the consistent misinterpretation by other countries of the acts and policies of Soviet Russia during the first quarter-century of its existence. This rule held good in the case of NEP, which the Western powers believed to be a sign that Russia was reverting to capitalism and would soon be willing to "rejoin the family of nations" and to behave in a normal and reasonable way. Such a theory was contrary to what was known, or might have been known, of the Bolsheviks' fanatic devotion to Socialism, and of the intense Russian (not merely Bolshevik) individualism and profound conviction that Russia was not a country but a continent, neither Europe nor Asia but itself, aloof and independent, irrevocably determined to blaze its own trail and be guided by its own interests. Paradoxically, too, the seal of Marxist internationalism which Lenin stamped upon his country contributed greatly to the Russian sense of differentness and isolation, and thus, indirectly, to nationalism. This, I admit, is almost equivalent to saying that Russia, even Soviet Russia, was and is, really and fundamentally, more individualist than socialist, more nationalist than internationalist. I do think that this may be said, with certain reservations and explanations, and that the statement is justified by the course of Soviet history.

Be that as it may, the French and British governments early in 1922 set a precedent by inviting Soviet Russia to attend an international conference at Genoa, where for the first time its representatives would confer on equal terms with those of other nations.

Franco-British motives were not wholly altruistic. The statesmen of the two countries had begun uneasily to realize that Germany could never meet the exaggerated financial obligations placed upon it by the Treaty of Versailles. They hoped, however, that Russia, whose potential wealth and resources were unlimited, might be induced by its urgent need of foreign credits to "recognize" all or part of its national indebtedness to the West contracted prior to the Bolshevik regime. The Russians evaded the somewhat ingenuous attempt to make credits conditional upon debt recognition by presenting a counter-claim for damages caused by Foreign Intervention whose total surpassed the debt figure. The result was a deadlock which was not broken at another conference, more specifically economic, held a few months later at The Hague, but the Genoa meeting proved far from unproductive or dull. Its first sensation was a news leakage, perhaps exaggerated and certainly premature, that the Soviet oil trust had made a sweeping "concession" agreement with the British Royal-Dutch Shell oil interests for the rehabilitation of the Caucasian oil fields. This news, which was said to have emanated from Czech sources in Genoa, provoked such roars of rage and pain from Standard Oil, which had a claim, by right of purchase, to the large Nobel interests in the Caucasian field, that the Russo-British deal died stillborn.

Undiscouraged, the Russians then played their ace of trumps, a pact of mutual non-aggression, friendship and economic collaboration with Germany, so extensive and closely woven as to be a virtual alliance between the two countries, which considered themselves, and did not hesitate to say so, "the victims of Versailles." This agreement, concluded in utter secrecy at Rapallo, near Genoa, burst like a bombshell upon the Franco-British leaders and their friends, amongst whom Beneš, the wily Czech, was caught napping like the rest. The Conference was blown from doldrums to smithereens, and the press of Western Europe raised a clamor that made Standard Oil's earlier outcry sound like the squeaks of a mouse. But nothing could be done, or anyway nothing done, and the partnership thus formed lasted ten full years to the profit and advantage, economically and politically, of both sides. In addition, the Russo-German Pact finally abolished the "cordon sanitaire" or "quarantine belt" by which the French Premier, Clemenceau, had sought to enclose Soviet Russia in 1919 and prevent the "Bolshevik virus" from spreading to Western Europe.

One of the Bolsheviks' first moves after seizing power in 1917 was the denunciation of secret treaties negotiated by previous Russian governments, the demand for general peace without annexations or indemnities, and the declaration that the Soviet Government regarded all nations as free and equal irrespective of their position as colonies or vassals of imperialist powers. Early in 1921 the Soviet Government set about implementing the latter declaration by concluding pacts of friendship and treaties on equal terms with its Eastern "Limitropes," Persia, Afghanistan and Turkey. These treaties contained "most favored nation" trade clauses. A similar treaty was signed in November, 1921, with the People's Republic of Outer Mongolia on terms which implied its recognition as a state independent of China. In point of fact the republic really exchanged Chinese for Soviet suzerainty. China was displeased, and refused to sign a Limitrope treaty until May 31, 1924, although in 1919 and 1920 the Soviet Government had announced its abandonment of all claim to the Boxer indemnity and of previous agreements infringing Chinese sovereignty, as well as its readiness to treat with China on terms of full equality.

In the course of 1922 the Russians consolidated their hold upon the Transcaucasian provinces, Azerbadjan (capital Baku, Russia's oil metropolis), Georgia (capital Tiflis), and Armenia (capital Erivan), which had been ruled since the Revolution by Menshevik or bourgeois-nationalist governments, and henceforth were united in a Caucasian federation with local autonomy for each member. This facilitated the defeat of a separatist movement in Central Asia, headed by the former "Young Turk" leader, Enver Bey. Enver had played a big part in the "Young Turk" revolt against the Sultan Abdul Hamid, and rose to great heights during World War I through his close connections with Germany. When Germany collapsed, Enver fell foul of his principal rival, Mustapha Kemal (later Ataturk), and sought refuge in Moscow, where for a time he appeared willing to co-operate in Lenin's plans for the development of the area stretching from the Volga and Ural Mountains to the frontiers of China, Afghanistan and Persia. But Enver's egoism and unbounded ambition could not brook a subordinate rôle. He dreamed of founding a pan-Turanian Islamic empire in Central Asia, and in 1921 crossed the Caspian Sea from Baku (amply provided, the Bolsheviks have alleged, with British gold and promises of support) to raise the standard of revolt in the Southeast. Late in 1922 he met a soldier's death in the final battle of a brief but bloody campaign.

Enver had doubtless counted upon help against the Russians from Turkey, where he still had influential friends despite his rivalry with Kemal. The Russians blasted his hopes by a striking gesture of friendship towards Turkey, which incidentally showed the British and French that the Soviet Union also could play the game of Intervention. Goaded beyond endurance by the harsh Treaty of Sèvres, which stripped Turkey to the bone, by the Allied naval occupation of the Dardanelles, Bosporus and Constantinople, and finally by the Greek invasion of Asia Minor, the indomitable Kemal had rallied his country to what seemed a hopeless struggle. In his darkest hour, in the late spring of 1922, when his shattered, exhausted and half-starving army had retreated far into the interior, the Russians proved the reality of the friendship pact they had signed the previous year by sending to Kemal's headquarters a military mission headed by Frunze, later Soviet Commissar of War. The mission was unaccompanied by troops, but it brought large quantities of clothing, supplies, food, equipment and munitions, and above all encouragement. Like Pilsudski at Warsaw two years before, Kemal turned savagely on his enemy and bloodily defeated the Greeks at Afium Karahissar. His victorious troops swept westwards and literally threw the Greeks into the sea from Smyrna and the coastal cities of Asia Minor, while another column moved northwards to command the southern shores of the Bosporus. The British Government saw that the Greek cause was hopeless, and soon afterwards withdrew its naval forces from Turkish waters. Kemal, who had cut the Treaty of Sèvres to tatters with his sword, pressed his advantage in the diplomatic field, and Turkey's independence and revival were assured by the Treaty of Lausanne.

The Bolsheviks had for some time been preparing a new political structure for the vast territory over which they now held undisputed control. More than eighteen months before Kemal's victory, Stalin, Commissar of Nationalities as well as General Secretary of the Party, had been instructed by Lenin to draw up for the Central Committee a program of federation or union for all the loosely knit Soviet republics. Stalin presented his report, duly approved by the Central Committee of the Party, to the first All-Union Congress of

Soviet Republics, which met in Moscow in December, 1922. Incidentally, this was the first time that the name of Stalin became known to the Western world, which had hardly noticed his appointment as Party Secretary. The office of Commissar for Nationalities, later abolished as unnecessary, was the only governmental (as distinct from Comparty) position held by Stalin until he became Premier twenty years afterwards.

On the proposal of Lenin and Stalin, the Congress voted unanimously to form a voluntary union of the Soviet peoples, to be known as the Union of Soviet Socialist Republics, or U. S. S. R. The word Russia was significantly omitted, and the sovereign federations or states which formed the Union were granted the right of free secession. [This clause surprised American correspondents in Moscow, who were told somewhat naïvely by an official of the Soviet Press Department, "You see, we are looking ahead to the time when Germany, France or England will wish to join the Soviet Union; their right of free adherence must be balanced by a right of free secession." He did not add that the dominance of a single-party (Communist) system in present or future member states of the Union would provide an all-binding cement to hold the Union in a monolithic block.]

The U. S. S. R., which did not formally come into existence until the following July, comprised (1) the Russian Socialist Federation, which had just been extended to include Eastern Siberia and the formerly semi-independent Far Eastern Republic (capital Chita); (2) the Caucasian Federation (capital Tiflis); (3) the Ukrainian Soviet Republic (capital Kiev, and later Kharkov); (4) the White Russian (Byelorussia) Soviet Republic (capital Minsk); and (5, 6, 7) the Central Asian Soviet Republics, Uzbekistan, Turkmenistan and Tadjikistan. There was no single President of the U. S. S. R., as the Act of Union provided that the office of president should be occupied in rotation by each of the presidents of the seven sovereign member states of the Union, to which others were later added.[1]

[1] The sovereignty of the constituent republics, especially in regard to language, customs and cultural aspirations, was guaranteed in the new Union. Each republic had its own parliament and council of commissars, but the Union reserved for itself the commissariats of Foreign Affairs, War and Marine, Commerce, Transportation, and Post and Telegraphs. The functions of these departments in the constituent governments were exercised by nominees of the respective Union commissariats.

On paper, the Union constitution gave the people of the U. S. S. R. democratic freedom and self-government, without distinction of race, sex or color. Every citizen, male or female, was entitled to vote on reaching the age of eighteen, with the exception of lunatics, criminals, former landlords, clergy, high Tsarist officers, and other political opponents of the Soviet system. The numerical preponderance of the rural electorate was counterbalanced by the proviso that twice as many votes were required to elect a rural delegate as were needed for the election of military and urban representatives. In practice, however, the Central Committee of the Communist Party, and in particular its inner junta, the Politburo, was the supreme authority in the U. S. S. R. All state officials, from members of the Council of Commissars down to local functionaries, were "proposed for election" by the Communist Center or by a provincial Communist caucus acting under the Center's orders. The electorate voted therefore for a list of party nominees, and these nominees in turn when elected voted for a list of higher party nominees, for instance the Council of Commissars. In other words, the function of the electorate and its chosen representatives was actually no more than to give a rubber-stamp approval to lists of persons selected by the Party, which of course was careful to entrust all leading posts to its own members.

The fact of the matter was that Lenin and his associates regarded the Communist Party as the tutor or guardian of the infant proletarian state which was not yet adult or experienced enough to govern itself and order its own ways. Lenin indeed is said to have declared that it would take three generations before the U. S. S. R. would be capable of genuine self-government and democracy; in the meantime it would learn democratic methods and principles under the guidance of the Bolsheviks. There is no reason to doubt the sincerity of Lenin and his successors in this respect. The two constitutions have done much to achieve their purpose of furthering the political education of the masses, whom Kerensky in the hour of defeat described as a "mob of newly freed slaves," and of familiarizing them with the methods of democratic election and the ideals of freedom.

Like NEP, the Act of Union and the new constitution were hailed abroad as signs of Russian stability, even conservatism, and desire for normal conditions of life. Correct enough, if "normal conditions of life" meant the peaceful development of Socialism and "conservatism and stability" meant that the Bolsheviks, strong and unchallenged, would keep their social and political conquests; which was by no means the interpretation of foreign statesmen. The latter might have known better if they had pondered a speech made by Lenin before the Moscow Soviet in November, 1922. He spoke of Russia's gains and achievements during the past two years under NEP, which, he said, had more than justified its purpose as an aid to economic restoration; but he repeated his historic phrase at the eleventh Party Congress in the preceding March, "Kto kovo" (literally, "Who beats whom?" or "Who will win?") about NEP being a life and death struggle between Capitalism and Socialism. To the Moscow Soviet Lenin declared that Socialism was winning, and that NEP, although it had not yet outlived its usefulness as a temporary expedient, had already accomplished its purpose. He concluded forcefully, "NEP Russia will become Socialist Russia." In other words, Lenin had introduced, and the Party had accepted, the New Economic Policy not as a *volte-face* but as an expedient. The Party had not yet abandoned its ideal of world revolution and a universal Socialist State, although now it might admit that the day of realization had receded into the distance, just as the early Christians towards the end of the first century A. D. reluctantly abandoned *their* ideal of the Second Advent in *their* time.

The conflict between idealism and reality, between Marxist internationalism and Russia's national interests, was to rage with growing intensity during the next fifteen years. Had Lenin lived, he might have been able to keep the two opposing forces in equilibrium and to use NEP as a balance of adjustment. But he was already stricken with mortal sickness, and his November speech to the Moscow Soviet was his last public appearance alive. In the autumn and winter of 1921 Lenin had suffered from severe headaches and insomnia, which at first were attributed to overwork in connection with the New Economic Policy and the Famine crisis. He was ordered to rest, but the symptoms persisted and in the early spring his physicians decided they were due to pressure of the pistol bullet which had lodged near his spine when the Kaplan girl tried to assassinate him three years before. They operated and removed the bullet, which had formed a small abscess, but far from improving, Lenin grew worse and had a paralytic stroke two weeks after the operation. For a time his life was in danger, but he rallied, the signs of paralysis disappeared and his general condition was so much better that he was able to resume work in the autumn. At that time I heard Lenin make two public speeches. He looked robust enough, but I noted a hardly perceptible thickening of speech, as if his tongue was slightly too big for his mouth, a common indication of paralysis; I saw too that his friends watched him anxiously, especially during the second speech, which lasted for more than an hour.

In December there was a renewal of headaches and insomnia combined with growing weakness, and again a complete rest was ordered, which proved unavailing, because in March Lenin had a second more serious stroke which completely paralyzed one side of his body and deprived him of the power of speech. His brain remained clear, and gradually as summer drew into autumn and autumn to winter, he was able by signs and labored writing to communicate ideas and instructions, including, it was said, a searching personal estimate of his closest associates, to which I shall refer later, known as "Lenin's testament." This and other messages which he was able to communicate were rewritten and read to him by his devoted wife and secretary Krupskaya, and finally emended and approved by him. Lenin continued to make slight improvement, until the afternoon of January 21, 1924, when a third stroke occurred and he died without recovering consciousness. His end was inevitable, but it may have been hastened by an outing that morning when he sat propped with pillows in a sleigh, watching a hunting party in the park of a mansion at Gorki, near Moscow, which had formerly been the residence of a millionaire businessman. Lenin's last reported words, enunciated with difficulty, were, "Vot sobaka," which might be translated roughly, "That's a good dog," as he pointed with trembling hand to a young hound which had just retrieved a bird.

Chapter 8

LENIN DEAD AND TROTSKY LIVING

LENIN'S DEATH WAS a tremendous shock to the people of Russia, most of whom believed that he was slowly getting better. His intimates must have known for nearly a year that the hand of death was on his shoulder, and could only hope against hope; but the masses seem to have shared the feeling once expressed to me by a friend of the Chinese leader Sun Yat Sen: "He was so strong and big in our eyes that we refused to believe that even Death could conquer him."

Lenin's funeral ceremonies were an amazing demonstration of popular mourning and affection. That his followers loved him I knew. I had seen the faces of a thousand delegates, workers, peasants and soldiers, light up and shine at the sight of him when he spoke at an important meeting in the Moscow Opera House; but that was nothing to compare with the last tribute of the Russian masses. Men and women travelled for days in the depth of winter to Moscow, where they stood five hours or more in a line two miles long with the thermometer at thirty-five below zero, waiting to pass through the great hall where Lenin's body lay in state. For more than seventy-two hours a never-ending human stream passed by the simple bier, until three-quarters of a million men, women and children had bidden their dead leader farewell. I venture to quote here the account of the final scene which I cabled to the New York *Times:*

"Moscow, January 28, 1924. The climax of an amazing week of national emotion was reached at four o'clock today under the ancient wall of the Kremlin, where, as bells tolled and guns thundered, Lenin's friends bore his red-draped coffin from the hall where it had lain for four days to the mausoleum, still covered by a wooden construction shed, in the Red Square under the shadow of the Kremlin wall.

"Massed bands played the 'Internationale' to slow time, and from the vast multitude in the Red Square rose in the icy air a fog of congealed breath, like a smoke sacrifice. So cold it was—35 degrees below zero Fahrenheit—that beards, hats, collars, and eyebrows were white like the snowclad trees in the little park close to the Kremlin wall. Few dared take off their hats as Lenin's body passed to its last resting place. The majority stood at salute with raised hands.

"In the streets leading to the square tens of thousands more, lined up under mourning banners, were awaiting admission. At the corners soldiers built log fires, round which each squad, relieved hourly owing to the intense cold, stamped and beat their arms against their bodies.

"The most striking feature of the last moment was its utter absence of ceremony. Lenin's disciples took the master's body and laid it in its appointed place. No word was said.

"The real obsequies had taken place in the Hall of Columns, where, at eight o'clock in the morning, the foreign diplomats and members of the highest Soviet organizations joined in the columned hall members of Lenin's family and a little group of closest friends that had been watching the body since midnight when the doors were closed to the public. The guard of honor, four strong, beside the body was doubled in the final hours to permit all the hundreds who claimed the privilege to take a turn, and the shifts were of five minutes instead of ten.

"Amid utter silence the combined orchestras of the Grand Opera House and Conservatory of Music played Chopin's 'Requiem' and selections from Wagner, followed by the Bolshevik funeral march.

"Even in the hall it was bitterly cold, and most of those present retained their coats and high felt boots.

"The huge pile of wreaths that last night almost hid the form in the centre had been cleared away, and there passed over the hall an almost physical manifestation of death's majesty. The Russians present sang the moving words of the funeral march and the 'Internationale,' which ended the ceremony.

"Then the hall was cleared of all except the members of the family and the guard of honor, and Stalin, Zinoviev, two workers, and two peasants raised the coffin, now closed and enveloped in a red cloth, for the final stage of the long pilgrimage. Through gray lines of troops, like pictures of medieval Russian knights, in peaked cloth helmets with flaps hanging low over their shoulders, the coffin was carried, with changes of bearers every fifty yards—still in the same proportion of two Soviet leaders to four of their humblest comrades—to the Red Square, where the whole garrison of Moscow was standing at attention.

"When the coffin was placed on the dais, Yevdokimov, a member of the Petrograd Communist Party, chosen because of his reputed loudest voice in Russia, read as an oration the declaration of the Federal Soviet Congress addressed to 'laboring humanity':

" 'Lenin is dead. But Lenin lives in millions of hearts, lives in the great union of workers, peasants, proletariat, and oppressed nations; lives in the collective intelligence of the Communist Party; lives in the workers' dictatorship which he erected, solid and menacing, on the boundary of Europe and Asia.

" 'The Old World is dying . . . The diabolical machine of capital, shaken and tottering already, is about to fall to pieces. But today capital in Europe is still holding out, and only one force, a gigantic liberator, victorious, can save the whole world. That force is the laboring mass—whose energy and class-consciousness guide and unite hundreds of millions of men. The leader of this mass humanity was our comrade Lenin. He held the key to the spirit of all workers and peasants . . . Before the mighty ones of this world he flung the simple and madly daring slogan, "All power to the Soviets," and the miracle was performed.

" 'We have lost in Lenin the loved captain of our vessel, but henceforth his work is set on the right road. Hundreds of thousands of disciples of Vladimir Ilyich firmly uphold his mighty banner. Already it is transfiguring the whole world. Proletariat of all lands, unite!' "

My dispatch concluded: "Another note of today's ceremony hardly less striking than its simplicity was the absence of Trotsky. For the last three days there had been a report that he was returning from the Caucasus where he was ill. More than once crowds assembled to greet him at the station, and official photographers were sent to wait chilly hours before the House of Columns to film his entry. To the last many believed he would come. A dozen times came a cry from the throng around the mausoleum, 'There's Trotsky,' or 'Trotsky's here,' as anyone in a military greatcoat faintly resembling Trotsky passed before us."

The absence of Trotsky was the absorbing question in that week of strain and sorrow to everyone in Moscow, whether Russian or foreign. It was a period of intense popular emotion and we all knew that to nine-tenths of the Russian masses Trotsky was second only to Lenin in popular esteem. He was said to be sick and travelling to a cure in the Caucasus, but nothing could condone his absence save the fact that he was so near death that it would have been fatal for him to make the return journey, which was not the case. Whatever may have been his reasons, Trotsky's failure to pay his last tribute to the dead leader horrified the people of Moscow as a want of respect and good taste. It was, moreover, a political error of the first magnitude and dealt a fatal blow to Trotsky's prestige, which his adversaries were quick to see and turn to good account. To this day I cannot imagine why he did not come. The night after the funeral I discussed the problem with my friend Rollin, the only French correspondent in Moscow at that time, who had held an important position in the French Navy as personal aide and adviser to the Admiral commanding the French forces at Constantinople and was one of the chief editorial writers of the Paris *Temps*, which ranks as the semi-official organ of the French Government.

Rollin agreed with me that Trotsky's absence was inexplicable. "From all I can learn," he said, "Trotsky is not even dangerously ill, although I won't accept the view that his illness is wholly, or mainly, diplomatic." He paused and rubbed his high, broad forehead. "Yes," he said, "it's extraordinary—worse than any surrender. How pleased Stalin must be!"

"Don't you think that rivalry stuff has been exaggerated?" I asked. "After all you must admit that the Bolshevik leaders are sincere, and surely Lenin's death will induce them to iron out any personal differences that may have existed before."

"For the time being perhaps," said Rollin sagely, "but that effect of Lenin's death may be no more than temporary and emotional. Unless I am mistaken, the divergence between Trotsky and Stalin is fundamental. I'll admit that both of them are sincere, but now that Lenin has gone there is bound to be a clash between them. Until now I would have picked Trotsky to win. I know that he is more popular than Stalin and I thought he was much cleverer, but now I have begun to doubt it. My God, what an opportunity to miss! Achilles sulking in his tent. *Quel idiot!* As if he couldn't understand that the whole strength of his position was his reputation with the masses as Lenin's chief aide and supporter. Surely you've heard the story that peasants in outlying villages talk with awe and reverence of the new Tsar called Leninandrotsky, who has come from the East to regenerate Holy Russia. As a matter of personal respect to Lenin, Trotsky should have risen from his death-bed to be present; it was his duty and obligation, and there isn't a man or woman in the whole country who doesn't think so. It is a blunder that will cost him dear. Think too of what he missed; if he had come to Moscow, he couldn't have failed to be the central figure in the funeral ceremonies. No one would have dared to interfere with him; he would have stolen the show, as you say in America, whether Stalin and the others liked it or not. But he did not come. Henceforth, I tell you, my money is on Stalin."

"So is mine," I said, "but it was already."

Trotsky's own explanation in his autobiography of his absence from Lenin's funeral is thin and unconvincing, and does small credit either to his heart or head. He declares that a code message from Stalin announcing Lenin's death was delivered to him in his private car at the station in Tiflis on January 21st, that is to say a few hours after Lenin died. He continues, "I got the Kremlin on the direct wire. In answer to my inquiry I was told: 'The funeral will be on Saturday; you cannot get back in time and so we advise you to continue your treatment.' Accordingly, I had no choice. As a matter of fact, the funeral did not take place until Sunday and I could easily have reached Moscow by then. Incredible as it may appear, I was even deceived about the date of the funeral."

This final accusation was as unjust as it was ungenerous. Lenin died on the afternoon of Monday, January 21st, and his funeral was originally set for Saturday, the 26th, but the number of people who wished to see him was so great—thousands came from places more distant than Tiflis—that it was postponed twenty-four hours. The journey from Moscow to Tiflis by ordinary express takes three days and three nights—allow four or even five days and nights in 1924 in winter-time. Trotsky's private car was in the station when he received the news on Monday night. Tiflis is one of the biggest railroad depots in south Russia and there is not the slightest doubt that the Red war-lord, whose authority was still unquestioned, could have ordered a special train and been back in Moscow within seventy-two hours. Trotsky's account continues theatrically, "The Tiflis comrades came to demand that I should write on Lenin's death at once. But I knew only one urgent desire—and that was to be alone. I could not stretch my hand to lift the pen." He then adds that he wrote a "few handwritten pages." Strangest of all, there is no word in Trotsky's recital of any surmise on his part, much less compunction, as to what people in Moscow might feel about his failure to return immediately. Any thought of the duty he owed to his dead comrade seems to have been as remote from his mind as perception of the political effects of his absence. Instead he writes of spending those days before the funeral lying on a balcony in the sun at Sukhum, a twenty-four-hour train journey from Tiflis which apparently caused him no physical distress—facing the glittering sea and the huge palms—and of his own "sensation of running a temperature" with which mingled, he says, thoughts of Lenin's death. To make the picture complete Trotsky quotes a passage from his wife's diary: "We arrived quite broken down; it was the first time we had seen Sukhum. The mimosa were in full bloom, magnificent palms, camellias. In the dining-room of the rest-house there were two portraits on the wall, one—draped in black—of Vladimir Ilyich, the other of L. D. (Trotsky). We felt like taking the latter one down but thought it would be too demonstrative." Later Madame Trotsky wrote: "Our friends were expecting L. D. to come to Moscow and thought he would cut short his trip in order to return, since no one imagined that Stalin's telegram had *cut off his return*." (This refers to the message from the Kremlin saying that the funeral would be on Saturday and that Trotsky could not get back in time.) "I remember my son's letter received at Sukhum. He was terribly shocked by Lenin's death and, though suffering from a cold with a temperature of 104, he went in his not very warm coat to the Hall of Columns to pay his last respects and waited, waited, and waited with impatience for our arrival. One could feel in his letter his bitter bewilderment and diffident reproach." On these extracts from his wife's diary Trotsky makes no comment at all.

Such a combination of personal callousness and political insensitiveness does more to explain Trotsky's downfall than a hundred books by Stalin's warmest supporters. To suggest that he was sulking is perhaps unfair. His autobiography states that he had an attack of influenza in October, 1923, which passed into a chronic fever aggravated (at this point he cites his wife's diary in confirmation) by his losing struggle against opponents in the Politburo. A month's stay at Prince Youssupov's former country house near Moscow brought no improvement and his doctor ordered a trip to Sukhum, which restored Trotsky's health but ruined his career. From that time onwards, although he had many devoted adherents in the Party, he had irretrievably "lost face" with the mass of the Russian people. His adversaries in Russia have not failed to question the genuineness of his illness at that time; they have claimed that it was sickness of spirit rather than sickness of body, that Trotsky had made an ambitious bid for Lenin's succession and that when he failed his wounded egoism turned on itself like a scorpion and poisoned him. They point to the long comedy of his plea to enter Germany "on grounds of ill health and for no other purpose than medical treatment" at the time of his exile from Russia, when no country save Turkey would give him harborage. Even there, from the pleasant island where he lived in the Bosporus, he poured out a continual stream of complaints about his health. In short, they imply, Trotsky was either a liar or a hypochondriac or both, but what they really mean is that he "worked himself into a fever," as the saying goes; and that may well be true. It is clear from his own account that it was not the state of his health which prevented him from taking part in Lenin's funeral. As for his sojourn in Turkey I can only say that two of my friends visited him on the Bosporus island and both of them remarked on his robust physical condition. In the spring of 1930 I went to Alma Ata in Central Asia, to which he had first been exiled. During his stay there Trotsky's sympathizers in Moscow wailed loudly that his health was being ruined by the extremes of heat and cold. He refers in his autobiography to the prevalence of malaria and leprosy. I saw the house where he lived in Alma Ata, which is far more comfortable and spacious than my own apartment in Moscow; I saw the pleasant villa in the mountains, where he spent the summer; and I heard everyone, from the local Gay-pay-oo men to the man in the street, talk warmly of Trotsky's hunting trips and how hard he worked and how cheerful and friendly he was to one and all.

A great man Trotsky, of that there is no doubt, a man of superlative mental ability, and a most competent executive withal; a man of proven courage, both physical and moral, a splendid writer and orator with the rare power of equal appeal to an intelligent and to a popular audience. In all history there are few careers so romantic as that of Trotsky: to have risen from so low to such a height, to have shone so bright in the sun, and to have done brave deeds in a quaking world—and then to have fallen again to nothing, to spend his declining years in spiteful twilight, and to meet at last a sordid and murky death. What a tragic fate for this man who was gifted with intelligence and force beyond his fellows, yet cursed by the folly of selfishness and pride.

To the Western world it seemed that the bitter and protracted conflict inside the Communist Party which followed Lenin's death, was mainly a struggle for power, for the inheritance of Lenin's mantle, between two rivals, Stalin and Trotsky. In reality the conflict began much earlier and covered much wider ground than a quarrel of individuals. I have already mentioned the deep-seated jealousy and ill feeling between the "Western exiles," the small group of Bolshevik leaders who had lived in Switzerland, France and England during the decade of repression from 1907 to 1917, and those of their comrades who had stayed in Russia as desperate champions of an illegal and "underground" movement. Secondly, there was a sharp divergence of views in the Central Committee itself, not so much about principles as about methods, persons and timing, that is, how the principles should be applied, and by whom and at what moment. Official Bolshevik records show that such divergences had always been a feature of discussions in the higher ranks of the Party, that they had existed, sometimes to a damaging degree, during the period between the abdication of the Tsar and the seizure of power in November, 1917. Nor did they cease with success, although Lenin appears to have realized, perhaps before the Revolution and most certainly after it, the vital difference between a more or less academic study of future possibilities and a council of war to decide immediate action. Lenin saw, as did Stalin, that a party in power must act rapidly and in unison.

As the struggle progressed, it was easily dramatized and personified as a fight between Stalin and Trotsky, who did indeed represent opposite poles and had moreover been long on unfriendly terms. I spoke earlier of their clash at the siege of Tsaritsin (Stalingrad), and other contemporary stories illustrate their mutual hostility. For instance, Trotsky once was holding a meeting of army commanders at the front, and had given orders to the sentry that no interruptions were permitted on pain of death. Stalin arrived from Petrograd as representative of the Supreme War Committee, brushed the sentry aside and interrupted Trotsky's conference.

Trotsky greeted him quietly, but when the council was over he had the sentry condemned to death for disobeying orders. The next day the local Red forces held a parade in honor of Stalin and his colleagues of the Committee. When it was over a firing-squad appeared on the parade ground, and sentence of death was read over the unlucky sentry.

Before Stalin could protest, Trotsky made a Napoleonic gesture. "This soldier," he said, "deserves death for disobedience to orders, because obedience, no matter what be the circumstances, is a soldier's first duty. But he has a splendid record of courage and devotion, therefore I have decided to exercise my powers as Commissar of War to cancel the verdict of the court-martial and dismiss him with a warning."

The troops roared applause, but Stalin went back to Petrograd with a sour report for Lenin about Trotsky's "aping the arrogance of a Tsarist general."

The two men were antagonistic in character, and Lenin was not joking when he once said, "Only I can drive this ill-matched pair of horses." Trotsky was brilliant in word and action, gifted with intuition, adept in the art of popularity, quick to seize an opportunity, but self-centered and intellectually arrogant. Stalin was slower-minded, forced to plod where Trotsky leapt, no less ambitious than the other but willing to submerge himself and wait. His essential quality was and is persistence, combined with a keen sense of the psychological moment. In those early days at least, and for many years afterwards, he never pushed himself forward, preferring to pull strings from behind the scenes, but he never lost sight of his purpose.

During the critical period just before and after the Revolution, Stalin sat outside the door of Lenin's office like a faithful watchdog. He always followed Lenin's lead without cavil or disagreement, but Trotsky was often quick to criticize or challenge. Later attacked as an ex-Menshevik, he was really "the cat that walked by himself," independent and self-sufficient. Such qualities were repugnant to Stalin, the loyal party man, arch-champion of unity and discipline, and Trotsky's popularity and cool assumption that he stood next to Lenin must have rankled in Stalin's heart. He gave no sign of his feelings, but sat patiently, biding his time.

In the autumn of 1923 economic difficulties—the scissors crisis—which Trotsky had foretold were used by him as basis for an attack on the policies or "general line" of the Central Committee. The official history of the Communist Party suggests that Trotsky was emboldened by Lenin's illness to make a deliberate bid for power as Lenin's successor. This may be an exaggeration, although Trotsky must have known that Lenin was doomed, but it is significant that he mobilized a powerful group of critics to sign a document called the "Declaration of the Forty-six." The declaration was a blow to the Central Committee, but Trotsky was rash enough to pursue his advantage by a letter which not only carried the attack further but established himself as leader of what was described by the Central Committee as an Opposition bloc. The word "opposition" or "factionism" produced a reaction. The Central Committee retorted fiercely that Trotsky was not a Bolshevik at heart and never had been, that he and his "Forty-six" were voicing Menshevik heresies as they had done before, and that most of them had already been castigated by Lenin for subversive or mistaken ideas. Trotsky then turned his guns against the "Party Apparatus," that is the Secretariat, which Stalin had controlled for nearly three years through his key position as General Secretary. This direct attack was a blunder, or anyway came too late, for Stalin and the Central Committee retaliated by calling a Party Conference at the beginning of January, 1924, to discuss the whole controversy. Between Congress and Conference there was this important difference, that the latter was formed of the leading party henchmen and bosses from all over the country, whereas delegates to a Congress were elected by their respective party organizations. Trotsky and his friends found to their sorrow what "Party Apparatus" meant, namely these very henchmen, hand-picked by the Secretariat during the past three years. Trotsky and his Forty-six were ignominiously defeated, and it is possible to assume that chagrin no less than fever induced him to take his fateful rest-cure in the Caucasus.

Chapter 9

"THIS ILL-MATCHED PAIR . . ."

LIKE OTHER PUBLIC men in other countries, Trotsky was to learn the extreme difficulty of bucking a party machine, especially when unsupported by any machine of his own. Without his knowing it, the machine had quietly planted a land mine under Trotsky's position, even before the Party Conference had demolished his hopes. With the ostensible purpose of "enlisting the vanguard of the proletariat," to cope with the stagnation and unemployment caused by the scissors crisis, the Central Committee _and_ Party Apparatus in the late fall of 1923 had issued an appeal for 100,000 "workers from the bench" to swell the Party ranks, which had been nearly halved by three successive purges. In response 127,000 persons entered the Party. One can be sure that they were carefully scrutinized by local secretaries before their admission. In the spring of 1924 came a similar appeal to tap the flood of loyalty and emotion called forth by Lenin's death. This time nearly a quarter of a million young and energetic enthusiasts flocked to join the Party, which thus had received in six months an accession of 375,000 new well-selected members whose great majority knew nothing of squabbles in high places and could be counted upon to support wholeheartedly the Central Committee and Party Apparatus of Lenin, their great dead leader.

It may seem that I am devoting too much space and attention to the struggle inside the Party, which raged with only brief periods of truce for almost fifteen years. That alone is enough to demonstrate the vital importance of this topic which dominated Bolshevik thought, occupied Bolshevik energy and, whether latent or aflame,

conditioned and affected Bolshevik policy at home and abroad.
Fundamentally it was a fight for unity, the core and essence of a
single-party system; but it was also, as I said before, a conflict of
opposing groups and methods, and finally a duel between two leaders, Stalin and Trotsky. This became evident in 1924 when Trotsky
attacked Stalin directly by his blast against the Secretariat, and Stalin
retorted, "Unless Trotskyism is defeated, it will be impossible to
convert present-day (NEP) Russia into Socialist Russia." As the
conflict progressed the personal element was stressed more and more
heavily, perhaps intentionally by the Stalinists, who found it easy
to picture Trotsky as a sort of Bolshevik Antichrist, or perhaps
naturally through the tendency of mankind to personify and drama-
tize an abstract and ideological struggle in terms of individual
antagonists.

In any event, the final issue was foreshadowed if not virtually
decided by the respective tactics of Stalin and Trotsky in 1924.
Stalin was using his Secretariat to enlist a strong body of supporters
in the Party ranks, and using too his own position as Party Secretary
to shift Trotsky's adherents from important posts and replace them
by men of his own choice. The most decisive of such shifts in personnel was the replacement of Sklansky, Trotsky's right-hand man
in the Commissariat of War, by Frunze, who later succeeded Trotsky
as Commissar. This and other similar changes were approved by the
Thirteenth Party Congress, in May, 1924, which Trotsky inexpli-
cably failed to attend—a political blunder scarcely less disastrous than
his failure to attend Lenin's funeral.

The truth of the matter was that Trotsky was prostrate and
broken, not by defeat at the Conference or, as he himself suggests,
by illness, but by the sickening realization of what his absence from
the funeral had done to him and his career. They say that Hell is
paved with good intentions, but the white-hot plowshares of opportunities missed and advantages lost make cruel treading for ambitious
feet. Trotsky lay on his balcony in Sukhum facing the sun and the
sea and the mimosa and palms and camellias, reading letters or receiving friends. Little comfort either brought him and no good medicine
for distress of soul. I have already suggested that the cause of his
illness was psychological as well as physical. In what torment he
must have writhed when letter after letter, friend after friend, told

him, albeit unwillingly, the plain and sorry truth. At first, I have been informed, he refused to believe that his tremendous popularity had not only faded but was changed in no small degree to resentment. Gradually, despite himself, he was forced to understand that this was the case, and, worse still, that he had missed the heaven-sent opportunity of confirming in the mind of the masses the position that he claimed of Lenin's right hand and destined successor. The cabal of his adversaries, of which he speaks so bitterly in his autobiography, might defeat him in the Politburo or the Central Committee, but they never could have robbed him of his hold over the masses. As Rollin said, Trotsky would have "stolen the show" at the funeral in the teeth of Stalin and the rest of them.

In twenty years of newspaper work I have been present at many scenes of national thrill and color—the day War was declared in Paris when a frenzied mob surged down the Grand Boulevard singing the *Marseillaise* and shouting "*à Berlin,*" and Armistice Night in Paris, and the Victory Parade—but all of them are dwarfed in my memory by Lenin's funeral week. I have known, too, popular figures and spellbinders of many races but never one to surpass Trotsky in the flame and power of his appeal to any audience. Lenin's funeral was literally made for Trotsky. Whether Stalin liked it or not, Trotsky could have delivered a speech in the Red Square that would have electrified not only Russia but the whole world.

In justice to Trotsky it may be supposed that Lenin's death had caused him deep personal sorrow. Nevertheless, that sorrow can have been nothing in comparison to the despair that he felt at seeing himself blacked out of the Russian picture in which he had played so prominent a rôle. No wonder that his health did not improve and that he took no active part in politics until the late autumn. Whatever he might write about being "deceived" as to the date of the funeral he must have known that he himself was responsible for his fatal blunder. By his own act he had ostracized himself, and there was no more spirit in him.

It is always possible that Trotsky did not return to Moscow for the Thirteenth Congress in May because he had realized, somewhat tardily, the effect upon his fortunes of the influx of new members to the Party, who were nearly half the total roster, at that time 736,000. In his memoirs Trotsky says that three-quarters of the Party were new members. What he probably meant was that two-thirds of the

Party were against him in 1924, because it was almost equally divided between him and Stalin in the middle of 1923, and most of the new members had been picked to support the Stalin program. Whatever were Trotsky's motives, the fact remained that his star was sadly eclipsed, and that he did not renew the struggle until fresh economic and political difficulties caused a new outbreak of heart-burning and discontent in the higher ranks of the Party. Incidentally, such outbreaks or flare-ups of opposition sentiment always accompanied, or perhaps were caused by, periods of difficulty and popular discontent. This may have been due to an inherent flaw in the single-party system, which by stifling all overt criticism in press, speeches or radio almost forced discontent to find its expression in the Central Committee itself. In default of another outlet this was inevitable, but unfortunately it led to the very "factionism" or intra-party Opposition which the single-party system was designed to preclude.

In 1924, however, it was not overt signs of discontent or immediate economic difficulty that called for Bolshevik attention. Rather the reverse, in fact: the causes of trouble were prosperity and progress, but of the wrongest possible kind from the Bolshevik viewpoint. To paraphrase the old distich:

> A preoccupied cat
> Lets mice thrive and grow fat.

In other words, the NEPmen, private traders and producers in the towns, and the kulaks (rich peasants) in the villages, were in a fair way to taking over the country, to the profound dismay of all good Bolsheviks who weren't too "preoccupied" by the Party Controversy. The peasant worker masses, too, who at first had profited by the NEP revival, were beginning to ask if the Revolution had been made for their benefit or to enrich a host of shoddy profiteers and grafters. It was high time for action, since the NEPmen were handling almost two-thirds of the nation's trade and a great volume of petty industrial production, while the production of factory-made goods and of iron, steel, coal, oil and copper (that is of state-controlled industry) was less than a third of pre-war level, and the kulaks were getting an ever bigger share in agricultural production through their ability to employ hired labor and hold down the poorer peasants under a weight of debt. Once alive to this danger, the Bolsheviks acted with typical energy. A vigorous campaign was launched against unscrupulous NEPmen and their accomplices or dupes in government service. The first fruits of the investigation were bitter as gall in Bolshevik mouths. Corruption and fraud were revealed on all sides to an appalling degree, and it is said that thirty thousand state officials were arrested in Moscow alone. Communists and non-Communists alike, they had been sharing the NEPmen's wealth by remission of taxes, by sale of permits and privileges, and even by diverting state-produced goods to private business. The Bolsheviks were aghast as they delved deeper into the muckheap, and the reminder by State Control organizations, like the Peasants' and Workers' Inspection Board, that they had for months been trying vainly to call the attention of the authorities to these abuses, did' nothing to mitigate the feelings of the Central Committee. The latter's first wrath was directed against grafting state employees, but it soon became evident that collusion between them and the NEP-men had almost reached the proportions of a conspiracy to wreck state business. The drive was accordingly extended against the NEP-men accomplices of dishonest officials. Heavy new taxes were imposed on private trade, and severe penalties—imprisonment as well as fines—were imposed on private individuals who bought or sold state-produced goods. Culprits were arrested in tens of thousands and their businesses liquidated.

The effects were disastrous for two reasons: firstly, the co-operatives and state trusts, both as producers and distributors, were thrown into confusion by wholesale arrests of their personnel and were therefore unable to take the place of the liquidated NEPmen at a time when the villages were clamoring for consumers' goods after a good harvest (in 1923). Secondly, even those sections of state business which remained honest had yielded to the temptation of putting prices on their goods which the peasants were unable to meet. It was in a minor degree a repetition of the scissors crisis of the previous year. To make matters worse, the recent introduction of stable money (the chervonetz issue) had brought upon the country all the inconveniences of deflation. Unemployment rapidly increased, and the authorities found that what had begun as a tardy investigation had become an economic débâcle. They realized for the first time that NEP and Socialism were not only incompatible but that the process of passing from the former to the latter would be neither painless nor easy.

Here was a situation made to order for Trotsky, who returned to
Moscow that autumn much restored in health and full of fight. He
issued a pamphlet entitled "The Lessons of October,"[1] which in its
way was a masterpiece of polemic writing. Starting from the premise
that NEP had been allowed to get out of hand in town and country
and had become a source of error and corruption, Trotsky made a
sweeping attack on the whole Stalinist platform, especially its assumption that it was possible to construct a Socialist state in a single
country. He declared that this theory was an abandonment of the
principles of Marx and Lenin, and insisted that the revolutionary
movement must be dynamic, that is in a state of continual expansion,
instead of static, which was equivalent to abandonment or even
betrayal of basic revolutionary principles. Going further, he challenged the policy of compromise with NEPmen at home and with
capitalist countries abroad. In short, he presented his case as a plea
for a return to Marxism pure and undefiled, and put himself forward
as a reformer seeking to chase hucksters, compromisers and backsliders from the temple of Marx and Lenin.

Trotsky's pamphlet was much more than a specious appeal to the
purists and fundamentalists in the Bolshevik Party and to the "Old
Guard" Bolsheviks. It was a definite bid for leadership and in addition confronted the Bolshevik Party for the first time with an issue
of vital importance. Was the policy of the Soviet Union to be dictated by the interests of Russia or by those of world revolution, by
nationalism or internationalism? Trotsky posed as the champion of
the latter and implied that Stalin had chosen the former.

The "Lessons of October" caused a tremendous furore, because
Trotsky had deliberately put his finger upon the sorest of points and
raised the most vexed of questions—what, after all, was the meaning
and purpose of the Bolshevik Revolution? Was it to create a new
Russia or to create a new world? Was it the elemental rupture by
the Russian life-tree of the iron ring of Tsarism that was restricting
its growth and progress, or the seed of a new tree that would over-
shadow the whole earth?

Stalin met the challenge coolly. He realized the cleverness of
Trotsky's maneuver which aimed at converting matters of practical

---

[1] This really means "The Lessons of the Revolution," because the Bolsheviks
were accustomed to speak of the *October* Revolution (October 25, old style,
instead of November 7, reformed calendar).

policy into an abstract, ideological—almost theological—discussion. He saw the horns of the dilemma on which Trotsky was trying to impale him—"Either you admit that I am right and you are wrong, or you are a backslider, a traitor to Marx and Lenin." The dilemma was shrewdly conceived, but Stalin managed to evade it. He maintained stoutly that Trotsky was using a doctrinal red herring to dodge the real issue, that it wasn't a question of Marxist faith and orthodoxy but of a temporary stabilization of capitalism and worldwide diminution of revolutionary sentiment. Soviet Russia, he declared, was the only land of Marxian Socialism in a capitalist world that might at any time become actively hostile; the two lessons of *Lenin's* October, the true *Foundations of Leninism* (as Stalin's counter-blast to Trotsky's pamphlet was entitled) were that the Bolsheviks *must* build a successful Socialist regime in the Soviet Union, which was not a single country in Marx's sense of the phrase but a mighty continent with unlimited resources and a huge proletarian population. They must not waste time and energy in Utopian speculations but devote themselves wholeheartedly to strengthening the Soviet Union against future attack and to making it a model of Socialist society for the rest of the world to imitate. In short, that the really revolutionary, really Marxist path or "Line," as laid down by Lenin (who also had been accused of backsliding when he introduced NEP) was the hard, often thankless day-to-day job of building a Socialist edifice on Lenin's Foundations.

As a political essay, Stalin's retort may have lacked the polemic brilliance and specious casuistry of Trotsky's thesis, but it cut through Trotsky's web of argument with the cold logic of fact, and offered a sound alternative to Trotsky's proposed dilemma. This gave reassurance to waverers in the Central Committee camp, who at first had been shaken by Trotsky's pamphlet. Stalin, besides, could count upon the solid support of the men who like himself had remained in Russia during the period of repression, whereas there were many differences of opinion and jealousies amongst his adversaries, the former "Western exiles." Some of them, like Zinoviev and Kamenev—notoriously a cautious, not to say timid, couple—were alarmed by Trotsky's boldness. Others, like Sokolnikov (who had just successfully conducted the currency reform as Commissar of Finance) and Bukharin, thought that NEP—under proper control, of course—might still be a valuable adjunct to national progress.

Others, like Rykov (President of the Council of Commissars) and Tomsky (head of the Central Council of Labor Unions), resented Trotsky's leadership and thought that he, as an ex-Menshevik and frequent critic of Lenin in the past, was no fit person to carry Lenin's torch. Then as later, Stalin ruled his opponents by dividing them, playing one against another, and was thus able to secure the appointment of Frunze in Trotsky's place as Commissar of War. Any complaints that might have been raised by the Army, in which Trotsky's popularity, though diminished, was still considerable, were allayed by the suggestion that he lacked faith in the existence of a strong, self-sufficient Russia, enabled by its army, navy and air fleet to stand alone in a hostile world.

Nevertheless, intra-party agitation continued throughout 1925 and reached a new climax in the early winter when it became known that the delegation from Leningrad (of which Zinoviev was Party Boss) to the Fourteenth Party Congress, scheduled for December, intended to oppose the policy of Stalin and the Central Committee. Kamenev had joined the movement of revolt, in which Trotsky seems to have taken no great part although he still remained the chief Opposition figure. Stalin retaliated by abruptly changing the personnel of the Leningrad Party Secretariat and of the Communist Youth Organization, in which opposition sentiment was strongest, and similar changes were made in the staffs of the Leningrad Pravda and Com-Youth Pravda. This sudden blow so staggered Zinoviev and Kamenev that they were meek as mice at the Congress and even proposed the expulsion of Trotsky from the Party. On a later occasion Stalin reminded them of this and said that he had refused to agree because "Expulsion from the Party is the worst penalty that can be inflicted upon a Communist." He added prophetically that if Zinoviev and Kamenev did not mend their ways they might find that supreme penalty inflicted upon themselves.

During the winter of 1925 and the first half of 1926, pressure upon the urban NEPmen steadily increased in severity, and it was clear that the authorities intended to force them gradually out of business. This had become a practical possibility because state and municipal stores and state-controlled petty industry, together with the stores and petty industry of the co-operatives, which ranked as a state organization, were now able to take over most of the business formerly handled by private traders and producers. In the villages, however, the kulaks and upper middle peasants still provided most of the food surplus needed for urban and military consumption and for export, and the production of state farms was still only a fraction of the private output. Many Communists, especially in the provinces, failed to realize this important difference between urban and rural NEPmen, and by midsummer 1926 their complaints on this score had reached such proportions that the Opposition was emboldened to venture another attack. Forgetful of their promises to follow the Party Line implicitly, Kamenev and Zinoviev once more joined Trotsky in an attempt to form a solid bloc of opposition to the Kremlin's agrarian policy. Although the Opposition had considerable support from the rank and file of the Party, Stalin met the new onslaught with his usual weapons, secretarial manipulations and control of press, public speech and radio. His opponents took the unwise step of holding secret meetings and using "underground" printing presses. Their excuse that they were "forced" to do so by Stalin's methods did them little good, for when it became known that they had held an "illegal" meeting in the woods near Moscow, Communist indignation was so great that Stalin was able to remove Trotsky, Zinoviev and Kamenev from the Politburo without a murmur of protest. Indeed, the six principal Oppositionists found it desirable to disavow their underground tactics and "factional meetings" and once more promised to toe the Party Line.

In 1927 urban NEP was to all intents and purposes eliminated, but the prosperous-peasant production still greatly outweighed that of the state farms, and Stalin therefore declined to change his agrarian policy at the behest of popular clamor. The Opposition perhaps overestimated the discontent thus caused, or perhaps they were growing desperate. At any rate, on November 7th, anniversary of the Revolution, they ventured a direct appeal to the public in Moscow, Leningrad and the other great cities from balconies or improvised platforms in parks and squares. This forlorn hope was an utter failure; the masses refused to be stirred. The Opposition orators were greeted with some booing and catcalls, and a few rotten apples were thrown, but there was no excitement or disorder. Nevertheless the gesture was flagrant, and by Soviet law tantamount to open rebellion. Once more Trotsky had played into Stalin's hands, and retribution followed swiftly. The Fifteenth Party Congress, which met in December, expelled Trotsky, Kamenev, Zinoviev and seventy-five of their principal adherents from the Communist Party. Their expulsion was speedily followed by exile to Siberia and Central Asia, and the same punishment was inflicted upon hundreds of their humbler followers.

This was the end of overt opposition to Stalin and the Central Committee by the so-called Trotskyist group. In 1929 Trotsky was exiled abroad, to Turkey. His associates and the smaller fry recanted individually or in groups during the next two or three years and were readmitted to the Party on probation after promising obedience in grovelling and abject terms. The last to "abjure his heresy" was Rakovsky, former Soviet Ambassador to Paris and London, who held out until 1933 and acknowledged his faults with more dignity than most of his comrades. Like them he was given a post of some consequence but devoid of political significance. Stalin had gained greatly in authority, not, however, without antagonizing many important Communists, and he was subsequently to find himself exposed not only to criticism but to an organized secret Opposition fully as dangerous as Trotsky's.

Chapter 10

CREDITS AND DEBITS

By the end of 1922 the Bolsheviks were able to take stock of their situation at home and abroad with a certain measure of satisfaction. They had fought the Civil War and Intervention to a victorious conclusion, and were at peace with all the world. In November the Japanese had reluctantly withdrawn from Vladivostok, and the whole vast area formerly ruled by the Tsar was now under the Red flag with the exception of the Baltic States, Poland and Finland, whose independence the Bolsheviks had recognized by treaty, and Bessarabia, seized by Rumania in 1918. Thanks to American aid and to their own efforts, the Volga Famine had proved far less disastrous than expected, and agricultural prospects were good. Thanks to NEP there was a great improvement in the supply of food and consumer's goods, and great headway had been made against epidemic diseases. Lenin, who had been at death's door in the early summer, seemed restored to health, eager and ready to begin the great task of Socialist construction. Friendly relations had been established with the Eastern "Limitrope" countries, especially Turkey, and a cordial partnership, involving full *de jure* recognition, had been formed with Germany at Rapallo. Other European powers had been forced to admit that the Bolsheviks were firmly in the saddle, and had become sufficiently interested in the possibilities of trade with Russia to have set up Economic Missions in Moscow and admitted Soviet trade representatives to their own capitals.

That was all to the credit side of the Soviet ledger, but there were debit factors whose influence would be profound and lasting. To begin with, there was a great gulf of mutual distrust, created partly by propaganda, ignorance and fear, but due also to years of bitter hostility, to memories of a separate peace on one side and intervention on the other, and to an almost diametrically opposite outlook on life and ways of living. This distrust was psychological rather than concrete, but then and later it worked like acid upon every move towards a better understanding. The second factor was the question of pre-Revolutionary national debts and of compensation claims by private foreigners and firms. Third, the Communist International (Comintern). These three factors combined to set between Soviet Russia and the West a two-edged "Sword of Severance," whose blade was so sharp and whose steel so durable that both sides to this very day have never failed to look the giftest of horses meticulously in the mouth, and to find worms of suspicion in the fragrantest of bouquets. Take, for instance, the negotiations at Riga in the summer of 1921 between Litvinov and Walter Lyman Brown, representing the American Relief Administration, which had been asked, remember, to extend its charitable aid to victims of the Volga Famine. Mr. Brown might have been excused for taking every precaution that American food should not be diverted by the Che-ka or the Red Army; but neither that nor Litvinov's blunt statement that "Food is a weapon" (to be used presumably in sapping Soviet loyalty and morale) contributed greatly to reaching the desired agreement.

A still more apt illustration was offered by the foreign attitude towards the Rapallo pact. In Paris particularly it was regarded as a deliberate league of two "outlaw" nations against the Treaty of Versailles, which perhaps in a sense it was, and the French view was confirmed—and glumly accepted in London—by Soviet support of Mustapha Kemal, not only in his war with the Greeks but during negotiations at Lausanne in the following year, when the Turks succeeded in tearing up the Treaty of Sèvres as one of the "unfair revenge-treaties" imposed by the Paris Peace Conference upon the losers in the World War. A large body of influential opinion in Paris, London and other European capitals viewed the Russo-German pact as an unholy alliance between the Soviet devil and the German "mad dog of Europe." It was not only a breach in the "sanitary cordon" which kept Bolshevism from spreading westwards, but set a detestable precedent in the matter of debts and claims. The Rapallo pact mutually waived all debts and claims unless and until a settlement should be reached by any third country, in which case the said settlement should serve as the basis for Russo-German discussion. Small wonder that bankers and industrialists everywhere who had lost huge sums through the Bolshevik Revolution should add their clamor to that of the political and military critics of the Russo-German deal. This joint outcry drowned the timid voices of those who suggested that Russia might prove a good market of supply and demand, and that anyway the Soviet Government was now a going concern which could not be suppressed or ignored.

What the Bolsheviks thought about the debt question was demonstrated at the Genoa and Hague conferences, when they coolly presented a counter-claim for damages caused by Intervention whose total surpassed that of all public and private claims against them. They had long ago given warning, they declared, that they would repudiate Tsarist debts whose purpose was to prepare an imperialist war and to strengthen the Tsarist yoke upon the necks of Russian masses. The same, they added, applied to the war debts of the Provisional Government, while the claims of foreign capitalist firms or individuals were marred by shameless exaggeration and the prior exploitation of Russia's national resources. In reality, they were probably less recalcitrant about debts and claims than their attitude seemed to indicate, because they were most anxious to obtain foreign help for their reconstruction program, both in the form of concession agreements and of long-term credits to finance their purchases abroad. In Soviet diplomacy, as in the Russian character, there is a streak of oriental bargaining, which asks more than it expects to get and offers less than it expects to give. This fact was overlooked by the French and British in 1922, as it often has been since by them and others; and the Soviet counter-claim was dismissed as an impudent attempt at evasion.

In 1923 and 1924 Europe's political pendulum swung against the reactionary conservative parties in favor of more liberal groups. In England Labour took office for the first time in history as the largest single party in the House of Commons, although without a full majority. One of its first acts was to grant *de jure* recognition to the Soviet Government on February 1, 1924, an example followed within a week by Italy and later by France and several other countries. Distrust of Russia was still widespread, but European businessmen showed a growing tendency to consider trade with Russia a possible remedy for the post-war slump. The Labour Government decided to tackle the debt problem by an ingenious formula. They suggested that all credits or loans to Russia should carry slightly more than the current interest rates—say 6 percent instead of 4 percent—and the excess figure (2 percent) should be devoted to amortization of the earlier debts. The Bolsheviks were willing to accept this face-saving device, which was later adopted by private American firms like the International Harvester, which had claims against pre-Bolshevik Russia but wished to do business with Soviet Russia. There was therefore nothing intrinsically unsound in the Labour Government's proposal, but it did not meet the approval of powerful financial interests in the City of London. For this and other reasons the Conservative and Liberal groups in the House of Commons combined to force a general election in December, 1924, and the former brought into play the third "debit factor" against the Bolsheviks, namely the Comintern.

Ten days before the date of election a London Conservative newspaper published a document purporting to be a letter signed by Zinoviev, President of IKKI (Comintern Executive Committee) and also member of the Comparty Politburo, instructing the English Communist Party how to conduct its pre-electoral campaign and even how to vote. The letter was denounced as a forgery (a view later accepted by consensus of unbiased opinion in England) but the mere fact that Zinoviev was in a position to write it, and that the IKKI did give instructions or "directives" to foreign Communist Parties, was enough to send a wave of indignation across England. Labour was badly defeated, and the project of Debt Settlement perished stillborn.

From its foundation in March, 1919, the Third Communist International (Comintern) has been Russia's "red rag to a bull" as far as the rest of the world was concerned. It was the embodiment of all that foreigners feared from Soviet Russia; to statesmen a means of disruption and intrigue, to financiers and businessmen a nightmare to poison their sleep with the fear that what had happened somewhere once might happen again to them, to labor leaders and unions a serpent in their bosom, and to patriots generally an unwarranted aggression and interference. I have written earlier (p. 64) that the Comintern probably did more harm than help to the Soviet state . . . that it never had much more than a nuisance value, and that its services in spreading Bolshevik doctrines abroad and in acquiring

information were largely nullified by charges of espionage and interference. I see no reason to modify this statement, although it would
doubtless be challenged by the Bolsheviks in Russia and by Communist Parties in the rest of the world. No one, however, can deny
that the Comintern was dedicated to the cause of World Revolution, which Lenin claimed had been betrayed by the Second International. The Bolsheviks, and the Soviet Government, have always
maintained that the choice of Moscow as headquarters of the Comintern no more involved Soviet Russia in its activities than the choice
of Amsterdam as headquarters of the Second International involved
Holland. The Comintern, they declared, was an aggregation of
Communist Parties, most of which had legal standing in their own
countries, and among which the successful Communist Party of
Russia was no more than "first among equals." The rest of the world
has firmly declined to accept this casuistic distinction and has persisted in regarding the Comintern and the Soviet Government as
vassals of a single overlord, the Russian Communist Party. That
party has always exercised a predominant influence in the Executive
Committee of the Comintern (IKKI) whose directives are binding
upon Communist Parties of other countries. Finally, it has never
been a secret that the greater part of the Comintern's funds, wherever used or for whatever purpose, was provided by the Russian
Communist Party, and there is an old adage that "He who pays the
piper calls the tune." Therefore, while power in Russia remained in
Communist hands it was hard for foreigners to reconcile the action
of the Comintern in any country with the good-fellowship between
that country and Soviet Russia.

Ill-feeling on this account was intensified by Comintern activities,
especially during the early years of its existence, in the colonial
possessions of foreign powers and in semi-colonial countries such as
China. The French and British were particularly incensed by the
creation of an oriental college in Moscow (later moved to Tashkent,
in Central Asia) where Asiatic students were "educated" under
Comintern auspices. The British claimed that the Soviet Government
and the Comintern worked hand in hand in Asia. The former re-
nounced and denounced unequal treaties, capitulations, treaty ports,
protected areas and unilateral tariffs, while the latter fostered not
Communism but nationalism and anti-foreign sentiment. Such slogans
as "Asia for the Asiatics" cut deep into talk of "the white man's

burden" and of the boasts of Western empires that their rule was
beneficent and disinterested. They also served to answer the question
which had long perplexed orthodox Marxists, why the working
masses of Europe had failed to revolt, as Marx had predicted, against
their capitalist masters. Lenin argued that the surplus profits from
the exploitation of colonies and semi-colonial countries like China
had enabled European capitalists to maintain their own "wage-slaves"
above the starvation level which would make revolution inevitable.
To free such countries from capitalist exploitation would therefore
further the World Revolution, in whose probability Lenin never
ceased to believe. He thus reconciled three apparently contradictory
forces: the nationalist aspirations of colonial and semi-colonial countries, the principles of Marxist Communism, and the ambitious desire
of new Russia to become a Great Power in the world. I shall refer
later to the operations of combined Soviet and Comintern policy in
China, but as early as May, 1923, its effect in British colonial possessions was so great as to draw from Lord Curzon, then Foreign Secretary of a Conservative Government, a note so sharply worded as to
be almost an ultimatum. There were other points at issue, but the
question of Communist propaganda in British colonies and the British
Isles (notably Ireland) was the principal grievance. The Soviet Government made its usual disavowal of responsibility for the Comintern, but accepted the British demands under protest. Nevertheless,
the propaganda ghost was not laid and continued to trouble Soviet
Russia's foreign relations.

For a variety of reasons this ghost found the United States a
"happy haunting ground." First of all, there is no country in the
world which resents outside interference so keenly as the United
States. This is not only due to tradition but to the very circumstances
which led to the creation of the Republic, the refusal of the American colonies to submit to English dictation. This feeling was intensified by Washington's warning to "beware of entangling alliances,"
by the Monroe Doctrine, which said in effect to Europe, "hands off
the American hemisphere," and by the whole course of American
history and thought. The average American could not fail to regard
Communist propaganda and the Comintern as a challenge and affront
to his patriotic instincts. Secondly, Americans as a people have the
highest respect for home and family, for religion and the Church,
and for the right of groups and individuals to own property, to

make money and use it for profit. Rightly or wrongly, they were convinced that the Bolsheviks wished to abolish all three of these time-honored institutions. In consequence, the principles of Bolshevism were so unpopular in the United States that a violent "anti-Red" campaign was conducted there by Attorney-General Mitchell Palmer in 1919-20. Widespread resentment was aroused by reports of Communist propaganda among the colored race, and unassimilated semi-foreign sections of the American population. Labor in particular never ceased its condemnation of Bolshevik tactics of "boring from within," by which Communist or near-Communist minorities sought to gain control of the unions and federations. The Comintern was doubtless the chief hindrance to American recognition of Soviet Russia, and proved a thorny point in the pre-recognition discussions at Washington in November, 1933. Despite the safeguards then obtained against Comintern interference in American affairs, the United States Government found it necessary to address a protest on this account to Moscow in 1935.

It is curious to reflect that Russia and the United States have always misunderstood or even mistrusted each other from what now is called an ideological viewpoint, but instead of clashing in international affairs have come to each other's support in time of need. How can one explain this paradoxical contrast of friendship and distrust? I should say by community of interests abroad and divergence of governmental systems at home. When Russia was ruled by Tsarist autocracy, America was a democratic republic; when Russia was Bolshevik, America was capitalistic. It took the Tsars thirty-three years to recognize free America; it took America sixteen years to recognize Soviet Russia. But at a critical period of the War between the States Russia sent fleets to the east and west coasts of the United States to counteract the tendency of influential circles in France and Britain (which had recently defeated Russia in the Crimea) to recognize the Confederacy. Similarly, the United States sent an expeditionary force to Siberia in 1918, not to oppose the Bolshevik Revolution but to keep an eye on the Japanese, and later at the Washington Naval Conference put pressure on Japan to evacuate Vladivostok and the southern part of the Siberian coast in 1922. It will also be remembered that the first attempt, though abortive, to reach an equitable settlement of the Russian problem was made by President Wilson and Colonel House in the spring of 1919, through the Bullitt Mission to Moscow, and that the American people supported Russian famine relief in 1921-23 with unstinted generosity.

The Japanese undoubtedly left Vladivostok and the southern part of the Siberian coast, which they had occupied since 1918, unwillingly. As it was, when they did withdraw in November, 1922, they retained the northern part of the island of Sakhalin, on the pretext that the families of Japanese soldiers "murdered" by red guerrillas in the previous May should receive compensation. The Russians replied with a long list of atrocities committed by the Cossack General Semyonov and other semi-bandit leaders operating with Japanese support, and negotiations dragged on until August, 1924, when the Japanese agreed to abandon the Russian (northern) half of Sakhalin in return for valuable oil and coal concessions. The settlement led to *de jure* recognition of Russia by Japan on January 1, 1925. By that time most of the independent states of Asia, including China (May 31, 1924), and of Europe had established diplomatic relations with Soviet Russia. The Western hemisphere still held aloof with the exception of Mexico, which recognized Russia on August 4, 1924.

It was generally assumed abroad that the catastrophic state of Russian industry in 1921 was due in one word to Bolshevism with all its attendant evils, indeed a statement was made to that effect by no less eminent an authority than Mr. Herbert Hoover, then Secretary of Commerce. The Russians attributed it to the effects of Civil War and Intervention. There was doubtless some justification for both views, but the underlying fact of the matter was that Russian industry had never been self-supporting but a "hot-house" growth fostered by high tariffs and governmental subsidies. Prior to World War I Russia had been essentially an agricultural country, and three-quarters of the goods consumed by its population were the product of petty industry or "homecraft." The average Russian village bought little that was produced at a greater radius than ten or fifteen miles—the nearest market town—with the exception of salt, kerosene, lamps and samovars, cheap cotton cloth called *sittits,* and in years of good harvest factory-made shoes and galoshes. Incidentally, sittits, shoes and galoshes were mostly produced in Poland or the Baltic States, which in 1921 were no longer part of the Soviet Union.

The War had given a temporary stimulus to the metallurgic industry and the production of coal and oil, but this artificial prosperity vanished under the combined effects of peace and disrupted trans-

portation. In the autumn of 1922 Lenin had said publicly that the
chief obstacle to Russia's industrial reconstruction was lack of cash,
that only 20,000,000 gold roubles were available when at least 100,-
000,000 were needed to start the work. He then expressed, or at least
implied, the hope that NEP would attract considerable amounts of
foreign capital through long-term credits or even loans. More than
once such hopes rose high, when Royal Dutch Shell discussed an oil
concession in the Caucasus during the Genoa Conference, when
Harry Sinclair opened similar negotiations later in Moscow, and
Leslie Urquhart, president of a great Anglo-Russian mining corporation in the Urals, visited the Soviet capital to discuss a concession
regarding his former properties. But in each case agreement proved
impossible. Despite the deadlock about debts and claims at the Genoa
and Hague Conferences, the Soviet Finance Commissar, Sokolnikov,
referring to discussions in Paris with a Franco-British financial group,
announced in the autumn of 1923 that "There are fair prospects of a
state loan being floated abroad." This also led to nothing, until
finally the breakdown of the British Labour Government's debt-
settlement scheme—whether due to the Zinoviev letter or not—
showed that Lenin's hope of foreign capital was doomed to disap-
pointment, and that Soviet Russia would have to pull itself up by
its own bootstraps. NEP had done much to restore the production
of foodstuffs and of petty industry's consumer goods, but large-
scale factory industry, especially heavy industry, metallurgy and
mining, needed stronger medicine.

The "scissors" crisis in the autumn of 1923 and the widespread
corruption revealed when the Bolsheviks began to investigate national business under NEP in the spring and summer of the following
year showed only too plainly where NEP had succeeded and where
it failed. NEP's true nature also became apparent, a palliative or
stimulant rather than a cure. Lenin had known that from the first;
after all, NEP was his own brain-child, and had his health not broken
and his followers not been too busy disputing among themselves,
NEP might have been so controlled as to be useful, which it was,
without being dangerous, which it became. As far back as October,
1921, Lenin had made an extraordinarily frank speech to a delegation
of workers' and peasants' instruction centers. He said, "The real
meaning of the New Economic Policy is that we have met a great
defeat in our plans and are now making a strategic retreat . . . a
defeat more serious than any we suffered from the armies of Denikin

or Kolchak. We thought that the peasants would give us enough food to insure the support of the industrial workers. We were wrong, so we had to retreat. It is inevitable that some of our comrades will not be pleased with the situation and will even get panicky, yet all our military successes were preceded by similar retreats, and the same state of panic was then noticeable. Afterwards we began a slow systematic and cautious advance finally crowned by victory. We must follow the same plan in the economic field."

Thirteen months later Lenin went further in a speech to the Comintern Congress, which curiously enough was devoted almost wholly to the Russian internal situation instead of foreign affairs. He said, "In February last year"—that is, just before the Kronstadt mutiny and the Tambov Province revolt—"the peasants that form the majority of our population, and even the inhabitants of the towns and cities, were protesting. Their masses realized we were trying to cut corners too sharply. The situation was critical, so we decided upon the necessary change of policy and instituted a new system more in accordance with their needs. Today instead of opposing us the peasant masses are with us, small industry and commerce are reborn and working for the general benefit and satisfaction. Only heavy industry is backward."

Lenin's last two sentences put the matter in a nutshell, and the truth of his words was doubly manifest by midsummer, 1924, when more than fifteen percent of the nation's industrial workers were unemployed, and the peasants, for whose sake, as Lenin admitted, NEP had been introduced, were preparing to harvest a greatly diminished crop. NEP restored the supply of locally made consumer's goods on which they had always depended, so why, the peasants argued, should they produce extra food for the towns and cities which could only repay them in worthless paper?

In consequence, the 1924 crop was much below the previous year and the general economic outlook sufficiently black to lend point and punch, as I said in a previous chapter, to Trotsky's pamphlet, "The Lessons of October." Nevertheless, the position was far from desperate; towns and cities everywhere had been repaired and refurbished, and public utilities put back into running order. Urban NEP, despite its abuses, had restarted the business machine and provided innumerable jobs; public health had greatly improved and the standard of living, even for the unemployed, had been raised above the bare subsistence level of earlier years.

Chapter 11

THE DARK BACKGROUND

THE PASSAGES QUOTED in the preceding chapter indicate that Lenin viewed NEP as a concession to the peasants rather than to capitalism. Many of his followers, and most foreigners, failed to appreciate this important point, because NEP's outward capitalistic appearance blinded them to its inner fundamental purpose. They forgot what Lenin always remembered, that the peasants were not only four-fifths of the total population, but that most of the soldiers and urban workers were either of peasant origin or only one or two generations removed from the villages. To city-raised Bolsheviks it might seem that the Revolution had been won, and maintained, by the workers, soldiers and sailors; but Lenin, and also Stalin, were aware that the peasants had played a vital part and that their support was essential to the success of the Soviet regime.

Throughout Russia's history the peasants have been a dark background, unknown yet ominous by sheer weight of numbers. From the Middle Ages, when Russia threw off the yoke of Tatar invaders only to begin another struggle against Western enemies, until the end of the nineteenth century the peasants played for the most part a passive rôle quite out of keeping with their numerical importance. On occasion, spurred by hunger and oppression beyond endurance, they rose like a devouring flood against foreign foe or native tyrant, but save for those moments of frenzy they lived and died indifferent and unsharing in the red pageant of their country's history. Because they were slaves, little better than animals, tied to the soil and sold as part of it.

Even their emancipation from serfdom in the middle of the nineteenth century brought little practical change; the scraps of land
they were allowed to buy were so loaded with rents and charges, and
their owners so handicapped by poverty and ignorance, that it was
almost as difficult as before for an individual to rise from the slough
of despond in which the whole peasant population seemed hope-
lessly bogged.

Prior to 1875 one cannot think of Russian peasants in terms of
farmers as America has known farmers. They were not farmers at
all in our sense of the word; they were scarcely farm-laborers—more
like farm-cattle. They lived huddled in drab villages, sharing their
huts with such livestock as they were lucky enough to possess; peck-
ing aimlessly at the land with tools and methods so primitive as to
maintain them near the edge of starvation unless seasonal conditions
were unusually favorable; condemned by ignorance, poverty, and
the apathy their existence engendered to a lifelong servitude. When
I speak of peasants it must be remembered that I mean peasants
en masse, as a huge body forming more than four-fifths of the total
population of Tsarist Russia. Among them, of course, especially in
outlying regions, were communities descended from soldiers, free
Cossacks, and Tatar nomads, or those bolder spirits who had chosen
flight, banditry, and rebellion and lived to tell the tale. There were
also settlements of foreigners, Germans, or Swedes, descended from
religious exiles, or introduced by some Tsar to teach an industry in
which he was interested.

These were ranked among the peasantry but were far above its
average in the social, cultural and material scale. There were not,
however, enough of them, at least not in European Russia, to leaven
the amorphous lump which Russian rulers, writers, and historians
considered "the dark people," the poor benighted peasants. True,
the genius of Tolstoy, that inspired madman, created toward the end
of the nineteenth century a legend of the Russian peasant as unreal
as Potemkin's feasting villagers one hundred and fifty years before.

Tolstoy, outromancing the French romantics with their "noble
savage," gave the world a picture of Ivan Ivanich, who loved God,
his Little Father the Tsar, and his landlord with sincere affection, a
devout, simple, honest, healthy, happy man. Tolstoy doubtless believed what he wrote, but there have been few greater and more
terrible errors in history, as history itself has shown.

It was not the love of God and the Tsar or respect for landlords which first began to raise the Russian peasant from his ancestral depths, but the harsh demand for labor of the materialistic industrial age which dawned in Russia in the second half of the nineteenth century—that and the compulsion of universal military service following the Crimean and Franco-German wars. Now at last Ivan Ivanich was released from his village prison, shown new sights and ways, perhaps taught fragments of useful knowledge, even though to his bewildered mind he was only exchanging the worse bondage of barracks or factory for the monotonous drudgery of peasant existence.

It is no mere accident that the demand for factory-fodder and cannon-fodder coincided with the release of the peasants from serfdom. No accident, either, that in this period there first appeared a figure whom the Bolsheviks have made world-famous—the kulak, the grasping "rich" peasant who squeezed his fellow-villagers in fingers harder than those of Tsar, landlord, or gendarme. The kulak was indeed the product of emancipation, the unconscious and, if he had but known it, the unwilling forerunner of another and greater emancipation.

During the period of serfdom a few rare individuals managed to rise above their peasant environment and become free citizens; others won liberty by flight and revolt. In both cases they left their villages behind them; in that stagnant atmosphere there could be drawn no breath of freedom. Now, however, there developed a steady flow of the strongest, most enterprising peasants, to industry and the army. Later, they returned to their villages and the land-owning instinct repressed by serfdom began to operate all the more fiercely because of that repression.

The kulak symbolized land-hunger in its sharpest form; he visualized for his poorer fellows the new aim that had replaced the bare struggle to live of previous centuries, the aim to own land for one's self, to add acre to acre, to grow rich, or what peasants meant by rich.

That the growth of the kulaks as a class involved and developed intense individualism, narrow conservatism, and a corresponding eagerness to exploit the weakness of poorer peasants around them, has been so vociferously proclaimed by the Bolsheviks that one is apt to lose sight of two important facts. First, that the kulaks, who after all were not "rich" in reality but simply self-supporting small farmers, were not all villains and squeezers, but as years passed began to represent the typical hardworking yeoman class that has been regarded as the backbone of many Western nations—the development of farming in France since the French Revolution is an obvious case in point. Second, that, whether they were cruel squeezers or kindly helpful neighbors, they were the object of envy and emulation to all the poorer peasants in the country.

The abortive revolutionary movement of 1905-1906 marks a definite point in the rural development of Russia. It was not only an uprising of the new (but lately peasant) proletariat of the cities, but an expression of the land-hunger of the would-be kulaks, that is, the independent land-owning masses of the villages; and for every factory seized or looted by urban workers there were parallel attacks on châteaux and the seizure of landlord's property.

For the first time the mass of the Russian peasants saw a goal ahead of them, no longer a dim possibility as remote as heaven, but reasonably near, perhaps in their own lifetime: the appropriation and division of big estates and the achievement of self-maintenance by each family on its own farm.

Defenders of the old regime in Russia have argued that peasant ownership was already so extended by 1917 that the partition of large estates added comparatively little to the number or volume of small holdings. But the point they forgot is that rent and charges on these holdings were so great that their owners, except the four or five percent of kulaks, were never self-supporting; that, in short, the mass of the peasants considered themselves cheated by the terms on which they had been allowed to own land since the emancipation; and that what they meant by their slogan of "land for the peasants" was ownership in fee simple—not just the addition of extra acres belonging to their masters.

And that, no less, was the program of the Social Revolutionary party, par excellence the peasant party in Russia, in the troubled summer of 1917.

The Bolsheviks have been pictured as riding to power on the joint demand for peace and land, but it is worth remembering that while they used both these and other methods of popular appeal, and did their utmost to hasten the process of disintegration in the army, their action in, and influence upon, the villages was relatively small. Their main effort was exerted upon the urban proletariat, by 1917 from half a generation to a generation and a half removed from village life; and it was in the urban centers that they won success.

For months before November 7th the peasants, led mainly by the Social Revolutionaries, had been driving passionately at their own goal of land expropriation, which grew steadily nearer as each accession of armed deserters from the army strengthened the hungry village and weakened the landlords' resistance. The Bolshevik revolution did little more than set the seal of fact and finality upon a process that was already near completion.

It may be said then that there were really two revolutions in November, 1917—the Bolsheviks' seizure of power in the cities and towns; the peasants' seizure of land, with all that it implied in outright ownership, in the villages. The two movements were united and made possible by a third revolution, that of the soldiers, which for the first time put the balance of physical power in the hands of the Russian masses against their masters. The Bolsheviks did not lead or even initiate the peasant revolution and were only partly responsible for the military revolution, but by a stroke of courage and statecraft they assumed leadership of both.

That lead they were able to hold by superior organization and the energy and character of their central committee or directorate, headed by Lenin, who knew well how utterly the individualistic land-grabbing of the peasants and the undisciplined desire for peace of the soldiers differed from the Bolshevik aim of Marxist collectivism, but whose first purpose was to establish and insure the unity of the revolutionary cause and make clear the essential factor that in town and village and cantonment alike it was a revolt of the proletarian many against the possessing few, of the propertyless masses against the masters and owners.

Throughout the years of struggle that followed, the Bolsheviks never lost the hold thus gained, though at times it wavered under the strain of military necessity with its requisition of men, animals, and food. But—and this is a point of vital importance—neither the ultimate victory over counter-revolution nor the exigencies of militant communism during the fighting period removed, or indeed materially affected, the fundamental contradiction between the Bolsheviks' goal of Marxist collectivism or socialism and the peasant goal of full land-ownership, without rent or any charges except the minimum taxation required for the protection of that ownership, which spelled individualism in the highest degree.

That problem, as Lenin knew, was still to be solved, and on its solution depended the success or failure of the socialist experiment to which he and his associates had devoted their lives. Its urgency became at once apparent in the winter of 1920-21, when for the first time the land had peace from civil and foreign war, and the peasants began to feel that the compulsion of military necessity had ceased to operate.

At that time the Bolshevik authority was fully established, the Red Army was a disciplined and coherent fighting force, and the urban proletariat was conscious of its triumph and loyal to its communist vanguard; but four-fifths of the population still were peasants, each holding jealously to the scraps of land they now felt they owned, most of them sharply resentful towards the food requisitions imposed by a war which had touched few of them directly, as it was fought chiefly along the scanty lines of national communication. To them now, as always, it seemed the government and the townsfolk were their enemies, demanding much and giving little. The Bolsheviks and the cities shouted victory, but the peasant idea of victory was different.

At this point it is necessary to make a brief explanation. There was, of course, no clear-cut distinction between the peasantry and the urban proletariat; the time-distance separating them—two generations at the utmost—was too short for that. What is more, the Red Army, still chiefly drawn from peasant sources, was a link of real value. But the differences were profound, nevertheless—differences of habit and outlook, differences of knowledge, and above all the difference of aim.

The peasants as a mass were still backward, dirty, ignorant, superstitious, conservative in the sense of hating the new and wanting to hold what they had got, and intensely individualistic. Though many among them were kindly, hard-working, and simple, they were still, as a whole, a slavish folk, timid and suspicious, incapable of self-government or useful co-operation. For centuries they had cowered beneath the whip, and now the whip was broken. They were the people of Russia, they had been told, and who should hold or bind them? Surely not the handful of Bolsheviks, decimated by bitter struggle; not the numerical minority of city workers, exhausted and well-nigh starving. Not even the Red Army, whose soldiers were their brothers. The peasants felt they could say: "The war was over, was it? Now let us see about taxes and requisitions!"

The spring of 1921 had hardly melted the winter snows before the clash came. The peasant revolt against Militant Communism burst forth in the Kronstadt mutiny and a flat refusal in Tambov Province to accept the practice of requisitions. The mutiny was crushed by superior forces from Petrograd, but the Tambov movement spread like a prairie fire. The Red Army refused to fire upon the rebels, and in Tambov some divisions made common cause with their "peasant brothers."

Lenin acted with characteristic flair for the facts of the situation. He rushed through the Communist Party Congress in March a decree abolishing requisitions as such and allowing "free trade" in the villages; then he spent the next four months in convincing his followers that the time was not ripe for a struggle with peasant individualism; that the kulak spirit and ideal was still too strong and prevalent, that Communism must retreat all along the line. In August his theories were embodied in the New Economic Policy, which restored private capitalism as far as the peasants were concerned, although keeping the control of finance, foreign trade, heavy industry and transport in the hands of the state. The clash had come, indeed, between socialism and individualism, and the peasants had won the first round.

But, said Lenin, the Bolsheviks had not abandoned the struggle, though some of them for a moment doubted him, and though a host of profiteers sprang up to reap rich if short-lived gains from private trading. The peasants, he said, were not enemies of the Bolshevik regime, but they were the most backward and ignorant section of the population, who must be taught slowly and carefully, encouraged to develop and realize the benefits of their own co-operative system, and led toward socialism by the use of machinery and the example of workers in the towns and cities.

It would be a long job, Lenin said, because the peasants had suffered much and were far behind the townsfolk in social consciousness; because the lesson of Militant Communism had been too severe and sudden, it was natural the peasants could not understand why their produce was taken and they received only promises in return.

"Give them tractors," said Lenin, "and schools and doctors and teachers, new tools and new methods; then they will change their old ways and leave the kulak to follow us."

Before the Revolution and after it (until the Collective Farm system was fully established) it was customary to divide the peasants roughly into three categories, the "kulaks" or richer peasants, the middle peasants, and the poor peasants. The first category, about five percent of the total, included those who owned animals and equipment, employed labor, and had sufficient reserves of food and money to survive all save the worst of crop failures. The middle peasants, some twenty-five percent of the total, could manage to farm their own land, without employing labor, and in an average year were able to exist without having to work for anyone else, either in the towns or their native village. The remaining seventy percent for the most part did not own draft animals at all, and either harnessed themselves and their families to the plough—no exceptional circumstance—or hired livestock and seed from the kulaks at usurious rates. Many of them were landless and spent their lives working for the kulaks in summer and at ill-paid unskilled jobs in the towns and construction camps in winter. Even those who had land rarely made ends meet without getting into debt and being forced to sell part of their labor in town or country at the cheapest rates.

Trotsky's "Lessons of October" attempt to put the intra-party controversy on to a purely theoretical basis and to portray Stalin and his Central Committee majority as nationalistic backsliders—heretics championing the program of Socialism in a single country—and traitors to the World Revolution ideal of Marx and Lenin did much to obscure, both at home and abroad, the real issues in the years 1925-27. These issues were: (1) the peasant question, that is, the production of food; (2) Industrialization. As I have said earlier, Stalin refused to follow Trotsky's "red herring," but the scissors crisis of 1923 showed him that the peasants were capable of greatly reducing the production of food if they did not receive goods or sound money in exchange for their produce. On this account the harvest of 1924 fell considerably, and grain exports, upon which the Soviet Government relied to bolster its still shaky credit abroad, were dangerously reduced. Accordingly Stalin took advantage of the emotional loyalty caused by Lenin's death and the great enrolment of new Party members to conduct a vigorous campaign throughout the villages for the

increase of the grain-sown area in the autumn of 1924 and the following spring. He was aided by favorable weather conditions, and
the harvests of 1925 and 1926 were excellent. By that time the
intra-party Opposition had taken a new tack. Instead of kowtowing
to the prosperous peasants—one prominent Oppositionist, Bukharin,
had actually issued to the villages the slogan "Enrich yourselves"—
the Opposition now (in 1926-27) demanded that the "kulaks"
should be expropriated *en masse*, as the urban NEPmen had been,
by heavy *retroactive* taxation. This demand won wide favor in the
ranks of the Party, but Stalin declined to accept it, because he knew
that surplus needed for export, to maintain purchases abroad, was
almost wholly provided by the richer peasants. He hoped that the
big state-owned farms would soon be able to fill the gap, but they
were not yet in a position to do so. Thus there was a close connection between the peasant question and industrialization.

The comparative failure of the "Concessions" policy as a means
of obtaining foreign capital, and the breakdown of Debt Settlement
plans, had convinced Stalin that the building of a self-supporting
Soviet industry, the development of railroads, mines and power
plants, and the construction of metallurgic factories to produce the
machines and machine-tools to make textile, agricultural and other
machinery, must be undertaken "the hard way" by Russia's own
slow efforts, buying what was needed from abroad by exports, and
gradually building up good-will and credit by prompt payment of
all obligations. In the autumn of 1925 he had a windfall in the shape
of an eighty-million-dollar credit from Germany to be used for the
purchase of German material, for a term of three years with a clause
permitting it to be "revolved" or renewed when the term was up.

This fortunate deal helped to stimulate credit in France, England
and, on shorter terms for the purchase of cotton, in the United
States. It still, however, was essential that all foreign bills should
always be met on time, no matter what hardships this might cause
at home. That this was done, even in the darkest period of depression, did much to restore Russia's foreign credit standing, and the
debt question quietly faded into oblivion except for some arrangements with individual foreign firms.

Not the least of Stalin's qualities is his ability to profit by experience. Thus, despite the bitterness of the intra-party controversy in
1926 and 1927, he did not repeat the earlier mistake of neglecting

public affairs, but on the contrary used the controversy as a reason for taking the masses into his confidence and winning their support through the press, public speeches, party and non-party meetings, and the growing power of radio. In view of what followed it is interesting to note that much of his success in the villages, and therefore or his victory over the Opposition, was due to his obstinate refusal to put pressure too soon upon the richer peasants. Patience, willingness to bide his time and await the psychological moment, is another outstanding quality of Joseph Stalin.

Chapter 12

UNITED EFFORT

THE YEARS WHICH followed Lenin's death were for Russia a period of intense activity and general progress, in which external circumstances played an important part. European countries were emerging from their post-war depression, and the victor nations were receiving reparation payments from Germany, made possible by a golden flood of loans from the United States, where business was booming. Europe thus shared American prosperity, and Germany in particular enjoyed a great business expansion which accounted for its three-year credit to Russia. The Russians further benefited by a world-wide rise of prices, especially in grain and other raw materials which they exported. Finally, the political horizon was clearer than it had been for decades, and the Locarno Agreement in 1925 held out hope that France, Britain and Germany would henceforth live in amity and co-operate for the benefit of all. Meanwhile, undeterred by difficulties ahead, the Russians embarked upon their program of industrialization. Work was begun upon an immense metallurgic "combinat" on the steppes of mid-Siberia in the coal and iron basin of Kuznetsk, and on an equal scale in the south Urals near the iron deposits of Magnitogorsk. No less ambitious was the project to construct on the Dnieper the world's largest dam and power station.

The Bolsheviks were disappointed by the failure of their attempts to get foreign capital for industrial reconstruction, but they cannot have been surprised and were certainly not dismayed. They faced the task of "making bricks without straw," of tackling a gigantic job with less than a fifth of the money needed to start it, as Lenin had frankly admitted. But there were factors in their favor by which the deadlock might be broken, and they were prepared to use them with ruthless energy. The first was precisely that, their own energy and ruthlessness. Men like Stalin, who had spent the best years of their lives in danger and difficulty, imprisonment and exile, could never be deterred by thought of the hardships their policies might inflict upon others. They knew that the Russian masses were accustomed and inured to hardship, and that the Revolution had released a vast force of energy with which miracles could be wrought if it was rightly employed. They had the feeling which Napoleon, another child of Revolution, shared with them, that nothing was impossible, no problem insoluble, no mountain too steep to climb. They were armored against adversity and peril because they could say with truth, "We met worse than this before and defeated it, so why should we doubt or falter?" Finally, with all its imperfections NEP had given the Russian nation a breathing-space and put some flesh on its bones.

The Bolsheviks, accordingly, set about their industrial reconstruction in a simple yet amazing way. They just *went ahead* with it, irrespective of money or obstacles. That is to say, they began in 1925 to execute the industrial program which had been approved by the Ninth Party Congress in March, 1920, when Soviet Russia was thrilled by its victory in the Civil War and ignorant that a new exhausting struggle with Poland was just around the corner. The Ninth Congress had welcomed Lenin's ambitious project for the Electrification of Russia, the building of huge dams and hydraulic power stations, the building of great metallurgic plants and the factories to make machines that would make machines, of a network of railroads and roads twice bigger than before, and a trebled output of mines and oil fields. For that purpose the Ninth Congress had also approved the formation of a State Planning Commission, called Gosplan, which should co-ordinate and direct the nation's industrial capacity from blueprint to finished product.

In 1925 and 1926 that program was still in embryo, and the Gosplan itself existed mostly on paper. But the Bolsheviks began work as if everything was ready, every "t" crossed and every "i" dotted. First of all they decided what was needed, so many railroad lines to be put in good running order, so many to be built, this number of mines to be restored to full output, that number to be opened, these metallurgic factories to be reconstructed, those to be built from the ground up. It did not stagger them that the plants to provide power for these new factories were not yet in existence, or that the machine-tool factories and tractor and automobile factories and the colossal industrial agglomerations that would produce harvesters and combines and multi-bladed ploughs and everything else needed to modernize agriculture were not even outlined on paper or more than a dream of the future. The Bolsheviks disregarded all that, supported by their own faith and energy and by the singular Russian faculty of believing that anything discussed and decided upon was already half accomplished. To use an un-Bolshevik metaphor, Lenin had realized, and taught to his followers, that the Russian masses were a bank upon which any check could be drawn, provided that they were told what the money was for and that it was being spent for their benefit. As Lenin said and repeated, the masses would do anything, suffer anything, and shrink from nothing, if they were rightly appealed to.

The hydro-electric dam project called Dnieperstroy, on a middle reach of the Dnieper River, in the heart of the industrial Ukraine, gave a magnificent and typical illustration of Bolshevik methods. To a backward and childish people which knew nothing of electricity and considered the ownership of one small horse a proof of prosperity and earnest of future success, Stalin presented the splendid vision of a mechanical giant that would have the strength of a million horses and harness the lightning of a thousand storms, that would make a great new lake to water the dusty steppes and bear ships for hundreds of miles across impassable rapids. All this would come from a dam, a monster of concrete and steel whose like the world had never seen, bigger and wider and stronger than even America, fabulous land of industrial marvels, had been able to construct. They, the new Russia, would build it as a monument to past struggles and to future hopes, a proof of their mighty Today and limitless Tomorrow.

Politically and psychologically the Dnieper Dam project, conceived by Lenin or perhaps before him but brought to birth and life by Stalin, was a stroke of genius. It played upon Russia's deep primitive love of fairy-tales and the miraculous, and on Russia's new-found pride in its bigness and unbounded horizon. The dam would be built, the Bolsheviks reminded them, not by angels or genii but by human effort, not for the profit of a few but for the benefit of the many. It would be a symbol of united effort and the first fruits of a creative era unparalleled in history. All the resources of Bolshevik propaganda were employed to popularize the Dam and to present it as a truly national enterprise. Every man, woman and child in Russia contributed to the Dnieperstroy, from the pennies of school-children to the week's or month's pay of workers and employees. This was fully understood by foreign observers in Russia, but none of us seemed to note something more significant still, that the Dnieperstroy was wholly Russian in concept, execution and purpose, without a vestige of international motive or idealism.

However, from a purely practical viewpoint there was a foreign note in the Dnieperstroy symphony; the Soviet Government enlisted the services, as consultant and supervisor, of an American, Colonel Hugh L. Cooper, who had had world-wide experience in dam construction. The agreement which Colonel Cooper made with the Soviet Government was not a concession like that which another American, Averell Harriman, made to develop the rich manganese deposits of Chiaturi, in the Caucasus, or an Anglo-American syndicate to work their former holdings in the Lena gold fields. Cooper had no financial investment in the Dam, which was built wholly with Soviet money. He was paid an ample fee for his services, but he assumed, under forfeit, full responsibility for the quality, volume and speed of the whole performance. Colonel Cooper knew exactly what that responsibility meant. He had built dams before in strange and difficult places for strange and difficult people, but his contract was drawn up with a thoroughness and care which Messrs. Harriman and the Lena consortium might have done well to imitate. His payments, in gold, were guaranteed beforehand; comfortable living quarters for his American personnel, and if necessary their wives, were provided ready and furnished before they arrived; they were entitled to bring in or receive, duty-free, any goods or supplies from America that they might want; and special arrangements were made about their mail and parcels. Finally, the Colonel's authority, and that of his subordinates, was absolute in supervising and approving or declining to approve every blueprint drawn and every yard of concrete poured. The result was an object lesson in American-Soviet co-operation. Actual work began in 1927 and was finished in 1932, almost two years earlier than originally estimated. It was at the time the biggest dam in existence, and on several occasions world records had been beaten for the volume of concrete poured in twenty-four hours. There had been throughout a minimum of friction between the Americans and Russians. Colonel Cooper and his hand-picked associates leaned over backwards to meet the Russians half-way and to make allowance for the differences of outlook and circumstance, of language and behavior which hampered and often nullified the work of other foreign specialists. For both parties to the contract it was an exceptional job, performed to their mutual satisfaction, and it is a pity that Colonel Cooper's professional duties—or other reasons—prevented him from continuing his collaboration with Soviet Russia on a much wider scale as Ambassador of the United States. More perhaps than any foreigner he had won the confidence, respect and liking of the hard and suspicious Bolsheviks.

I have devoted much space to the Dnieper Dam, not only because it was so successful and of such enormous value, but because it was a national achievement, accomplished despite terrific difficulties by an untrained army of men and women workers. It was only the first and largest of a thousand great enterprises which were to transform the face of Russia, and for which it served as example and inspiration; but it proved to the Russian people and to the world that if wisely led and rightly stimulated they could do anything. The Dam was far more than a feat of industry and engineering; it gave hope and faith and pride in themselves and their own possibilities to the nation which Kerensky had contemptuously described as a mob of enfranchised slaves.

There was one item in the Dam's construction which had a profound and tragic significance. A number of special chambers were prepared at vital points in the power plants, sluices and the body of the dam itself, ready in advance to be filled with high explosives to blow the whole thing to pieces. Consider what this meant in terms of courage, and of foresight. Before it was even finished, this work that was the nation's pride and joy, thus to prepare for its destruction! And calmly to destroy it, before ten years had passed, when the long-anticipated onslaught struck Russia from the West.

Stalin and his friends may well look back upon the five-year period which followed the death of Lenin as decisive in his life and in his country's history. Inside the Party he was fighting opponents

armed with greater dialectic brilliance and a closer companionship
with Lenin than he could boast. In Russia there was a monstrous
complex of economic and social problems; and abroad, distrust and
hatred on every side. Against all that Stalin had his own strong will,
patience and political acumen, and the wholehearted support of men
who trusted him and on whom he could rely. He had belief in the
Russian people, in its desire for knowledge and progress and its
resistance to any hardship. And by a curious quirk of Fate, which
had not been kind to the Bolsheviks, conditions abroad were such
as to give him aid and opportunity to maneuver. These were circumstances beyond Stalin's control which doubtless facilitated the
accomplishment of the work on the Dnieper River, on the two
immense metallurgical plants in Siberia, on other industrial enterprises and the huge state farms, all of which were conceived and
planned, and some of the spade work done, as early as 1925 and 1926.
But foreign conditions were not responsible for Stalin's success in
defeating his Party opponents, in boldly planning and starting the
job of making bricks without straw, and finally, in 1928, of preparing
an outline of "planned economy," the program of Socialist construction for the next five years. That would seem task enough to absorb
the energies of any group or government, but the Bolsheviks found
time and strength to conduct a foreign "adventure"—perhaps this
phrase is too strong—of no small interest and importance then and
for the future.

As Russia lies between Europe and Asia, in moments of weakness
it has been attacked from West or East, and in moments of strength
expanded westwards or eastwards. As its strength increased, it
seemed that a law of growth had been imposed on Russia, to see-saw
from East to West in alternate surges of effort, like the blinded
Samson striving this way and that way to break the bonds which
bound him. In the summer of 1920 Lenin had a moment's vision of
westward expansion, to drive on through Poland into the heart of
Europe and plant the Red flag of Russia upon the citadels of Berlin,
Vienna and Budapest. That dream was blasted at Warsaw, and
Russia recoiled like a spring to gather strength and tension. In the
years which followed, the barrier of European capitalism grew
stabler and more solid against Russia, but Russian influence was

spreading in the awakening countries of Asia, Turkey, Persia, Afghanistan, India and China. Russia was looking eastwards, and its slogan, "Asia for the Asiatics," found an echo in the East. Like any tide, there was ebb and flow in the waves of this Russian expansion. Turkey won independence at Lausanne, Persia was liberated, and Afghanistan dared to defy the British; but the Russian flood was checked in India and the Franco-British islands by Curzon's ultimatum. There remained China, half-free, half-slave, wise and ignorant, conquered and unconquerable, divided against itself.

Like Russia, China had known a great Deliverer, and there had been a link of fellowship and understanding between Sun Yat-sen and Lenin; but after the former's death his country had fallen prey to the internecine struggles of selfish and reactionary war-lords. Nevertheless, the seed of freedom was bearing fruit and the Chinese nation was ready to hear the Moscow Gospel. Stalin, like Lenin his master, a subtle opportunist, must have welcomed the chance of confuting by action in China the Trotskyist charge that he was betraying the cause of World Revolution. Actually, whether Stalin knew it or not, he was swimming with the tide of Russia's eastward surge when in 1925 he sent military and political advisers, Army Commander Blucher, called Galen, and Borodin to Canton, where Sun Yat-sen's brother-in-law, Chiang Kai-shek, had headed a new nationalist movement for Chinese unity and freedom from foreign control.

The Russo-Chinese agreement of 1924 had established a Soviet ambassador, Karakhan, in the former Imperial Embassy of Pekin, then ruled by the Manchurian war-lord Chang Tso-lin. The other Western diplomats, except the Germans, were outraged by the presence of "this Bolshevik" inside the Legation Quarter of the Chinese capital. As I said earlier, their countries at home were passing through a phase of liberalism and they could only rage impotently while Karakhan, Galen and Borodin carried on what was subsequently alleged to be an ingenious combination of diplomatic, military and Comintern activities. Blucher-Galen and his Staff aided Chiang Kai-shek to build an army for the Nationalist Movement from the nucleus of the Whampoa Military Academy at Canton, whence he pushed northwards in 1925 and the following winter, gaining strength and adherents as he went. Early in 1927 Chiang

Kai-shek took the important city of Hankow on the Upper Yangtse, and occupied Nanking and the Chinese section of Shanghai in March.

Meanwhile Borodin and his civilian assistants organized an equally successful propaganda campaign whose keynotes were "Asia for the Asiatics" and "Down with Unequal Treaties," in accordance with the Communist International's policy for colonial and semi-colonial countries. At Hankow the British were induced, if not compelled, to abandon their jealously guarded extra-territorial rights and foreign circles throughout China were alarmed and angered by the wild-fire spread of anti-foreign sentiment. They suspected, perhaps with reason, that Borodin and the Nationalist Movement as a whole were receiving financial assistance from Moscow through the Soviet Ambassador, Karakhan, at Pekin. The Manchurian dictator, Chang Tso-lin, may at first have viewed the Nationalist progress without disfavor, as being likely to weaken some of his rival war-lords in South Central China. Chiang Kai-shek's capture of Nanking and Shanghai, however, was more than Chang Tso-lin had bargained for, and led him to pay attention to foreign complaints. In March, 1927, his soldiers entered the sacrosanct Legation Quarter of Pekin, perhaps at the request, and certainly with the knowledge, of the foreign diplomatic corps and raided the premises of the Soviet Embassy. A great number of documents were seized and several Chinese Communists and other refugees were arrested. The Soviet promptly withdrew Karakhan and broke relations with Chang Tso-lin, who retaliated by publishing selections of the seized documents, which purported to show not merely the interlocking action of the Soviet government with the work of Galen and Borodin, but the transmission of funds to the latter from Moscow through Karakhan.

At this juncture Fortune, who had favored the Bolsheviks in China for two years, began to frown upon them. The British, infuriated by the loss of their settlement in Hankow, used the Soviet Embassy documents to put pressure upon Chiang Kai-shek and to persuade other foreign representatives to join them. It is possible that Chiang Kai-shek himself had been alarmed or at least made restive by the growing influence of the Russians and the "Left Wing" in the nationalist movement and may have listened readily enough to suggestions that he was acting as their cat's paw. He could see, too, the economic and political advantages of being on friendly terms with the powerful interests, both native and foreign, who had made the International Settlement of Shanghai a world stronghold of Big Business. At any rate, he broke suddenly with his Left, or Communist Wing, and drowned their attempts at resistance in blood. Galen, Borodin and their Russian subordinates were forced to flee back to Russia. This *coup de théâtre* in China had its parallel in London, where the Conservative Government had not forgiven the Bolsheviks for financial support by the Russian Miners' Union to the striking miners of Great Britain in the previous year. The coal strike had even led to an attempted general strike, which failed dismally but had given the City of London some unpleasant moments. In May the British police raided the premises of Arcos, the Anglo-Soviet Trading Corporation, in London and submitted the whole building to a minute search. No "incriminating documents" were published, and it is generally believed that none were found. On the other hand, the British authorities appear to have been convinced that such documents, or a document, alleged to be connected with the Northwest Frontier defenses of India, had been in the Arcos safe but had been removed or destroyed before the raid. After a brief and acrid exchange of notes the British Government recalled its ambassador from Moscow and broke diplomatic relations with the U. S. S. R. on May 24th, and they were not renewed until a second Labour Government took power in England two years later.

Chapter 13

THE FIVE-YEAR PLAN: A WEAPON

In EVERY HISTORICAL analysis one is forced to consider the influence of two factors, Personality and Luck. There is such a thing as truth, that is, the facts as they happened, which the historian tries to record, but he must seek to discover whether and to what degree those facts were used and brought into being by an individual and, conversely, influenced that individual in his choice of policy and conduct. This sounds obscure, but it can be simplified, as follows. Was it France or Napoleon from 1794 to 1814? Was it Germany or Hitler from 1933 to the present day? Is it England or Churchill since 1940? And last but not least, has it been Russia or Stalin?

The Bolsheviks have answered this question by what they are pleased to call Marxian dialectics, a dogmatic copy of ancient Greek Sophistry. The Bolsheviks say that circumstances produce the personality, that the leader is the product of environment, need and opportunity. This can be put more simply, that if there's a horse and cart and a road along which to drive, the driver will be provided. Provided, one must ask, by What, or even by Whom? Marx never answered that question, but Hegel, his teacher and source of inspiration, would, I suppose, have replied that God or some superhuman force would provide the driver. Carlyle, on the other hand, took a more practical view, that the "hero" or leader, an exceptional man, no more, saw a cart and a horse and a road and jumped to the driver's seat. Many people will prefer Carlyle, with a reservation about the phrase "jumped to the driver's seat." How

146

easy was this jump, or how difficult? How fast was it made or how slowly?

There is, too, the other factor, Luck. I make bold to state that no one with any experience of life can deny the existence of luck, the importance of luck, and the fact that it comes in waves when everything goes right and ebbs away in waves when everything goes wrong. Why this is so no one knows, but everyone knows it is true. Everyone, that is, except Stalin himself . . . or at least he won't admit it. I once asked him if he believed in luck. I didn't put the question very seriously, but thought it would be a sort of human interest touch at the end of an interview. To my dismay he became indignant and replied sharply, "Do you think I'm an old Georgian granny to believe in things like that? I'm a Bolshevik, and I don't believe in gods or devils or any form of obsolete superstition."

His eyes were hard and angry, and I was much taken aback. So I hastened to explain that Napoleon had believed in his Star, and Cromwell had a belief that important things happened on his birthday, that it was his "lucky" day, and . . . in short, that I meant no offense by my question.

Stalin smiled, but repeated firmly that luck had no part in his considerations. I venture to disagree with him.

Stalin undoubtedly has become the driver of the Russian horse and cart. But he did not reach that position by a single leap, as Minerva, Goddess of Wisdom, is said to have leapt spontaneously from the head of Jove. Stalin reached the position of mastery by long laborious effort, and it is perhaps all the more to his credit that luck turned against him at a highly critical moment.

In the last two chapters it has been seen that luck, by which is meant in this case extraneous circumstances outside Stalin's control, played strongly in his favor. The spring and summer of 1927 brought a change. His Chinese adventure went sour and the rupture of relations with Britain reduced to a trickle the flow of foreign credit upon which his daring industrial program depended. That was bad enough, but he could find consolation in the excellent harvest. Not, however, for long, because the harvest was scarcely reaped when it became evident that big trouble was impending with the richer peasants.

In Tsarist days Russia had sustained and attempted to expand its infant industry not only by tariffs and foreign loans but by export of grain, which had amounted to nearly ten million tons annually in the pre-war period. Tsarist economists called this an average exportable surplus, but critics were found bold enough to say that England and Germany could eat cheap Russian bread because Russian babies were starving. Which once led Lenin to declare that Tsarist Russia was itself a "semi-colonial country" whose masses suffered to keep the living standards of European workers high enough to avoid revolutionary trouble. This exportable surplus came from the big estates, which on the whole were fairly well managed. The Revolution broke down these estates into thousands of tiny peasant holdings, not more than fifteen or twenty acres per family, of which only a very small proportion in the hands of richer peasants, who themselves rarely farmed more than fifty acres, produced a surplus. War and civil war had taken terrible toll of the Russian land in men and animals, in supplies of grain for food and seed. With the best will in the world, and all the stimulus in the world, it was impossible that the new farm system could produce an exportable surplus of more than two or three million tons. In the autumn of 1927 stimulus and goodwill failed simultaneously. The Soviet Government had eliminated the NEPmen traders, but had failed to fill their place, and the peasants were now being asked to deliver their grain surplus at low fixed prices in return for little save promises. This requires explanation. The unpopular "requisitions" of the Militant Communism period had been replaced by a system of "grain collections," as they were called, which actually represented a combination of taxes and rent to be paid by peasants, averaging about fifteen percent of the total crop. These collections were bought by the State at fixed rates much lower than those of the open or free market, but in return the villages received salt, kerosene and other consumer goods at fixed prices equally below free market rates, so that the balance was not uneven. In the fall of 1927, however, the supply of "fixed-price goods" dropped almost to zero, with a corresponding reluctance on the part of the peasants to deliver "fixed-price" grain. An awkward tangle for Stalin to unravel at a time when his prestige was lowered by events in China, by the rupture with England, and by the ever-present need to meet foreign credit obligations.

It is interesting to note that Stalin pursued the same tactics which had served him well before. This may be a natural human impulse or an attribute of great men, as Foch repeated at Montdidier in March, 1918, when the road to Paris seemed open to the Germans, his desperate maneuver which had won the Battle of the Marne, the same maneuver, incidentally, which his pupil Weygand used against the Bolsheviks before Warsaw in the summer of 1920. Stalin now saw himself attacked by Trotsky, Kamenev, Zinoviev and their ultra-Bolshevik "Left" friends, who charged that he had failed to attack the rural NEPmen (the kulaks) and demanded their immediate suppression and the forcible seizure of their grain. Stalin knew that this demand was unpopular with the powerful "Right" group in the Party led by Rykov, Bukharin and Tomsky, all members of the Politburo, and respectively President of the Council of Commissars (Rykov), Editor-in-chief of the Party newspaper *Pravda* (Bukharin), President of the Central Trade Union Council (Tomsky), who believed that peasant individualism should be encouraged, at least for the time being, as a matter of national expediency. Some of the "Rightists" had gone so far as to advocate a Soviet state whose foundation should be thousands of self-sufficient farmers like those of France after the Revolution there. They had strong support in the villages, amongst the members of the former Social-Revolutionary Party, and in the Army. Accordingly Stalin, as before, played one group against the other, and not only maintained his majority in the Central Committee but unleashed such a blast of "Right" dynamite against Trotsky and the Left as to paralyze their activity. Through Bukharin, Rykov and Tomsky, Stalin controlled all the organs of propaganda: press, speech (including right of meeting and assembly) and radio. The Trotskyists found their position untenable and were forced to make their rash appeal to the people on November 7th and to take the other illegal step against the bloc of Stalinists and Rightists which led, as described in an earlier chapter, to their defeat and exile.

Stalin had scored a political and personal triumph over his most dangerous opponent, but it hadn't brought an extra ton of grain into the "State Collection" depots. By the end of January, 1928, while the trains were bearing the disgruntled Trotskyists to seclusion in Central Asia and Siberia, the grain situation had reached a desperate urgency. Stalin acted with characteristic opportunism, energy, and disregard for his recent supporters of the Right. Faster than the trains his orders were flashed to Party leaders and government officials throughout the country to take "extraordinary measures" to insure one hundred percent delivery of the grain collections. A quota was given to every local Communist chieftain, with instructions to fill it at all costs, and the whole mechanism of the Party, the Communist Youth League, the Army, the OGPU[1] and other government organizations, was immediately set to work. Free markets were closed, peasants were prevented by force from selling grain to private dealers and compelled to deliver it at fixed prices to the state collectors. Simultaneously, however, an effort was made to increase the supply to the villages of salt, kerosene and consumer goods at low fixed prices.

Thanks to the "extraordinary measures" enough grain for urban and military requirements had been collected by midsummer, but no surplus was available for export (two million tons in the previous year) and it was found necessary to import 150,000 tons, with the result that the annual foreign trade balance showed a heavy deficit. Even this limited success was not attained without causing a terrific furore in the country. The leading Trotskyists were in exile, but their friends at home and abroad cried indignantly that Stalin was now executing the very anti-kulak policy which Trotsky had advocated for the past two years. Their cry was echoed in tones of horror by the Rightists, who charged, with some justification, that Stalin had fooled them and used them simply as a catspaw to defeat the Left. Meanwhile, in the villages the prosperous peasants, who had come to regard themselves as privileged because they produced the surplus food, did not yield tamely to the "extraordinary measures." Supplies of grain that were known to exist disappeared—buried to evade the state collectors—and arson, that age-old weapon of the Russian peasant, increased alarmingly, as did "accidents" to Party officials and volunteers.

Stalin watched the gathering storm without dismay. After all, the prime object of assuring the food supply of the towns and armed forces had been attained, but he was aware that the state farms did not yet produce enough grain to take the place of the richer peasants. Finally, he had to maintain his majority in the Central Committee. Accordingly he made a strategic retreat. In July he sum-

[1] State Political Administration, as the former Che-ka was now known.

moned a special plenary session of the highest Party executives, which voted a resolution deploring the "extraordinary measures dictated by necessity," and promising that they should be abolished and never repeated. Stalin personally reiterated this pledge in two speeches. He could doubtless afford to do so, but the plenary session nevertheless marked a serious setback for him. His authority, which had seemed firmly established six months before, had not only been successfully challenged, but the policy of pressure on the richer peasants had been abandoned. True, that policy had been forced upon Stalin by circumstances, and to a man of his cautious nature the sudden severity of the "extraordinary measures" may well have seemed unwise or at least premature, but it had been *his* policy and he had been forced to disavow it.

Stalin had in fact reached a crisis in his own career and in the development of Russia, which now was at the parting of the ways. Either it must become, as rapidly as possible, an industrial state, able to modernize, mechanize and radically change its backward agricultural system, or be content to remain an agricultural state exporting great quantities of foodstuffs, as in Tsarist days, in the hope that it could thus gradually build up a native industry. The former course was much more difficult, and its first steps, although not unsuccessful, had already roused widespread anxiety and charges of over-industrialization. It would clearly be easier and more generally acceptable to follow the Rightist policy of creating a strong system of individual farming through which the sale of surplus food abroad would provide the means for a slow but steady growth of industry. On the other hand, this involved dependence upon foreign markets, that is upon foreigners, and kept the country in the condition of a semi-colonial state, as Lenin had described it, whose cheap food would be used to bribe the wage-slaves of Western capitalism. Viewed in that light, the "easy way" was at once an abandonment of Bolshevik ideals and of new Russia's belief in itself and its own strength and independence.

Stalin fully realized this, but he was handicapped by his lack of personal popularity. Many of the older Bolsheviks resented his harshness towards the Trotskyists and repeated a statement dictated by Lenin before his death—Stalin himself once vouched for its authenticity—that "Stalin is a rough fellow whose ambition may cause a split in the Party." During the years of Tsarist repression,

1906-1917, Stalin had been denied the personal contact with Lenin enjoyed by the coterie of "Western exiles." A hard, reserved man of non-Russian (Georgian) origin, he had never had much appeal for the rank and file of the Party, and the Opposition movements against him, then and later, overt and covert, were in no small degree personal. He had, however, a strong loyal group of his former co-workers in Tsarist Russia, and he and they had better firsthand knowledge than his adversaries about the feelings and wishes of the masses and the character and capacity of local Party leaders. His control of the Party Secretariat gave him vast influence through a framework of "key" appointees.

Stalin used this control to strike the first blow in a campaign which he had carefully prepared with his closest friends, Molotov, Kuibeshev, Kirov, and Voroshilov. It was a superb piece of state-craft in which Stalin forsook his wonted caution for perfectly timed audacity. The first blow was the appointment of Molotov to the key position of Moscow Party Secretary in place of Uglanov, one of the noisier critics of over-industrialization. Stalin accompanied the change by an attack upon faint-hearted men who lacked confidence in their country and advocated a "petit-bourgeois" policy of compromise. He did not openly assail the Rightist supporters of peasant individualism, but they knew that the cap fitted them, and Bukharin replied with a specious editorial in the *Pravda*, which "viewed with alarm" the drive for industrialization and "voiced doubts" about the tendency to put pressure on the richer peasants.

Then Stalin unmasked his major batteries in the form of the Five-Year Plan, upon which Kuibeshev had long been working with a large and busy staff. The Plan as such was no novelty. It was known to have been in preparation, and something of the sort had been contemplated by Lenin as far back as 1920, when the State Planning Commission (Gosplan) was formed. But Stalin produced it at the psychological moment as the sign or symbol for which his country was waiting. The Plan met a need of which everyone was aware. The problems facing Russia were so great that they could not be solved by short-term methods, by haphazard makeshift, but required a detailed program covering a period of years. Secondly, it enabled Stalin to answer the Trotskyist criticism that he had betrayed the principles of Marx and Lenin, because he could now declare that he was reviving on a more practical and hopeful basis the policy which Lenin had advocated at the Ninth Congress of the Party in the spring of 1920, a policy postponed by the war with Poland and other considerations, but never forgotten by Stalin. Thirdly, the Plan demolished—one might almost say devoured—a two-year plan proposal put forward by the Rightists for the gradual development of individual farming by improvement of methods, seed and equipment, and wider use of fertilizers.

Above all, the Plan had a tremendous popular appeal to the young Soviet Republic. It was the biggest, boldest, newest thing in the whole wide world, a vast comprehensive program such as America had never dreamed of nor Britain ever attempted. The Russians as a race have almost a veneration for theories and plans. This was a super-theory to cover one-sixth of the earth's surface in every detail of its life and progress. It was grandiose and inspiring, yet full of facts and figures, precise to the last half-rouble. To the Russians a plan conceived is already well begun, a blueprint written on paper is a project half-accomplished. Here were a thousand blueprints of a thousand projects, minutely mapped and outlined. The Bolsheviks had boasted, and the Russian people had listened, that the word "impossible" was expunged from their vocabulary. Here was proof of their claim. The Plan bespoke unlimited confidence in the Russian people and faith in their capacity to accomplish miracles. That, I think, was the cardinal factor, that the Plan was an example of the courage, hope and faith in which impoverished, ignorant, bewildered Russia was so rich.

As a political maneuver its effect was as startling as the descent of Moses from Sinai with the Two Tables when he found the children of Israel dancing around the Golden Calf. The Russians were not dancing, but from Stalin's point of view they were following foolish leaders and strange gods. The Plan resolved their doubts and swept the country, and almost overnight it seemed that the whole basis of discussion had shifted. The Plan had been presented in two "variants," maximum and minimum, and now, instead of arguing whether industrialization should be slowed or speeded, the kulaks cajoled or chastised, the question was whether the maximum or the minimum should be adopted. Before that point was even settled, the Plan went into effect on October 1, 1928, amidst a thunder of speeches and newspaper articles booming extravagant applause. In the following spring the Central Committee of the Party and the

Congress of the U. S. S. R. voted the maximum variant by an over-whelming majority. Before that, however, Stalin cemented his victory by summoning a second "plenary session" of Communist executives in November, which violently condemned defeatist and petit-bourgeois deviations and warned the Rightists that "Kulak agents inside the Party" would no longer be tolerated.

Another factor which influenced public opinion in this crucial period was the public "demonstration" trial of a score of Soviet engineers and technicians employed in the coal mines of the Shakta region of the Donets field. Almost all of them had worked for private owners before the Revolution. They were charged with sabotage by omission and commission, and with illicit contacts with their former employers, from whom some were said to have accepted bribes. The trial lasted two weeks, and most of the accused were found guilty of treason and shot; but except to them and their families that was a point of secondary importance. What mattered more, then and for the future, was that the trial was held in the great columned hall of the former Nobles Club of Moscow, which held four thousand spectators, and that ninety percent of these spectators consisted of picked delegates from cities, towns and villages who were rapidly shuttled through for a session or two. This meant that fifty thousand Party henchmen went out to tell their comrades about "bourgeois treachery" and the danger of compromise with capitalism or its minions. Secondly, without any direct statement to that effect, the prosecution subtly implied that there was some sort of connection—not exactly collusion or connivance, but at least a spiritual connection—between these "wreckers" and the intra-Party oppositionists who also in their manner were sabotaging Stalin's efforts to build Socialism in Russia.

Foreign observers at the trial, of whom I was one, were somewhat puzzled by the apparent readiness, even willingness, of the accused to admit and sometimes actually to stress their own and each other's sins. We were unaware that in Soviet Treason Trials the accused were not brought into court until their guilt had been established by preliminary inquiry, which was in fact a sort of trial in camera. Then and later treason prisoners were thus convicted in camera and the public trial was not held until they had been so convicted and admitted their guilt. This, incidentally, was no new procedure in Russian law, but it had a confusing effect upon foreigners, who did not realize that the public trial was indeed a "demonstration" held chiefly to acquaint the mass of the Russian people with the circumstances of the case and, as a minor consideration, to apportion the exact degree of guilt and fix the penalties.

Viewed in retrospect, the Shakta trial threw interesting light upon Stalin's political technique. Like later, more celebrated treason trials, it was no accidental happening but a calculated means of influencing public opinion. The picked "audiences" at these trials automatically became channels for spreading, at a given moment determined by the authorities (i.e. Stalin), certain views and opinions which the said authorities wished to have impressed upon the nation. This "eye-witness" reporting by word of mouth and vivid personal description proved much more effective than newspaper or radio propaganda. It illustrates Stalin's knowledge of Russian psychology, and more particularly the shrewd timing and premeditation which have carried him to power.

Chapter 14

THE PLAN IN OPERATION

THE FIVE-YEAR PLAN was greeted abroad with a skepticism as great as the enthusiasm which it roused in Soviet Russia. Foreign economists ridiculed the idea that a bankrupt, backward agricultural state could afford the capital investment in industry called for by the Plan. Most of them dismissed the Plan as a gigantic rabbit drawn from Stalin's hat to dazzle the ignorant Russian masses. They thought, of course, in terms of capitalist economy and did not understand the methods and possibilities of a highly centralized authoritarian state. In Russia the question of money as such was unimportant except insofar as foreign purchases were concerned, which had to be paid in gold or its equivalent, that is by exports. Inside the Soviet Union, however, costs were reckoned in terms of time and human effort, in manpower-hours, which were relatively inexhaustible, plus the utilization of Russian raw materials, also produced by manpower-hours. In other words, it wasn't what Russian workers were paid in money that counted, but what they actually received in food, shelter, clothing and so forth. If they received enough to keep them working, the money cost mattered little. Actually, during the Plan and in subsequent years, Russian workers did not receive much more than a bare subsistence minimum of food, shelter and clothing, but they had other real, if intangible, inducements to stick to the job. Free medical treatment and education for themselves and their families, opportunities hitherto unknown for recreation, the stimulus of competition, with rewards of publicity and kudos, medals, travel holidays gratis, and, more concretely, prizes of cash and goods, all this was "payment" for Russian workers, and last but not least, the carefully fostered belief that they were performing a patriotic duty and the hope that their efforts would bear rich future fruit for themselves, their children and their country. Foreign economists made a similar error about totalitarian Germany in the years 1933 to 1938, when they confidently predicted the collapse of a system which according to their lights was already bankrupt, although they might have remembered that even nations of capitalist individualism, like the United States and Britain, had successfully ignored orthodox economic rules under the stress of war. It was not, perhaps, an accident that the Five-Year Plan period was presented to the Russian people almost as a war with all that war demands in devotion and self-sacrifice. There was a steadily increasing use of war metaphors and phrases—the "coal front" or "oil front" or "grain front," "shock brigades," the "storm" of positions, and the term "*hero* of Soviet labor" as a decoration for meritorious service. To complete the analogy, there was heavy and tragic loss of human life, and even actual fighting with bloodshed.

None of these criticisms reached the Russian masses, and if they had it would have been water off a duck's back. For them the Plan was a repetition on a far wider scale of the Dnieper Dam story, a truly national effort which had nothing to do with world revolution or the Communist millennium. The Plan was proclaimed in the name of Socialism, and Socialist it was, but the work was the work of the nation, done by Russians for Russia, and it is therefore possible to say that the Five-Year Plan was the first peacetime expression and accomplishment of the Russian nationalism—as opposed to Marxist internationalism—which became apparent and grew stronger in succeeding years.

Despite the scorn of foreign economists, conditions abroad as well as at home were not unfavorable to the Plan. In the winter of 1926-27 profitable sales contracts for Russian oil had been negotiated with two of the Standard Oil subsidiaries in the United States, which helped to compensate for the loss of English business due to the rupture of diplomatic relations. In the following autumn (1928) the American General Electric Company signed a contract with Amtorg (the Soviet trading corporation in America) to supply electrical machinery on terms which safeguarded American interests but did in fact involve five years' credit. These were important breaches in the foreign "credit blockade" which virtually disappeared a year later, in the autumn of 1929, when a second Labour Government replaced the Conservative administration and renewed diplomatic relations with the U. S. S. R. About the same time the Russians won considerable foreign prestige, especially in the Orient, by a remarkable two days' raid into Manchuria, whose war-lord, Marshal Chang Tso-lin, had been blown to pieces in his train and succeeded by his son, the "Young Marshal," Chang Suey-liang. The Young Marshal had renewed relations broken by his father with the Soviet Union, but had been causing a lot of trouble to the Russian-owned Chinese Eastern Railroad which ran across Northern Manchuria from Manchouli through Harbin to a point due west of Vladivostok. Exasperated by Chang's refusal to listen to their protests, the Russians suddenly "invaded" Manchuria with two columns of infantry-supported tanks, cavalry, motorized artillery and planes, which met at a point not far west of the North Manchurian capital, Harbin. The invasion was wholly bloodless, and the Russian bombing planes dropped sacks of soot instead of high explosives. Then quick as they had come the Russians went away, leaving the Young Marshal—and the rest of the world—to think the matter over. It was a unique operation in military history, an "invasion" of less than forty-eight hours which did no harm and hurt no one. It brought the Young Marshal to heel in no uncertain manner, and the smoothness, celerity and co-ordination of the Russian staff work opened eyes in Japan and elsewhere.

Inside Russia the first flush of enthusiasm for the Five-Year Plan carried the October grain collections—no longer enforced by "extraordinary measures"—far above the previous year, and the autumn sowing *campaign*—note the military word—ran well ahead of program. The "Right Troika," as Rykov, Bukharin and Tomsky were termed, from the Russian word for three-horse sleigh or carriage, had not yet recovered from the stunning effect of the Five-Year Plan, and the spring sowing campaign of 1929 was no less successful than the autumn's. Another card in Stalin's favor was the "perpetual prosperity" boom in the United States, with its attendant rise in the price of foodstuffs and raw materials such as Russia was exporting. Russia took advantage of this to place as many orders abroad as possible for machinery it required, on terms of credit that ran from ninety days to five years. In America notably its orders were greater than they had ever been, and although the price of their purchases was high the food and raw materials they had to sell were also fetching maximum rates. The Russians themselves were surprised by the ease and success of the first six months of their Five-Year Plan, and in rural areas notably Communist zeal began to outrun discretion. Crop prospects in July and August were so good that Party leaders in the countryside began to think that the "battle with the kulaks" could be won in short order.

The Plan had been deliberately restrained in regard to the socialization of agriculture, which the Bolsheviks hoped to achieve by grouping the little peasant holdings into large Collective Farms on the basis of two or three hundred such holdings per Collective. The Plan required that only about a third of the nation's agriculture should be included in the "socialized sector," as it was called, by the end of the fifth year, that is September 30, 1933, and of this a considerable part was to be huge state farms, veritable "food factories," so that the proportion of peasant holdings to be collectivized was only about a quarter of the whole. In the autumn of 1929 Communist zeal ran far ahead of such modest figures; local Party chieftains talked glibly of hundred percent collectivization and began to engage their respective districts in "Socialist competition" as to which should have the highest number of Collective Farms in a given period.

In 1928 the sown area of the Collective Farms was less than 3,500,000 acres. In 1929 it was over 10,000,000 acres, and in 1930 it was proposed to raise it to nearly 40,000,000 acres, an exaggerated figure far ahead of the program set for that year by the Five-Year Plan. The Plan's first year, which ended on September 30, 1929, was therefore claimed by the Soviet press as a triumph and conspicuous refutation of foreign criticism. To add to the joy of Moscow and the other large urban centers, meat, which had been rather scarce in the preceding autumn and winter, suddenly became plentiful at agreeably lowered prices. Stalin himself celebrated the Plan's first year in a signed article entitled "A Year of Great Change," in which he declared, "The new and decisive feature of the present Collective Farm movement is that the peasants are joining the Collective Farms not by groups, as before, but by villages, districts and large areas. What does that mean? It means that the middle peasant has rallied to the Collective Farm movement. That is the basis of the radical change in the development of agriculture which represents the most important achievement of the Soviet Government."

These were hopeful words, an unconscious tribute, perhaps, to Mr. Hoover's era of optimism and "perpetual prosperity," the days of "two chickens in every pot, two cars in every garage." Before Stalin's article was written, the American bubble had been pricked, and had he but known it, a hand had already scratched words of warning on the Soviet wall.

Moscow's jubilation was contagious, and for that reason I venture to quote a dispatch I sent to the New York *Times* on October 3, 1929. Looking backwards, I do not see how it could have been written otherwise.

"Moscow, October 3, 1929.—October 1 began the new Soviet fiscal year, which furnished a truly remarkable phenomenon. Newspapers without exception devoted their first three pages to adulation of the Five-Year Plan, which now enters its second year, after a considerable first year's success—so considerable that it is taken as warrant for a notable expansion for the coming twelve months over the original estimates.

"What is most interesting is that this Five-Year Plan has become a sort of Bolshevik sacred cow, against which it is blasphemy to speak. It is, indeed, the completion of the Communist religion—a paradise or millennium that hitherto was lacking.

"It seems to be established that no religion can really be a success without an idea of heaven. From Communism this idea was hitherto lacking. Now it is supplied—at least temporarily—by the Five-Year Plan.

"Thus the *Workers' Gazette*—the most popular of Moscow newspapers—devotes its front page to a picture of an express train (the Soviet state) rushing along a railroad labeled the Five-Year Plan, through five cities and countrysides (one for each year) of growing beauty, until it reaches—in the year 1933—a splendid terminus, which, by the way, closely resembles the present New York City.

"What is this but the same spirit that animated William Blake's famous 'To build a new Jerusalem in England's green and pleasant land,' humanity's incurable yearning for heaven? Like the inspired fanatic, Blake, the Bolsheviks prefer a heaven upon earth to any nebulous conjecture of unknown vistas after death.

"Their 'paradise in five years' has captured the popular imagination, which will no more be disappointed when the fifth year is ended than a mountain climber who finds that the peak he has scaled is but a step to further heights.

"From a strictly dispassionate standpoint, the Bolshevik Five-Year Plan is a superb political invention. It gives esoteric stimulus to a people whose roots are deep in mysticism, and yet corresponds to the severely practical surface of orthodox Marxism, which denies the gods and devils of religion and immortality, to concentrate uniquely upon economic facts.

"So 'Pyatiletka,' which is the popular and official name of the Five-Year Plan in Bolshevik theology, can boast of such a real achievement as 13,700,000 tons of oil production in the year just ended, 40,600,000 tons of coal, and 76,200,000 tons of grain. (In the previous year, 1928, oil production was 11,500,000 tons, coal 30,000,-000 tons, and grain approximately 69,000,000 tons.) For 1930 it is planned to increase these figures respectively to 16,200,000 tons, 51,600,000 tons, and 88,900,000 tons. (In each of the three years mentioned the grain figures were really the roughest of estimates, and the figure set for 1930 proved to be absurdly high. The oil and coal figures were more accurate, but here, too, the Plan failed to attain the 1930 program.)

"No country in the world ever made so swift a forward jump as Russia plans this year, but I for one would not dare to say that it cannot be accomplished. There are obstacles in plenty. The class war which the Bolsheviks have thrust on the villages to break individual ownership and bring the peasants to collective farming has in many cases become a war indeed, with arson and assassination as the opponents' weapons.

"Currency expansion is racing forward—2,500,000,000 roubles of paper money is in circulation today, as compared to 1,750,000,000 roubles a year ago, without much increase in the gold reserve. But Pyatiletka needs it.

"That is answer enough, and the prices of essential commodities are held down by rigid rationing. Moscow housewives have to stand in line before drygoods stores to buy cheap textiles. The *Workers' Gazette* tells them bluntly that textile exports have increased threefold to help pay for Pyatiletka. It is the same with other commodities, but the word of power—Pyatiletka—conquers all complaint."

This dispatch was, of course, passed by the Moscow censorship, and on that account it is interesting to note that the censor allowed me to refer directly to class war in the villages. I remember that we had some discussion on this point, and that I finally induced him to let it pass by saying "If the Plan is as successful as you all claim, the class war—which is, you know, the official phrase used by the *Pravda* and your leaders in their speeches—will easily be won. I think you are too optimistic, and that is why I want to mention this point." My dispatch, however, shows clearly enough that I did share the prevailing optimism.

The Right Troika—Bukharin, Rykov and Tomsky—were, as I have said, overwhelmed by the enthusiasm which greeted the Five-Year Plan. They had been maneuvered into a position where any note of criticism sounded antipatriotic or like an example of the cowardly defeatism of which Stalin had accused them. Accordingly they were mute, although not unobservant, until the summer of 1929, and when they did break silence with the suggestion that the country was living in a fool's paradise and that in the villages especially all was far from the best in the best of all possible worlds, they met the fate of those who have told unpopular truths from the days of Cassandra onwards. They declared that the policy of rushing rural socialization, of hoping to defeat the kulaks overnight, was little short of suicidal, and backed their statement, all three of them—Rykov, Bukharin and Tomsky—by an offer (or threat) to resign not only from the Politburo but from the Central Committee of the Party. For once they showed real courage, no matter what Stalin had said of them, but their gesture accomplished little against the flood of optimism. In November a plenary session of the Central Committee removed Bukharin from the Politburo and issued a sharp warning to Rykov, Tomsky and others as deviators from and would-be diverters of the Party Line. Perhaps after all they *were* cowardly, and their spurt of truth-telling was only a flash in the pan, because they all recanted in most abject terms and signed a declaration acknowledging the correctness of the Party Line. It was a complete surrender, all the more tragic to those who made it because for once they were right. But it seems to have destroyed them morally and politically, since they proved unable, a few months later, to take advantage of the situation when Stalin himself was forced to admit the errors of the optimism which the

Troika had denounced. Henceforth these men were little more than supers on the Soviet stage. Before the end of 1930, Rykov had ceased to be President of the Council of Commissars (replaced by Molotov on December 20, 1930), Bukharin to edit the *Pravda*, and Tomsky to direct the Central Council of Trade Unions. Tomsky some years later died a natural death, but Rykov and Bukharin were to have a final moment of hideous limelight . . . before they were shot as traitors.

The downfall of the Troika marked the end of serious opposition to Stalin within the upper hierarchy of the Bolshevik Party. There was later a movement called the "New Opposition," organized by some of the younger Communist executives, but it had no great importance and was crushed with comparative ease. One may say that from the beginning of 1930 onwards Stalin's authority was established and supreme. From then he was indeed the driver of the Russian cart, and mighty rough driving he found it. The Five-Year Plan was gigantic in scope and in conception, its first year was successful beyond expectation, but it asked more of any nation than any nation has ever given in peacetime. It asked no less than a complete transformation from backward agricultural individualism to mechanized collectivism, from hothouse subsidized industry to self-sufficient industry on the greatest, most modern scale, from the mentality of feudalism, far behind the Western industrial age, to socialism still ahead of it.

At this point I am almost inclined to wonder whether the Marxists are not right after all, that the Occasion does produce the Man. To make so prodigious a change in such a country in so short a time required iron will, unflinching courage and . . . ruthlessness. Stalin possessed all three of these qualities, but he had learned from Lenin the rarer courage of daring to retreat, and the willingness to admit that he might not always be right. The world has grown accustomed to regard dictators as masters of tide and thunder, who can say, "Do this," or "Make that," and their orders must be obeyed. This was never the case in Soviet Russia, where even Lenin was only "first amongst equals," and despite his moral ascendancy was more than once forced to tell his followers, "All right, this is how I see it, and this is what we must do. If any of you can prove that I am wrong or show me good reason why we shouldn't do it, I am willing to listen. In the meantime I am tired, so let me sleep." Lenin spoke those words on the eve of the Bolshevik Revolution in 1917, when there were still doubts and fears and men of little faith. The story goes that he wrapped up his head in a scarf and lay down to sleep on a bench ... at that eleventh hour. Later they woke him up and said, "Comrade Lenin, we have talked it over and we know that you are right."

"I thought so," said Lenin cheerfully, and "pressed the button" which changed the face of the world.

Stalin was less sure of himself than Lenin. Instead of saying, "I am right unless you can prove me wrong," he would ask the advice of others and gradually form a composite opinion and decision. Once that opinion was formed, however, he was much more rigid than Lenin about subsequent misgivings or opposition. Perhaps he was in reality less sure of himself in those days than Lenin had ever been. He could not brook opposition or attempts at interference with his plans. Of all his plans the Five-Year Plan was the greatest, and it was therefore significant and a good omen for his fortunes and those of Russia that he was able to undertake the gigantic task of carrying through the Plan without being seriously hampered by critics from Left or Right.

Chapter 15

PORTRAIT OF A STRONG MAN

ONCE MORE I am faced by the consideration of the folly or wisdom of interpolating a more or less personal narrative in my historical interpretation of Soviet Russia. As this interpolation concerns Stalin, and as, after all, the history of Soviet Russia since Lenin's death has also been the history of Stalin, I have decided to write the following chapter.

When in 1923 I learned that Lenin could not long survive and began to wonder about his successor, I remembered a conversation in my office in Moscow two years before. A Russian friend had said to me, "Stalin has been appointed General Secretary of the Communist Party."

"What does that mean?" I replied.

"It means," said the Russian impressively, "that he now becomes next to Lenin, because Lenin has given into his hands the manipulation of the Communist Party, which is the most important thing in Russia."

In 1923, therefore, of six possible candidates I picked Stalin as Lenin's successor, for the reason that he was Party Secretary and therefore able to manipulate. Henceforth he was in a position to play both ends against the middle, as he adroitly did. After choosing Stalin, I talked about him irreverently the way we talk about horses. I said, "I'm betting on Stalin," just the way you say that you're betting on Whirlaway or any other horse, and when they've won once or twice you talk of them as "your" horse, although they may belong to Mr. Whitney or Mr. Woodward or someone else. But to you they're *your* horse, as Stalin was *my* horse, because I had bet upon him. And once, later, he said to me, "You have bet on the right horse." He said it without a smile, but I knew and he knew that somehow or other my phrase about betting on Stalin had come to his notice, so I replied:

"Yes, I did, and think it will go on winning."

He grinned, because even dictators can be human.

"How did you get the name Stalin?" I asked him. I knew that he had had many alias names before, and thought that as Lenin took the name Lenin to commemorate a massacre of workers on the Lena River, so Stalin had chosen his because he had worked in a steel plant or something of the kind. The Lord of the Kremlin puckered his brows and smiled almost with embarrassment.

"I don't quite know," he said. "It started with some of my friends. They seemed to think that it suited me."

Today it is right to say that J. Stalin—as he always signs himself, not "Stalin" alone—has greater personal power than any man alive. Yet he would be the first to qualify this statement by declaring that his power resides in his position rather than in himself. He would say that not Stalin the man, but Stalin the Party Leader, is master of All the Russias, greater than any Tsar. In a sense this is perfectly true, because Stalin forms, so to speak, the top and crown of a vast pyramid, the Communist Party and its junior affiliates, whose foundations are set solidly across the length and breadth of the Union of Soviet Socialist Republics.

Foreigners seem to believe that the Communist Party in Russia is only a small percentage of the total population. They see the figures —say three million Communists and "candidates" in a total of 193,000,000—but they forget that the population total includes every living man, woman and child on the day the census was taken. In addition to the adult Communist Party, there are at least ten million members of the Communist Youth Organization, youngsters between the ages of fifteen and twenty-two, and another twelve million "Young Pioneers," Red Boy Scouts and Girl Guides from eight to fifteen, not to mention many millions of younger children born to Communist parents, who must be added to any list that counts the whole population by noses. You thus reach a mighty host of thirty to thirty-five millions, pledged, one might almost say, to serve the Red Cause from birth, which brings the final total almost to twenty percent. On that monolithic mass is based the rule of Stalin. He is the apex of the pyramid and the supreme chief of an army more disciplined and obedient than any soldiers, because there is interwoven in their militant training a central cord of almost religious fanaticism, so strong and real that close observers can sometimes venture to speak of the "Bolshevik hierarchy," like an order of priesthood in which Stalin is high priest, and can compare the Communist Party to the followers of Mohammed, or even, in more hostile mood, to the drug-crazed zealots who executed the orders—and enemies—of the semi-legendary Old Man of the Mountain, lord of the Assassins. From this "religious" angle, which must not be denied nor neglected, Stalin is the core and symbol of the Communist Party faith, the holder, guard and transmitter of a mystic inner Something known as the Party Line, which is and has been from the outset the expression and inspiration of Bolshevik policy and belief. The world has known no such combination of spiritual and temporal power in the hands of a single man since the days of the mightiest Popes whose thunder of excommunication could be and often was enforced by the lightning of war. Perhaps Stalin's greatest achievement has been to mobilize and direct Bolshevik fanaticism and self-devotion in unison with Russian patriotism and contempt for death.

Once upon a time, as old tales say, there was a certain Chinese Emperor who deemed that some of his most powerful subjects were lacking in the proper respect due to himself as Son of Heaven, and after much thought decided that the reason was his own insignificance of feature, unworthy of his exalted station. So he summoned the chief of his craftsmen and bade him fashion a mask closely resembling the imperial lineaments but with a trifle of added sternness and dignity. This he wore for a month and noted with self-gratulation that his great lords listened more attentively to his words, and that there was less strife than heretofore in the courts of the women.

Again he summoned the master craftsman and ordered a second mask, closely resembling the first, but yet more dignified and stern. A third followed and a fourth, each with more notable effect, until finally on the fifth day of the fifth month, which by fortunate chance was the imperial birthday, the fifth mask struck awe and wonder in the hearts of all beholders, so that henceforth the Son of Heaven spoke only with a soft and gentle voice, scarcely above a whisper, and the mightiest among his lords and the fairest among his ladies bowed low in solemn reverence, then leaped instantly to do his bidding.

This ancient fable contains a lesson that has not been lost on modern rulers, especially those whose power is based on their own achievement rather than on the "divine right" of birth. Who shall compute what Mussolini owed to the savage glare of force and determination in which he set his heavy Italian jowl, or what old Clemenceau gained from the grim rigidity of his Mongolian features? Masks, both of them, to impress beholders, for nearly all men, save only the very greatest (those rare integral souls of whom Mohammed said, "Once in a thousand years Allah chooses a servant to lead mankind with whom he speaks directly and allows to see his face like Moses, or me, his prophet"), have moments of doubt and weakness, when they must hide their true selves from their followers in order to win to power and hold it fast.

Many of their masks are not facial; they retire behind a screen of mystery, or aloofness, or reserve, until they seem to the masses, and even to those near them, to be treading the heights, alone upon a mountain top. And gradually a legend is created to serve their purpose, "Silent Cal," "Murphy, the Imperturbable," "Foch, the Devout Warrior," and "Stalin, Man of Steel, the Recluse of the Kremlin." It is not all a play, of course, for no man achieves greatness and retains it but by unusual qualities of mind or body, and with the passage of time the element of artificiality grows less, as oft-repeated acts form habit and habit crystallizes into character, as Aristotle proclaimed two thousand years ago. Thus the legend merges into truth and Napoleon becomes "The Man of Destiny," whose fate is the fate of France, and Stalin stands out to the world as the Communist Party, which rules all the Russians yet cannot unseat his mastery though he spur it ever so sharply. Because his legend has grown too great, too real, he has become flesh and bone of a living organism; the horse and rider are transformed to Centaur; he is indispensable and they cannot remove him without a risk they dare not take. That, today, is the last secret of Stalin's power; should opposition grow strong and noisy, he can meet it in the final instance, as Lenin once met it in the days of Brest-Litovsk, by the threat to retire and leave them to their own devices. Which they cannot bring themselves to accept. And he knows it, as Lenin knew it, and they know it, as those who intrigued against Tammany Bosses Croker and Murphy knew it. The leader is identical with the cause.

But what of Stalin himself, and how has he performed this miracle of transmutation? What is the man behind the legend or the mask? Is he human, like the rest of us, or some strange mechanism, some robot—soulless, or, stranger still, an echo or phantom, compacted into human shape and seeming by the thought and will of millions of zealots for this newest and harshest of religions, Communism?

The truth, as always in this crazy patchwork life of ours, lies vague and diffused between all three conceptions. There is the Man —Stalin; the Mouthpiece—Stalin; the Machine—Stalin; and in all of them, uniting and animating all three, the "inner God," as Plato called it, of Stalin, which is will power.

It has long been my fancy, after wide experience of men and cities, that there is somewhere a key to persons and problems, to unlock men's characters and reveal the secret of events, if only one can find it. In the case of Stalin, the remote reticent lord of all the Russians, he gave me the key himself. He said he became a revolutionary because he could not stand the Jesuitic repression and martinet intolerance of the Orthodox Church seminary where he spent some years. Those are his own words, and came right from his heart, although he gave other reasons, about his poor birth and surroundings and revolutionary friends, all in the proper Marxist manner.

But the truth of it, the key to young Joseph Dzhugashvili, later Stalin, was that he had in him a fire of revolt against tyranny and would brook no master. He was wild and hot-blooded and impatient, as Georgians are, and inside him hating bitterly the Russian conquerors and their Orthodox Church, which was, in his land of superstitious peasants, a valuable tool of government.

Joseph Vissarionivich Dzhugashvili was born in 1879 in the little town of Gori in the uplands of Georgia, where his father was a cobbler. Among the Georgians, themselves a subject race conquered by the Russians, names ending in -idze or -adze were considered a mark of local nobility, whereas names ending in -illi betokened the lower classes. The boy Joseph, known as "Soso" to his family and friends—this was his first alias—was a bright and sturdy child. At the age of seven he survived an attack of smallpox, the only serious illness of his life, which left him pock-marks all over his face and neck, but so small and fine as to be unnoticed save at the closest distance. Eight years later, to the great delight of his mother—a most religious woman who retained her faith until the day of her death and was buried with Christian rites—young Soso won a scholarship at a religious seminary in Tiflis. And was expelled in his third year for "subversive" views and behavior. In this connection my friend H. R. Knickerbocker tells a story that is not without its pathos. He interviewed the old lady shortly after her first and only visit to Stalin in the Kremlin, and Knickerbocker said how proud she must feel that her son was sitting in the seat of Peter the Great. To which she replied, a trifle sadly, "Yes indeed, but if he had not been naughty at school he might by now be a bishop."

So young Soso went off to school with rough homespun clothes and a cake, no doubt, and a goat's milk cheese in his bag, and his mother's prayers. And he felt, too young—because when you are young it hurts—that his mother's hopes and prayers were founded on quicksand, that in the eyes of his Orthodox Church teachers the glory and wonder, even the material advancement, of priesthood had become a crude matter of playing the Tsarist game in the conquered yet untamed Caucasus. If he would sell his soul to the conqueror, he might go far and high and be paid in the golden guineas of fame and comfort. If he stayed true to his "inner god," though it broke his mother's heart, he must revolt.

That, perhaps, was Stalin's first battle and first self-conquest. He has now become a legend of hardness and icy decision. Stalin, the man of steel, of whom Lenin cried on his deathbed, as did David of Joab, son of Zeruiah, "This man is too hard for me," and Lenin added, "He is too avid for power and his ambition is dangerous." Stalin repeated this himself in open congress of the Communist Party, and said quietly: "I told you then and I repeat it now, that I am ready to retire if you wish it." But it is easier to play politics as a full-grown man than risk at seventeen breaking a mother's heart. Stalin took that risk and it hurt him—who can doubt it?—and drove him in upon himself for comfort and encouragement. Then, at his life's crisis, he heard of Lenin, another young rebel, and, though the world knew it not, one of Mohammed's "chosen leaders." Lenin was a beacon light to him.

Stalin made it clear to me that at his first meeting with the Master —at Tammerfors, Finland, in 1905—he decided to hitch his wagon to Lenin's star. "Lenin," he told me, "differed from the rest of us by his clear Marxist brain and his unfaltering will. From the outset he favored a strong policy and even then was picking men who could stick it out and endure."

It was in 1929 that I first interviewed Stalin. I was required to submit him a copy of the dispatch I was going to send to the New York *Times*. In it I had used the conventional phrase that Stalin was the "inheritor of Lenin's mantle." He scratched out those words and replaced them with "Lenin's most faithful disciple and the prolonger of his work." He also told me later that in any critical moment he tried to think what Lenin would have done in the circumstances, and to guide his own actions thereby. Stalin is a great man now as the world reckons greatness, but Lenin was different— Stalin knows it—one of the very rare and greatest men. Stalin always regarded his leader with deep, almost dog-like devotion, and never on any occasion challenged Lenin's views or failed to support him wholly.

In his heart I am certain Stalin has a profound jealous dislike of what is defined in Moscow as "bourgeois culture," the mental agility of trained minds which is so baffling to those who do not possess it. Baffling and humiliating, as many a self-made American executive who has not been to college dimly feels, though he hates to admit it even to himself. In Stalin's case it derives partly from his hated schooldays; partly from his genuinely "proletarian" origin, which contrasts with the "bourgeois" birth of the rivals he has defeated successively; partly, perhaps principally, from the fact that he is not gifted with great intelligence and creative ability. Lenin once said of him that he was the highest type of mediocrity, and did not mean it unkindly. For there is virtue in mediocrity—did not Aristotle set it the highest?—and it is no easy task for a revolutionary leader to steer the middle course. Robespierre, whom Lenin considered the most brilliant of the French revolutionaries, met his death in Thermidor because he swung too far to the left—though not, Lenin added, until Marat's murder had cut him off from contact with the masses whom Marat controlled. Stalin held the middle road when the Trotsky Opposition tried to pull the Communist Party to the Left and again when the Troika Opposition urged it to the Right.

Stalin's utter single-mindedness, ruthless perseverance and genius for political organization brought him to the topmost peak of individual power in the world today, but he has "the defects of his qualities," as the French say, and one of these defects is envy of quicker brains which can leap where he must plod and produce new ideas beyond his own imagination. In comparison with the mental finesse of Trotsky, Stalin is crude, yet when it came to political maneuvering he showed a patience and dexterity with which his cleverer opponent, who at the outset had a position of equal strength, found himself, to his surprise and dismay, wholly unable to cope.

Stalin has been reproached, by Trotsky and others, with the desire to surround himself with mediocrities. I am certain he would say, "Better a dull man I can trust than a bright man I'm not sure of," but there is more to him than that. He reminds me of Foch, who had within him a core of bright, burning faith and idealism. Foch was a military genius as Stalin is a political genius, but when Foch adventured into world affairs and the realm of ideas and came in contact with the brains of wider capacity than his own special chess game, he was less successful.

Stalin is like that, too; he has the same steady, unwinking gaze as Foch, the same soft voice, the same patience, and, especially, the same faith within him and the same selfless devotion to his cause. And the same limitations, but in addition an idea, born perhaps from his own consciousness of intellectual mediocrity, that he is not the "chosen *leader*," the "successor" of Lenin, but the disciple, the chosen *vessel*, through whom Leninism and all that it implies will henceforth be given to the world. In short, the mouthpiece.

In the opening years of the twentieth century, prior to the Russo-Japanese War, the revolutionary movement in Russia made great headway, especially in the oil fields of Baku, where strikes and armed conflict were a common occurrence, Stalin flung himself into this struggle with great energy, despite his comparative youth. When the Social Democratic Party in 1902 split into two factions, the majority Bolsheviks who favored Lenin's policy of active armed revolution, and the minority Mensheviks who preferred more devious methods of compromise and appeasement, Stalin, I need hardly say, had supported the Bolshevik program. Lenin then opposed the practice of individual assassination advocated by the anarchists and some other revolutionary groups. He did, however, countenance what was known as "expropriation," that is, the seizure by violence of Tsarist wealth. This game was especially popular in Georgia and the South Caucasus, whose bolder tribes still longed for the freedom they had only lost in the past half-century, and thus Stalin first came into prominence as a revolutionary by engineering a coup against the treasure of the Bank of Tiflis which was being removed to Moscow for safer keeping. The heavy horse-drawn wagons were attacked by bombs, the guard was surprised and shot down, and the assailants captured several million dollars' worth of gold and securities.

Although Stalin planned the coup, its actual leader was a young Georgian known as Kamu, whose career was as extraordinary as its end. Most of the participants escaped abroad, and it is worthy of remembrance that Litvinov was arrested in Paris, while trying to negotiate some of the securities, on a charge made by the Tsarist Government that he was disposing of stolen property. The French Government took the view that the "crime" was political, and Litvinov escaped extradition and made his way to England, where he lived unmolested. Kamu, arrested in Germany, found himself less fortunate, and to avoid being handed over to the Tsarist police, feigned madness with such success that he deceived the German doctors and lay low in a lunatic asylum for several years. Discharged as cured shortly before World War I, he made his way back to Georgia and played a thrilling part in the revolutionary movement. On one occasion he was captured and confined in the fortress of Tiflis which overlooks a river. On the eve of execution he forced his body through a narrow window, falling ninety feet into the river, across which he swam and made good his escape. He was the hero of a hundred such hairbreadth exploits during the revolutionary period and the Civil War, until his name had become a legend in Transcaucasia. Then one day in the early '20's he was riding a bicycle down a steep street in Tiflis, and swerving suddenly to avoid a child, fell off and broke his neck.

Stalin also succeeded in evading the clutches of the police, and in December, 1905, went as a delegate to the Bolshevik Conference at Tammerfors, in Finland, where he first met Lenin. This conference was important because it decided to carry out the Bolshevik policy of violent revolution, by trying to combine all strikes and labor outbreaks into a mass general strike backed by the use of force and the slogans "Down with the Tsar" and "All Power to the Workers and Peasants."

During the years which followed, Stalin's life was a long tale of illegal "underground" work, arrest, imprisonment, exile, escape and re-arrest. He did manage to attend the Fifth Congress of the Bolshevik Party, in London in May, 1907. An article which Stalin wrote about that Congress, called "Notes of a Delegate," set the seal upon his Bolshevik orthodoxy, as opposed to the compromise views of the Mensheviks and other temporizing groups. In it he stressed Lenin's belief that the urban workers, the true proletariat, must be the leaders of any real revolutionary movement, even in a country like Russia which was more than three-quarters agricultural.

About the middle of 1907, however, the weak Tsar Nicholas II found a pillar of strength in his First Minister Stolypin, who set himself to liquidate all sedition in a most Russian manner. By his orders rebellious workers and peasants were slaughtered by tens and hundreds of thousands, until the hangman's rope was known by the phrase "Stolypin's necktie." But Stolypin's policy was not wholly destructive. He aimed at building a strong class of prosperous farmers, the "kulaks," who would hold their poorer and weaker brethren in order and become, by their own self-interest and natural conservatism, the chief pillar of the Tsarist State. Had Stolypin lived five years longer, he might have achieved his purpose; but he was slain by an assassin in September, 1911. As it was, he succeeded in breaking the movement of revolt in Russia and driving its leaders into prison or exile, in Siberia or abroad. The official Kremlin history of the Russian Communist Party refers to the "dark period of the Stolypin reaction" and says frankly, "The first Russian revolution thus ended in defeat."

The "Stolypin reaction" provided a touchstone of great future importance between two sets of Bolshevik leaders, the "Western exiles" and those who, like Stalin, remained in Russia to bear most literally "the burden and heat of the day." Lenin, it is true, belonged to the former group, but Lenin was somehow different, a man in all Bolshevik eyes of superlative character and transcendent ability. At no time, during his life or after his death, did any Bolshevik raise his voice to suggest that Lenin was living in relative comfort abroad while the Bolsheviks in Russia were groaning in Tsarist prisons. Lenin always was above such criticism, especially to Stalin, "his most faithful disciple." But no such distinction was made about the other Western exiles, who won no favor in the eyes of Stalin and his associates, Molotov, Voroshilov and the rest of Russia's present rulers, who stayed home to fight a lost cause against the minions of Stolypin. For them it might be said that "the iron entered into their souls," as they were tracked by police, betrayed by spies and provocators, imprisoned, exiled and hanged. While Lenin lived the "Westerners" held power and pride of place; but after his death the conflict amongst his followers was inevitable, and it is interesting to note that not one of the "Westerners" holds power in Russia today.

The clash of personalities, between Stalin and Trotsky, and of groups, between the Westerners and those who had fought it out in Russia, had to come after Lenin's death. It came, and Stalin won. Thenceforward, he put into practice his own policies, based always, as I have said, on his idea of what Lenin would have wanted. He forced, at great cost, the industrialization, or collectivization, of the farms, and drove headlong on Lenin's path towards making Russia an industrial and mechanized rather than an agricultural country. To do this, Stalin found it necessary to abandon "Communism" so called, which offered no incentive to the average man, and to revert to a system which is almost equivalent in method to Capitalism. I should say that the present state of affairs in Russia is State Capitalism, much as the Bolsheviks dislike the latter word, because Industry, Commerce and new construction are financed by central banks and their branches, as in a Capitalist country. There is complete difference of wages between the worker who gets the equivalent of fifty dollars a month and his boss who gets one thousand. In other words, greater reward for greater service. There is extra payment for overtime, and if any enterprise has a successful year, its workers receive bonuses. The same applies to the Collective Farm system, so that I can say that Russian methods today are not far remote from those of Capitalist countries.

Stalin thus stimulated production in Soviet industry and agriculture because he was the first of world statesmen to perceive that sooner or later Hitler's Nazi Germany would make a bid for world dominion. Stalin saw that from the outset, from 1935, when Chamberlain, and Bonnet in France, and even the United States, had small idea of Hitler's wild ambition. From then onwards Stalin swung Russia towards what I might call "preparedness," in the American sense. Deliberately he reduced the production of consumer goods, which the Russian people so greatly needed, in favor of factories to produce the matériel of war, and located those factories in areas east of Moscow, far from hostile attack, in the Urals and mid-Siberia and along the east Siberian coast.

Meanwhile, he used all the power of the Communist Party to stimulate the idea of patriotism among the Russian people, that their country was their own, for which they must fight and die. There were motion pictures of a Tsar, Peter the Great, and of a great noble, Alexander Nevsky, who had defeated invaders, and by tens of millions of copies there was reprinted the book of Tolstoy, "War and Peace," which described the victory of another Tsar, Alexander I, against the invader Napoleon. By every means of propaganda which the Communist Party in Russia controlled, that is, by every means, because they control them all, the lesson of patriotism was taught. Simultaneously the Red Army became an object of popular veneration. Its soldiers were better fed, better clothed, better housed, than the mass of the civil population. And taught a trade or profession, and given good jobs after their term of service was ended.

Under the German threat, Stalin was swinging towards nationalism, trying to build, and succeeding to build, a strong power to meet the invasion which he foresaw.

Chapter 16

THE AGRICULTURAL FRONT

ON THE DAY before the Soviet Five-Year Plan reached the triumphant end of its first year (September 30, 1929) there occurred a distant event, outside Russia's orbit and control, which nearly blasted the Plan's first-fruits into dust and ashes. The New York stock market crash on September 29th was hailed by the Moscow press with sardonic or gleeful headlines, but if they had known it the consequent worldwide depression was to put the Soviet Government in the tightest of financial spots and was partly responsible for the length and bitterness of their struggle with the peasants. During the Plan's first year the Russians had placed orders abroad for machinery, tools, etc., on terms of credit ranging from six months to three years, which they proposed to pay by the export of foodstuffs and other raw materials. The orders had been booked at boom prices, but the price of raw materials slumped catastrophically. Russian gold production was still too low to be of any great help, yet the Russians knew that their hard-won credit must be maintained at all costs: no matter what the sacrifice, their bills must be paid on time.

Pay them they did, although Russian "paper" was sold at a forty percent discount in New York and London, and the Russians were sometimes driven to desperate expedients. Thus on one occasion it is said that they bought a large consignment of sugar on ninety days' credit and immediately sold it elsewhere for cash, at a loss, to raise funds for a bill about to mature, which comes close to the dubious practice known as "check-kiting." This was doubtless an

177

isolated instance, but it illustrates the critical nature of the Russian position. For the next three years the Russians were forced to sell their products at any price on a falling market. Food and lumber urgently needed at home were thrown pell-mell into their gulf of debt, and with them art treasures, jewels, antiques, anything that could help their foreign balance. In Moscow and the other great cities an ingenious method was devised to tap the reservoir of foreign currency and gold hoarded inside the country. Stores were opened called "Torgsin" (meaning Trade with Foreigners) where all manner of "deficient" goods, from food to razor-blades, soap and clothing, unobtainable elsewhere in stores and markets, were sold exclusively for foreign money, precious metals, or jewels. No exact figures of the Torgsin returns are available, but they may be estimated at an annual total approaching $100,000,000.

As might be expected, foreign producers of raw materials, notably oil, grain and lumber, raised a hullabaloo about "Soviet dumping," which was depicted as a sinister attempt to undermine capitalist economy and administer the coup de grace to its sadly shattered organism. This was absurd, because the Russian oil and grain trusts were no less eager than their capitalist competitors to sell at higher prices, but they had no choice in the matter. Foreign producers, especially the lumber interests, then raised a different cry, that Soviet dumping was not only heinous in itself but was made possible by the use of "forced," that is convict, labor, in the Russian lumber camps. It cannot be denied that the Russian lumber industry was being provided with a more than adequate and rapidly growing number of involuntary workers; but this, too, was not the reason why Russians sold lumber abroad at rates below their competitors' costs. Soviet credit must be maintained, that was the story in a nutshell.

It is no exaggeration to say that the lumber camps, and for that matter other public projects, like the Leningrad-White Sea canal, were receiving a more than adequate supply of involuntary workers. Bolshevik enthusiasm for the Five-Year Plan had greatly surpassed the relatively modest program originally assigned for the socialization of agriculture, which required that only a third of the cultivated land should be "socialized" by September 30, 1933. Part of this area was allotted to *State* farms, so that the proportion of peasant holdings to be grouped in *Collective* farms would not be more than a quarter of the total. This was far too slow and small for Communist district leaders, who set out on the path of wholesale collectivization in the earliest possible time. The first three months of the Plan's second year, October-December, 1929, saw peasants being dragooned into Collectives by millions all over the country, whether they liked it or not. It was not only a point of pride with each district leader to obtain the greatest number of Collective farms, but the dragooning process simplified, for a time, the grain collections, which had become all the more urgent because of the world slump in prices accompanying the American depression. The peasants were at first dazed by the hurricane of appeals, orders and innovations that beat upon their heads, but they soon began to rally and ask with growing indignation what it was all about. Many of the younger and poorer villagers could see the advantages for them and their communities of collective farming, but after all the kulaks were something more than hated oppressors; they were the strongest and most successful families, and in many cases were united to their less prosperous fellows by ties of blood.

Farmers everywhere are conservative, and there was a strong feeling in the Russian villages that the old and tried ways were preferable to new experiments. The peasants didn't like to be told how they should live and work by Party officials whom they regarded as interlopers and "city slickers," who were full of talk and bright ideas but had never worked on the land. Above all they resented being made the subject of Communist competition, as if they were serfs or animals—if I heard this complaint once during that period I heard it a thousand times, and I suppose it was really an echo from the old days when the landlords could sell their serfs with the land. At any rate, there began a sharp and savage reaction, all the more difficult to handle because it was sporadic and unorganized, against the collectivization program. The peasants, not only the kulaks but the middle peasants too, hid and even burned their grain, declined to plough and sow, and—greatest protest of all—began killing off their animals, the horses and oxen which pulled their ploughs and harrows. That, if the "city slickers" had known it, was a symbol of open war. In the villages of Russia ownership of animals was the hallmark of prosperity, and the peasant's "little cow" or "little horse"—always the affectionate diminutive—had been immortalized in a thousand folk tales. Rural Party leaders might boast that 73.7 percent of their district had been "socialized," but they failed to add in their reports that the number of cattle in the said district had diminished by more than half.

Somewhat belatedly, the Moscow authorities began to see that the "class war in the villages," of which they had spoken so glibly, was war indeed, and that their opponents were considerably more numerous than the four or five percent of real kulaks in the peasant population. Indeed it was not long before the word "kulak" ceased to have its specific connotation of a labor-employing peasant who ground the face of the poor, and was applied to any recalcitrant villager who opposed collectivization. Nevertheless, the Kremlin adhered obstinately to its phrase "liquidation of the kulak as a class," and Stalin himself wrote a signed editorial in the Army newspaper *Red Star* in January, 1930, on the anniversary of Lenin's death, which ran as follows:

"It is necessary to smash in open combat the opposition of this class and to deprive it of the productive sources of its existence and development—the free use of land, the means of production, the right to hire labor, etc. The present policy in the country is not a prolongation of policy, but a violent change from the old policy of limiting capitalist elements in the villages to a new policy of liquidating the kulak as a class."

Prior to this statement it had been assumed, at least by foreign observers, that the process of liquidating the kulaks would mean their reduction to the average peasant status by deprivation of their land and other privileges, after which they would enter the collective movement as poor or middle peasants. Nothing could be further from the truth. Stalin proposed to stamp them out root and branch, so that the place where they had been should know them no more. Not only were they refused admission to the collectives, but they were being expelled if they managed to join.

Almost simultaneously the Moscow press carried a resolution adopted by four hundred and fifty delegates from the collectives of one of the counties of Moscow province. The delegates resolved to "devote all efforts to this achievement by the end of spring—that not one kulak, priest, NEPman, or trader be left in our country."

Further to illustrate a brutal truth, I venture to quote a dispatch cabled by me from Moscow on January 26, 1930:

"An article in today's *Red Star* concludes as follows: 'What will become of the kulak after his liquidation as a class? To us it is all one—let him fall under the first passing automobile or spend the rest of his life in exile—anything, provided he disappears from our midst.'

"The fact is that the revised policy puts the kulaks, private traders, and servants of the religious cults up against a wall. In the urban centers the NEPman, or small capitalist, is deprived of his apartment, his property, including his furniture, and is even forbidden to live in any large city. It is done legally on a taxation basis, but it amounts to expropriation, differing only in form from the nationalization of apartments and other property, which occurred in the early days of the revolution.

"The same things happen to the kulaks in the villages. It is a wholesale and ruthless carrying out of what the word 'liquidation' means in Russian. In answer to your correspondent's inquiries, the authorities said the 'dispossessed classes' might gradually regain their standing as citizens by work in the lumber camps or on construction projects where the labor demand exceeds the supply."

The month of February, 1930, must have smitten the villages of Russia like a cyclone. Stalin's words on the anniversary of Lenin's death were interpreted everywhere by Communist District leaders as carte blanche to go full speed ahead. The process of consulting the rural population about collectivization became a farce, and new collective farms sprang up everywhere like mushrooms overnight, into which the peasants were hustled wholesale. Not only the holdings of land and the kulak's equipment and livestock, but clothing and household goods, the poor man's horse or cow, even his pig and chickens, were pooled in the common stock. The confusion was indescribable, and the peasants' laments rose loud, but the urban newspapers continued blithely to register new "victories" on the Collective front, and to paint the rosiest picture of the Five-Year Plan's success in the agricultural sector. They exulted in the fact that meat had become cheaper and more plentiful, without pausing to think that this was due to the slaughter of peasant cattle, and their songs of triumph and self-praise drowned the wailing of the peasants. Even Stalin's sharp ears seemed deaf to his people's cries. One of the flaws in the dictatorial system is that the leader is surrounded by yes men, who cannot credit evil news, much less let it reach his ears. No word of criticism may be voiced by his servile press, no hostile senators or representatives rise to question his policies. A year or two earlier in Russia the Right Opposition trio, Rykov, Bukharin and Tomsky, had dared to contest the wisdom of a headlong rural program. Now they had been bludgeoned into silence, or perhaps themselves shared the prevailing Communist belief that the peasant problem was not so hard or complicated as had been supposed, and that a "firm hand and no nonsense" would bring the peasants like sheep into the Socialist fold.

Perhaps Stalin himself was misled for a time by such wishful thinking, but on March 2nd the Moscow newspapers published a signed statement by him entitled "Dizziness from Success." He stated that more than fifty percent of the peasant holdings in Russia had now been collectivized, and continued: "Our success already is producing a dangerous spirit of glorification and over-confidence. Communists are beginning to feel and say, 'We can work miracles—nothing is too hard for us.' Optimism is good, but to let it turn our heads is bad. Some of our comrades have already had their heads turned and have begun to make errors, which are not only not practical and non-Leninist, but they are actually playing into the hands of our enemies. This tendency must be checked immediately."

Stalin went on to point out the two principal dangers of an over-confident attitude as, first, the idea that collectives can successfully be established in regions as yet economically unsuitable, such as Turkestan or the extreme northern part of Russia, and, secondly, that collectivization must be pushed immediately to the extreme of communism and even pigs, poultry, and dwellings shared in the collective. It was a dangerous mistake and playing the enemies' game, said Stalin, to try to collectivize "by military force" unsuitable regions.

It was equally wrong, he said, to attempt suddenly to change the artel system—the artel is the typical peasant collective under which land, horses, cows, equipment and seed are united for the common benefit, but homes, sheep, goats, pigs, and poultry remain individual property—into a one hundred percent commune in which everything is shared with everyone. Stalin slashed at "those comrades who seem to believe that a communist Utopia can be established in the villages by bureaucratic ordinances," and he warned them that the untimely attempts at super-socialization must be stopped at once.

The basic success of the collective movement, he said, lies in the fact that it is largely voluntary on the part of the peasants. To force them further would be a fatal and autocratic error and would imply a rupture between the Communist Party and the masses it controls, whereas in reality its strength and its whole reason for existence are based upon a close connection with and work for the masses.

"Some of our comrades," concluded Stalin sarcastically, "think they can start a collective by pulling down church bells" (that is, demolishing the churches) "and then they call themselves r-r-revolutionaries (with three r's)."

The effects of Stalin's article were immediate and extraordinary, far beyond what he had written, although not, perhaps, beyond what he intended. Peasants everywhere assumed at once that Stalin was telling them they did not have to stay in the collective farms, or to be collectivized, if they did not wish to. What they wished was shown by the fact that in the province of Moscow alone the percentage of collective farms (that is, of grouped rural holdings to replace the individual small-holding system) dropped from sixty to twenty-seven. Not only near Moscow but throughout the country peasants literally fought for copies of the *Pravda* and other newspapers publishing Stalin's statement, paid a dollar or two for a paper that cost three cents, and brandished them in the faces of the District Communist leaders, saying, "That means we can quit the collectives; we can have our own cow back again, and our clothes and pigs and chickens." In the villages near Moscow there were actually processions of peasants who had thus recovered their "little horse" or cow. They were not kulaks but poor humble folk, and some of them carried candles, blessed by the priest, in these processions, as if to symbolize their defiance. That was the peasants' answer to the dragooning they had endured.

The reaction of the villages to Stalin's statement was not confined to the province of Moscow: it was repeated throughout Russia and made clear to the Kremlin how unpopular had been its policy of enforced collectivization. Like all dictators, Stalin had "lived in an ivory tower," too remote and aloof from the people he ruled, and he had only changed his policy in the final nick of time to avert a worse catastrophe than the Kronstadt mutiny and the Tambov revolt of 1921. The truth of the matter was that the Communist

Party as a whole had misunderstood the peasant problem. Its the-
oreticians had rigidly divided the peasants into categories, the kulaks,
the middle peasants, the poor peasants, and the *batraks*, landless
men, poorest of all, but had failed to realize that every village was
a small world in itself, composed of interdependent units.

To explain the peasant question requires a big digression, but it is
so important that I must attempt it. Karl Marx had written and
believed that social revolution would first occur in a highly industrialized country where the workers, finding that they had nothing
to lose but their chains, would suddenly take over factories and
other means of production from a small minority of bosses. Russia
was anything but an industrial country; in 1917 more than eighty
percent of its population was engaged in agriculture of the most
backward and primitive character except on a few large estates.
This eighty percent, the peasants, did not really *own* their own
land, like farmers in the United States or Western Europe. It belonged to the village as a community, not to the individuals, and
the name for this community was "*Mir*," which is the Russian word
for world. The "*Mir*"—roughly and incorrectly translated by Westerners as "village council"—was indeed his world to the Russian
peasant. It, not individuals, owned the village land, which it allotted
to individual families for a term of years. In some cases this term
was five years or less, in others it was longer; but almost everywhere
the family which farmed the land knew that it didn't *own* it and
that sooner or later it would pass to someone else, by lot or rote as
the case might be. It was a most destructive form of agriculture,
because every man's interest was to get as much as he could out of
the land while he worked it, without trying to improve it, by
fertilization or crop rotation, for the benefit of someone else. The
Russian peasants did not much like their system, but they were
ignorant and conservative—the two words are not necessarily synonymous—and did not know how to change it. After the Revolution
one of their strongest demands, as I have said earlier, was for
"documents" to guarantee for each man the ownership of his land
whether he had received it by allotment from the *Mir* or had seized
it from the estate of his landlord. Lenin refused to give the peasants
such documents, because he was a Communist and knew that the
Mir system of Russia provided a better basis for Communism—or
anyway Collectivism—than Marx had ever dreamt of with his revolt
of class-conscious industrial workers in Western Europe.

To dispassionate theorists like Lenin and Stalin, and their fellow-Communists, it seemed not only logical but simple to transform the *Mir* system, which already recognized the predominance of the community over the individual, into a socialized system, that is a Collective Farm. In a sense no doubt they were right, and it was the *Mir* spirit which made possible a Socialist revolution in a country that Marx would never have picked for such an experiment. But Lenin and Stalin and the rest of the Bolsheviks were mostly townsmen who did not understand the terrific land-hunger of the Russian peasants, the almost instinctive need of the man who works the land to own it for himself and improve it for his children. That, in a word, was the crux on which the peasants and Stalin split in 1930. Like Lenin before him, Stalin's strength and weakness was that he was a Bolshevik, that is a man to whom personal possessions—which doesn't mean personal power—are indifferent, or even something to be disdained. He could not understand that the poorest peasant, the lowliest of *batraks*, had a feeling for the land on which he worked and wanted it for himself.

From the earliest days of the Soviet Revolution the peasants of Russia—rich peasants, middle peasants and poor peasants—had wanted to own their land outright, as they could not do under the *Mir* system. Again and again they begged Lenin to give them a document, a title to their land. He refused, and Stalin, as always, followed him, because both the Bolshevik leaders felt deeply that Socialization, or Co-operation, that is the Collective Farm system, was the only final solution of Russia's agricultural problem. The Bolsheviks were willing to give, and did give, outright ownership of land, inalienable and for ever, to the Collective Farm, as a corporate personage or legal entity. Beyond that they would not go: individuals, peasants or townsmen might rent land on a fifty years' lease, but they could not own it outright. Thus the question of outright ownership of land became for some years (1928-1932) a bone of contention between the Kremlin and the villages. The Russian peasants had the traditional conservatism of farmers all the world over, reinforced by ignorance and, at first, by the lack of machines, fertilizers and modern methods which ultimately made the collective farm system a success. They opposed the Kremlin's innovations by passive resistance and sabotage. The rich and middle peasants killed off their cattle rather than surrender them to the collective pool. They hid their stocks of grain and refused to plough and sow the land. It was a cruel and prolonged struggle, which involved great loss of human life and reduced the livestock of Russia by fifty percent; but, as I shall tell later, its worst effects were caused by an extraneous circumstance, outside the Kremlin's control, the danger of war with Japan.

Stalin's "Dizziness from Success" article came in time to prevent disaster of a violent and catastrophic nature, but it could not alter the fact that the die had been irretrievably cast between the Kremlin and the villages. Henceforth it was one or the other, collective farms or individual holdings. Seen in this light, Stalin's pronouncement was rather a palliative or breathing-space than a fundamental change of policy. In a more shallow and less permanent manner, his "retreat" from collectivization in March, 1930, was a tactical maneuver, like Lenin's NEP in 1921. Lenin once remarked that Bolshevik progress must be three steps forward and two steps back. That was, partly, his excuse for, or explanation of, NEP. Nine years later Stalin might have made the same explanation about his "Dizziness from Success" article, with the difference that he began to step forward again much sooner than Lenin had done. Because Stalin now had a new and powerful weapon to use in his conflict with the peasants.

More clearly than his followers, Lenin had foreseen that the success or failure of the Bolshevik attempt to socialize Russia would ultimately be decided on the "agricultural front," and had said in a moment of inspiration, "A hundred thousand tractors in our Russian villages spells Socialism." On October 1, 1928, when the First Five-Year Plan began, there were about 25,000 tractors in use, many of them purchased abroad, and the annual production in Russia was only 3,300. By the end of 1931 production had risen to 50,000, and Lenin's figure of 100,000 in use had been attained—it rose to 149,000 in the following year—which was a great reinforcement for the cause of collectivization. The suicidal slaughter of draft animals and the destruction of equipment by recalcitrant peasants could now be met from the Bolshevik side by mechanized traction, by many-bladed ploughs and huge harrows no animal teams could have pulled, and even by harvesting combines. In addition, the State Farms, whose production two or three years earlier had been sadly limited, were now sufficiently well organized and mechanized to provide for the needs of the urban centers and construction camps, and the Army.

The autumn of 1930, therefore, and the year 1931, brought a renewal of the collectivization campaign, but it was now conducted in a less arbitrary and haphazard manner than before. Social distinctions in the villages were observed more reasonably, the voluntary principle (of joining collectives) was maintained, and there were no further attempts to pool dwellings, household goods and clothing. Finally, there was the great inducement of mechanical traction and modern equipment. Initial defects in the use of mechanization, due to local ignorance and unfamiliarity, were corrected by the establishment of MTS Depots, as they were called, Machine Tractor Stations, owned, operated and serviced by the State instead of by the collective farms. Not only was the efficiency of tractors thus increased, but they could be moved from district to district in accordance with climatic conditions, which proved a considerable economy. There was, too, another point of advantage in the Tractor Stations: they gave the State additional control (later developed further and used at a yet more critical moment) over the collective farms.

The improvement in the agricultural situation, due to the tractor "intervention" and to more cautious methods of organizing the collective farms, was accompanied by remarkable progress, despite the world depression, in all branches of industry, construction work and electrification. In July, 1930, less than six months after Stalin's "Dizziness from Success" article, the Sixteenth Congress of the Communist Party adopted a resolution to "Finish the Five-Year Plan in Four Years," that is by the end of 1932, actually four and a quarter years. Foreign observers then and later offered the criticism that total production figures were not reached ahead of time, sometimes not fully reached at all in the four-and-a-quarter-year period, but the Russians paid greater attention to the *rate* of progress than to its volume, and argued that if a given number of tractors and ploughs or tons of coal and oil could be produced in a given period, this proved that the Plan *was* being fulfilled ahead of time. It is certainly true that the end of 1930 showed that more than half the cultivated area of the country had been included in the "socialized sector" (State and Collective Farms), a higher figure than had been proposed for the whole of the Five-Year Plan.

_____ *Chapter 17* _____

"MAN-MADE FAMINE"

THE KREMLIN'S DIFFICULTIES were far from ended, and there were still cases of gross misconduct, or worse, among those engaged in carrying out its agricultural program. Thus in the autumn of 1930 no less than forty-eight officials of the Agricultural Department were summarily executed for sabotage, theft and oppression of the peasants on a scale so flagrant as to be equivalent to treason against the State. Nevertheless, the Bolsheviks were beginning to draw new strength from the employment of their own young men as trained experts in industry as well as in agriculture. It was the same process that had occurred earlier in the Red Army. Initially the Kremlin had to depend principally upon experts and technicians drawn from the ranks of "class enemies" or upon foreigners hired from abroad. The former were not always to be relied upon or suffered from Bolshevik mistrust, while the latter were hampered by their ignorance of Russian language and Russian ways, although both groups often rendered valuable service.

Early in 1931 Stalin made a speech on this subject at a conference of industrial managers. He said that the history of Russia recorded defeats by many enemies on account of the country's backwardness, and continued: "We are fifty or a hundred years behind the advanced countries. We must make good this difference or else we shall be crushed. In ten years we must recover the distance we now are lagging behind. Bolsheviks must master technique, must themselves become experts. If you are a factory manager you must look into everything, let nothing escape you; you must learn and go on learning." Stalin's words did not fall on deaf ears. Thenceforward the term "expert" ceased to have its "bourgeois" or "class enemy" connotation, and the distinction between the Bolshevik managers, who had authority without knowledge, and the non-Bolshevik experts who lacked authority, began to disappear. This change was not effected quickly or easily, but it gradually tended to remove a grave source of confusion and inefficiency.

Stalin's phrase about lagging behind became a popular slogan, "To catch up and surpass America"—not "advanced countries" but America—"in ten years." Not for the first time he had exposed a chink in the Bolshevik armor. They were trying to make bricks without straw, like blind men leading the blind, and their efforts were sorely misspent and retarded by their own ignorance and lack of technique. Foreign advisers in every branch of Russian endeavor were loud in their complaints against the inability of Communist managers and directors to understand the simplest problems. Many of the foreigners threw up their jobs in disgust and declared that the Russians were incapable of handling modern machinery, but others were more far-sighted and admitted that the Russians were eager to learn and did learn quickly enough. The chief trouble, they said, was that there weren't enough teachers to go round.

At all events, 1931 was distinctly a year of progress at home, and abroad the Soviet Government continued to meet its financial commitments. The leaven of education was working in the Russian dough, public health was improving, and athletic games, hitherto confined to the Army and the larger towns and cities, were being extended to the countryside as part of the collective farm program. Nine-tenths of the Russian population had never known sports or games, either as participants or spectators. It was an old saying that the Russian peasant had only one amusement, to get drunk on Saturday night and beat his wife. Track sports, football and hockey were unknown, horse-racing and tennis reserved for the privileged minority. Now, football, hockey and track teams from the urban factories and Army depots were sent out into the villages to play with and instruct the peasants. For the younger peasants it was a revelation, for young and old alike a novel entertainment. Simultaneously the radio was bringing unheard-of amusement and instruction to collective farms, each of which had a loud-speaker in its local hall. These "imponderable" factors, little less than tractors and giant ploughs, were winning the peasant masses, as they had already brought fresh joys and interests to factory workers and soldiers.

Suddenly the whole picture was changed, and the peasant question, in particular, embittered by an event outside the Kremlin's calculations or control. In September, 1931, the Japanese on a trumped-up pretext seized the Manchurian capital, Mukden, and within a few months extended their conquest over the whole of Manchuria, including the Chinese Eastern railroad, jointly owned and operated by the Russians and Chinese. Russia and Japan were brought to the verge of war because the Russians were convinced early in 1932 that Japan proposed to follow its Manchurian action by a drive through Outer Mongolia to the Russian area south of Lake Baikal, with the purpose of cutting off the Maritime Provinces of Eastern Siberia from the Soviet Union. The Russians faced this threat alone; far from having confidence in the Western Powers to check Japanese aggression, they believed that London at least was encouraging Japan to invade Siberia.

I do not say that the Russians were right to think this, or that their conviction that Japan was about to attack them was wholly justified. But human action, of nations or individuals, is based upon what men think rather than what they know. The Russians thought that Japan was about to attack, and understood, as the world did not, how weak was their own position. To a degree which the Japanese fortunately never suspected, the Russians were entangled in the success of their Five-Year Plan. Because it had done so well in the first two years, they had expanded it until now their whole country was tense and taut as a bow-string, with every ounce of its weight, every effort of its mind and body, devoted to the Plan. "Tomorrow," they were saying, "we shall have great factories and power plants, steel mills to rival Krupp, and chemical works like du Pont. Tomorrow our agriculture will be modernized and mechanized." Tomorrow . . . but what of today? Today it was only half done, the peasants only half won to collectivization, success only half assured. Transportation, ever Russia's weakest link, was groaning under the strain, and if transport was overloaded, so were gasoline, coal and iron. Everything was overloaded, the peasants and the workers and the rulers of the Kremlin, like a team in a tug-of-war, heels dug deep in the ground, giving its uttermost strength to haul its opponent across. The opponent was the Plan, which must be pulled up to the mark, but now came the danger of war, like a sword to sever the rope and leave both the Plan and the Russians prostrate in disaster.

Stalin met the peril with guile and determination. He and his Soviet Russia have proved their merit since then, but Stalin was never so great as when he did what he now did . . . and never so vilified as for doing it. Russia's position was desperate—must I say that again? Japan, as Russia believed and as was probably true, was on the verge of invasion, and the Red Army had not enough food reserves, irrespective of other supplies, to fight a war; but the Japanese didn't know it, and Stalin's bluff succeeded, at frightful cost to his country.

Although I had been the New York *Times* correspondent in Moscow for more than ten years, I don't for a moment pretend that I knew what was going on. I did not know, for instance, that the grain reserve of the Red Army was greatly depleted, that much of it had been taken to feed the towns and construction camps and pay foreign obligations in 1930 and 1931. Like other foreigners, including the Japanese, I thought that the measures adopted by the Kremlin to hasten the grain collections in the spring of 1932 meant simply that Stalin had decided he could rush through the fight for rural Socialism and win it by quick ruthless action. That indeed was the note of the Moscow press, with the obbligato of triumph about the Five-Year Plan in Four, and the great Dnieper Dam, the biggest in the world, to be completed in the summer, two years ahead of time. The Bolshevik habit of secrecy and distrust, acquired in years of conspiracy and prosecution, of living devious lives under "alias" names, and watching always for police spies in their midst, served Stalin well at this time. There was a gasoline shortage in Moscow, even for diplomats and other privileged foreigners; the Five-Year Plan demanded it. Their facilities for travel were restricted; the railroads could hardly bear the strain of the Five-Year Plan. There came stories from the provinces that the peasants once more were dismayed and bewildered by collectivization methods; that was due to the Five-Year Plan. But no word of the danger of war, no suggestion that the Army needed gas and grain to be able to fight a war, not to mention boots and clothing which vanished from Moscow's stores. Foreign observers in Moscow were fooled, but so were the

Japanese, and it was only many months later that I learned what had really happened in the spring of '32.

What happened was tragic for the Russian countryside. Orders were given in March, at the beginning of the spring sowing period in the Ukraine and North Caucasus and Lower Volga, that two million tons of grain *must* be collected within thirty days because the Army had to have it. It *had to be collected*, without argument, on pain of death. The orders about gasoline were hardly less peremptory. Here I don't know the figures, but so many thousand tons of gasoline *must be given* to the Army. At a time when the collective farms were relying upon tractors to plough their fields.

That was the dreadful truth of the so-called "man-made famine," of Russia's "iron age," when Stalin was accused of causing the deaths of four or five million peasants to gratify his own brutal determination that they should be socialized . . . or else. What a misconception! Compare it with the truth, that Japan was poised to strike and the Red Army *must* have reserves of food and gasoline.

It is probable, as I shall explain later, that the Kremlin was deceived by its own agents about the quantities of grain that might be available, that is hidden but to be produced under pressure, in the Ukraine, Caucasus and Volga regions. Whether this was so or not, the fact remained that not only kulaks or recalcitrant peasants or middle peasants or doubtful peasants, but the collective farms themselves, were stripped of their grain for food, stripped of their grain for seed, at the season when they needed it most. The quota had to be reached, that was the Kremlin's order. It was reached, but the bins were scraped too clean. Now indeed the Russian peasants, kulaks and collectives, were engulfed in common woe. Their draft animals were dead, killed in an earlier phase of the struggle, and there was no gas for the tractors, and their last reserves of food and seed for the spring had been torn from them by the power of the Kremlin, which itself was driven by compulsion, that is by fear of Japan. The peasants did as they had done before at the time of the Volga famine in 1921, as peasants do in China when famine blasts their land, as happened in Oklahoma and its adjoining states in the year of drought and dust storms. They fled from their barren fields in the hope that somehow or somewhere they might save their lives and their children's by work in towns or construction camps. Or fled without any hope, only because they knew that it was death to stay. The number of these "fugitives" cannot be estimated, but it must have totalled millions. Their living standards were so reduced that they fell easy prey to the malnutrition diseases—typhus, cholera and scurvy, always endemic in Russia—and infected the urban populations. In Moscow itself there were outbreaks of typhus in 1932 and 1933, although the authorities tried to play them down, and the total death rate must have been appalling.

Russia was wasted with misery, but the Red Army had restored its food reserves and its reserves of gasoline, and cloth and leather for uniforms and boots. And Japan did not attack. In August, 1932, the completion of the Dnieper Dam was celebrated in a way that echoed round the world. And Japan did not attack. Millions of Russian acres were deserted and untilled; millions of Russian peasants were begging for bread or dying. But Japan did not attack.

In November, 1932, the Soviet Government felt strong enough to propose to the Japanese a pact of non-aggression, which was promptly refused. Nevertheless, the Russian bluff had worked; the Japanese and the rest of the world had been impressed by the Dnieper Dam achievement, which was guaranteed by Colonel Cooper and a score of American, British and German newspaper correspondents. The shortages of food and commodities in Russia were attributed, as Stalin had intended, to the tension of the Five-Year Plan, and all that Japanese spies could learn was that the Red Army awaited their attack without anxiety. Their spearhead, aimed at Outer Mongolia and Lake Baikal, was shifted, and their troops moved southwards into the Chinese province of Jehol, which they conquered easily and added to "Manchukuo." Stalin had won his game against terrific odds, but Russia had paid in lives as heavily as for war.

In the light of this and other subsequent knowledge, it is interesting for me to read my own dispatches from Moscow in the winter of 1932-33. I seem to have known what was going on, without in the least knowing why, that is without perceiving that Japan was the real key to the Soviet problem at that time, and that the first genuine improvement in the agrarian situation coincided almost to a day with the Japanese southward drive against Jehol. My dispatches refer constantly to "food shortage" and to "trouble in the villages" and to the "difficulties of the present situation." Then in January their tone changes, and I write of a "new wave of energy" and of "the Bolsheviks being galvanized into action." All that was true enough, but I didn't know the reason. The reason was that somewhere around Christmas the Japanese decided that Jehol would be easier than Siberia, and turned their faces south. They didn't actually move until February, but Moscow must have heard of it, and in January, therefore, the Kremlin heaved a deep breath of relief, knew that the peril was past, and began at once to repair, if possible, the damage.

In the first fortnight of January there were three important happenings, to show that the tide had turned. It was announced that "political sections," as they were called, would henceforth be attached to the Tractor Stations; that a new and special drive to aid the spring sowing campaign would be conducted in the Caucasus; and Stalin made a speech. All three were intimately connected and part of the same pattern. "What is wrong," Stalin asked in effect, "on the agrarian front? We are wrong, my comrades—we, not the peasants nor the weather nor class enemies, but we Communists, who have the greatest power and authority the world ever saw, yet have made a series of blunders. That is what is wrong. We thought that once the Socialist form of collective farms was instituted our whole job was done, and the collective farms would run themselves socialistically. We miscalculated the new tactics of hostile forces of boring from within, instead of engaging in open warfare. For that *we* are to blame"—he repeated this sentence a dozen times—"not the peasants."

Stalin perhaps was letting off the steam of his suppressed anxiety, but he also was putting his finger upon a tender spot. Because in December the Communist Party had held one of its periodic "purges" in the Caucasus, one of the chief grain-producing areas of Russia, and had found a parlous state of affairs. Apparently every type of "class enemy," from generals who served under Kolchak to former landlords, had wormed their way into the Communist Party of the Caucasus, and were doing their utmost to exasperate a situation that already was intolerable. More than one-third of the Party members of the Caucasus were expelled as a result of this purge, and their expulsion showed that Stalin had now discovered a most dangerous fly in the Collective Farm ointment. He and his fellow-Communists had failed earlier to understand that although the Collective Farm in form and principle was a Socialist fortress, it might also become—and in many cases did become—a fortress for anti-Socialists. In union there is strength, and a thousand united peasants could be much more dangerous than a thousand individualist peasants. That was what Stalin meant by saying that the Communists themselves were at fault, and that was the weakness he corrected by attaching the political sections to the Tractor Stations.

The decree about political sections stated simply that in each of the thirty-five hundred Tractor Stations throughout Russia there would henceforth be a directorate of three men selected from Communists of not less than twelve years' Party standing, with power to override any local authority, and responsible to the Kremlin alone. As I have said before, mechanical traction had become a vital factor in the Russian villages. Stalin's new decree about the political sections put it right in the Kremlin's hands.

That was only part of the story. The Tractor Stations were powerless without gasoline, no matter who controlled them, and the fields of the Caucasus and the Ukraine could not be sown without grain. Here the picture was completed by the order that fifty thousand Communists and a hundred thousand tons of grain, and everything else needful, should be mobilized immediately for the spring sowing campaign in the Caucasus. Because it shows that the gasoline *was* available now, that there *was* grain for seed, that help *could* be given, in food and seed grain both, to the starving, desperate population of the Caucasus and the Ukraine and the Lower Volga, Russia's fabled "bread-basket," which had been stripped to supply the Red Army with food to fight Japan. That is the core of the story, which we American reporters in Moscow had been unable to understand. It meant, to say it succinctly, that Stalin had won his bluff: Japan moved south, not north, and Russia could dare to use its best men—did I not say that the Communists of twelve years' standing who formed the political sections included soldiers?—and perhaps, too, its Army food reserves, and the Army gasoline, to save what might be saved.

In April, 1933, I travelled through the Ukraine to Odessa, and by accident met on my way a number of delegates to the Kiev conference of the "Political Section" leaders. I learnt enough from them to round out the picture. A Red Army brigade commander—in those days the word "general" was still taboo in Russia—told me: "We had a communal farm in the Ukraine attached to my regiment, that is,

that when the boys had finished their military service many of them
joined this farm, which we had 'adopted' and regarded as our foster-
child, or whatever you care to call it. Two hundred of our youngsters, and their wives and families, started the farm, called after our
regiment, the Fifteenth Rostov Rifles. We gave them a galloping
start, tractors and farm equipment and seed grain, by regimental
subscription. The local authorities provided land and buildings and
foodstuffs and other help. That was in '29, and by '31 the 'Communa'
was flourishing. You see, the boys were disciplined; there was no
trouble about kulaks or private interests or who should be boss.
They were getting along fine, and used to send back to the regiment
parcels of fresh eggs and butter and honey and plum brandy. Everything went well until a year ago. Then the whole set-up changed.
We began to get letters asking for food. Can you imagine that, that
they asked food from *us?* We sent what we could, but I didn't know
what had happened until I went to the farm, only a month ago. My
God, you wouldn't believe it. The people were almost starving.
Their animals were dead—I'll tell you more, there wasn't a cat or a
dog in the whole village, and that is no good sign. They had tractors,
kept in good order because our boys have gone through the Red
Army and know how to take care of machinery. But they had no
gasoline. Instead of two hundred and fifty families there were only
seventy-three, and all of them were half-starved. I asked them what
had happened. They said, 'Our seed grain was taken away last
spring.' They said to me, 'Comrade Commander, we are soldiers,
and most of us are Communists. When the order came that our farm
must deliver five hundred tons of grain, we held a meeting. Five
hundred tons of grain! We needed four hundred tons to sow our
fields, and we only had six hundred tons. But we gave the grain as
they ordered; and then came another demand, for more gasoline
than we had. We gave the gasoline, because we were soldiers and
Communists, but now you see the result.'"

"What was the result?" I asked the brigade commander.

"Barren fields," he told me. "Do you know that they ate their
horses and oxen, such as was left of them? They were starving,
do you know that? Their tractors were useless; and remember,
these folks weren't *kulaks*, weren't class enemies. They were our
own people, our soldiers. I was horrified," he said, "but now of

course it's all right. I got them gas for their tractors and seed grain for their fields, and food and whatever they needed; I mean that it's all right now."

"Why did it happen?" I asked.

He looked at me rather strangely, and doubtless thought me a fool that I didn't know why it happened. He thought I knew so much that I ought to have known about that, to have known about Japan. He said slowly, "Oh, you see there was a tension at that time; we were just in the most difficult period of the Five-Year Plan, and so . . . and so . . . but now of course things are better. We are able to give them the food and the grain and the gasoline for their tractors."

You'd think I might have guessed, but it's always easy to guess, afterwards when you know, and always so hard when you don't.

That spring brought sharp improvement to the troubled land of Russia, with the Army's aid and the political sections, and men who could send their reports direct to the Kremlin, to Stalin himself, regardless of local villainy and hate. Hate and villainy there were, not only in the provinces. In Moscow itself, in the center, there was treason and corruption. Treason, that is the word, which Stalin henceforth must remember. His Japanese foe in the East had feared to strike in Siberia, but in the West a new enemy, Adolf Hitler, was building his strength, eager to seize the oil fields of the Caucasus and the rich black grainland of the Ukraine. On March 12, 1933, the OGPU announced that thirty-five persons, arrested in a counter-revolutionary plot connected with agrarian difficulties, some of them high officials of the Agricultural and State Farm Commissariats, had been found guilty and shot. These executions involved a fantastic story of espionage. The "hero" of this romance was Feodor M. Konar, lately Vice-Commissar for Agriculture of the Soviet Union, who as such had access to the meetings and minutes of the Council of Commissars, when his chief was absent on leave or business.

In 1920 Konar was expelled from the Party on the ground that he was responsible for the failure of the Soviet government established in Polish Galicia during the Soviet-Polish War, but somehow he managed to explain matters and was reinstated. There was some confusion, he said, between him and another man named Polashchuk.

In the following year he went to Moscow to live with his brother. The latter also was a member of the Communist Party and specialized in the affairs of the Communist International. Both were supple citizens who displayed particular ability in stepping exactly upon the center of the "party line." That was an achievement in itself during the troublous years of the intra-party opposition.

Konar specialized in agriculture and steadily advanced in rank and importance, and was appointed Vice-Commissar in charge of State Grain Collections. Meanwhile, his brother made frequent trips abroad on Communist International business, mainly to neighboring states.

The apartment of the two men became the center of the "true blue incorruptibles" of the Kremlin policy, and though most of their friends were men of secondary standing they were on excellent terms with the men of higher rank.

Suddenly, by sheer accident, according to the general belief, it was discovered that Konar was also on "excellent terms" with a prominent foreign diplomat—on far too excellent terms, and an order went out for his arrest.

The story went that he was indignant when the OGPU guards summoned him. "It is absurd," he said of the order for his arrest. "I'll telephone" (to the OGPU headquarters) "at once." Then they showed him the signature on the warrant, and he buried his head in his hands.

Inquiry and Konar's own confession brought out that for thirteen years he was a secret agent of Poland and that he was, in fact, responsible for the betrayal of the Galician Soviet because he *was* Polashchuk.

He revealed, too, that his "brother" was not related to him by blood but was brother-agent in the same service, whose trips abroad served admirably to give the information Konar was unable to transmit directly to his diplomatic friends in Moscow.

Further investigation showed that there was a double conspiracy —not merely for the transmission of Soviet secrets to a foreign power, but to strike at the most vital point of the Soviet socialization program in diminishing the food supply and driving the peasants to ruin and hostility by deliberate mismanagement and sabotage of the grain collections.

The case was considered so grave that the whole presiding council of the OGPU participated in the judgment. The evidence was utterly damning and for the first time in the OGPU's history the verdict was delivered without the court's retiring for consultation.

Still another exception was made. The sentence was carried out immediately, instead of giving forty-eight hours' grace for a possible pardon by the President of the Republic.

Chapter 18

YEAR OF SUCCESS

DESPITE TREASON IN high places and the war danger and the hardships inflicted upon the Russian people by hunger and disease, it was officially announced that the First Five-Year Plan had been completed by the end of 1932, and that the Second Plan would immediately begin. This was not entirely correct, but the measure of success was remarkable and the three main purposes of the Plan were well on their way to accomplishment. Russia was being transformed from an agricultural to an industrial state; agriculture was being mechanized and modernized; and both these gigantic operations were being carried out under the aegis of Socialism.

In October, 1928, when the Plan began, there were 1,500,000 unemployed in the U. S. S. R. By December, 1930, unemployment had disappeared, and by December, 1932, the number of industrial workers and employees had risen from 11,500,000 to more than 22,000,000, and the average monthly wage had more than doubled. The gross production of industries had increased from 15.7 billion roubles in 1928 to 34.3 billion roubles in 1932, and there had been a total capital investment in industry and agriculture of 60 billion roubles. Most significant of all, the "socialized sector" of agriculture had won great preponderance over the *individual* peasants. In 1928 the latter had sown 97.3 percent of the total crop with an average holding of only 11 acres; in 1932 they sowed only 22 percent, with an average holding of 7 acres. The rest was sown by State farms (10 percent) averaging 5,000 acres each, and by more than 200,000 collective farms (68 percent) with an average unit of 1,000 acres. The collectives now included two-thirds of the peasant population, and nearly half their land and that of the State farms had been ploughed and reaped by mechanical traction. In the circumstances this was an extraordinary achievement.

In reality most of 1933 was spent in tightening up loose ends of the First Plan and bringing backward branches of industry and construction into line with the rest. This lag was minimized because the Russians were still unsure of Japanese intentions, but it undoubtedly existed. There was another more serious reason for delay in getting the Second Plan started; it had to be redrawn in two important respects: greater stress must be laid upon war industries, and they must be located as far as possible in regions safe from enemy attack. The First Plan had not neglected the requirements of military defense, but the international horizon had been fairly clear when it was framed, whereas in 1933 the situation was changed. In addition to the Japanese danger, which had not wholly vanished, there was the rise of Hitler. In 1928 Germany and Russia had been on good terms and were co-operating closely for their mutual benefit. Much of Russian industrial training, and even of Red Army training, had been aided by German experts; but in 1933 Germany had become a potential enemy instead of a friend. On that account Russia's great industrial region, the Donets iron and coal basin, could no longer be considered safe in any long-term planning scheme. Plants that might have been built there and mines that might have been opened must be shifted to the Urals and Central Siberia.

In short, the purpose and locality of the Second Plan were considerably changed. War preparedness took precedence over the peaceful industrial program, and it was decided to speed up the industrial development of the areas remote from potential attack. This was in keeping with the Government's policy of developing Siberia, but it involved great changes in planning. The Russians did their best to combine military and civil needs by pressing the construction of tractor factories, for instance, which could easily be converted to the production of army tanks, and chemical plants which could produce fertilizers or high explosives as required. At this time, too, they puzzled American construction engineers employed to supervise the building of their new factories, by demanding much greater strength and solidity than seemed necessary. The Americans learned, or guessed, that this extra margin was provided in view of possible conversion of the factories to war production.

The first sign of improvement in the agrarian situation came from the North Caucasus, upon which the Kremlin had concentrated its efforts as being the southernmost and therefore earliest sown of the major grain-producing regions. On April 6th, 1933, the *Pravda* stated that the daily sowing figures for April 1st, 2nd and 3rd were respectively 86,000 acres, 118,000 acres, and 158,000 acres, as compared to a daily average of 40,000 in the previous year. The *Pravda* declared editorially that this was proof that the mass of the peasants was at last rallying to Socialist farming with "the invaluable help and leadership of the political department of the machine tractor stations." On April 20th the Moscow press announced that a total of 25,000,000 acres had been sown in the North Caucasus, Ukraine and Lower Volga regions, as compared to 8,000,000 acres in the previous year. Weather conditions were unusually favorable, but the gains were really due to the political sections of the tractor stations, whose commanders cleared out inefficiency, laziness and graft in the collective farm managements without regard for local "pull" or connections. They also were able to provide adequate supplies of grain for seed and food, and there was now no shortage of oil and fuel for the tractor caravans which moved in an orderly procession from south to north in accordance with the ploughing and sowing period of each region. There was a new spirit among the peasants, who began to say, "Moscow has not forgotten us. They have sent men with whips to chase the dogs that were biting us." A further incentive was given them by a decree establishing fixed ratios for State grain collections with the right of peasants, whether individual or collectivized, to sell their surplus on the open market (that is, at higher rates) as soon as the collections were completed.

The favorable prognostics of the spring were justified by the greatest grain crop in Russian history, and the grain collections were actually completed before the end of the year, by December 14th, two and a half months earlier than ever before. Their total figure was not given, but I had been informed by the chief of the political section of the tractor stations of the Ukraine that it would be about 24,500,000 metric tons. As the needs of the urban population, construction camps and Red Army would not surpass 17,500,000 tons, that would leave 7,000,000 tons for reserve or export. It was difficult to estimate what percentage of the total crop the grain collections formed, as conditions varied in different regions. It was probably between one-fifth and one-quarter, which would put the total grain harvest at a record figure of more than 90,000,000 tons. It seemed clear that the Kremlin had won the long and cruel struggle to modernize and socialize agriculture.

In September of that year another correspondent and I made a long motor trip through the North Caucasus and the Ukraine. We travelled without "guides" or any official interference and varied our itinerary at will, which contrasted sharply with the previous year, when permission to make a similar trip had been flatly refused. We saw that the harvest had been splendid, of that there could be no doubt; but there were large areas, especially in the Caucasus, where miles of ugly ragweed had replaced the rich wheat of earlier years. There were many deserted villages as token of past woe, although in the Ukraine we were told that a large proportion of refugee peasants had already returned to the land, and we knew that the horde of peasant beggars, so prevalent nine months before in Moscow, Kharkov and Rostov, had entirely disappeared. We were much struck by the inability of local authorities to give us vital statistics or figures about the exodus of peasants, and at first thought this was due to prevarication. Later we found that in most cases they simply didn't know, because few of them had held their jobs for more than six months. This was interesting evidence of the workings of the Party "purge" in the previous spring, and of the thoroughness with which the political sections of the tractor stations had done their duty. As a matter of fact, the shocking state of affairs revealed by the initial purge in the North Caucasus was not paralleled in the rest of the country, where the purge was held later. We learned that only ten percent of Comparty members were judged unworthy in the Ukraine for instance, as compared with the Caucasian figure of thirty-five percent expulsions.

In Kharkov, then the Ukrainian capital, we talked with Alexander Asatkin, chief of the Ukrainian section of the tractor stations. He said that the crops had surpassed the highest expectations, and on some collective farms had actually reached sixty bushels an acre. The "socialized sector" of Ukrainian agriculture, he told us, was eighty percent of all the cultivated land, served by 646 tractor stations with an average of forty machines each. In reply to our question about mass emigration the previous year, Asatkin said: "There undoubtedly was a considerable outward flow from the villages to the Donets Basin and other industrial centers, but when they saw that the sowing program had been accomplished, the tide flowed back again." He denied that the death rate had been as high as ten percent, but showed no indignation at the question. The Ukrainian population was then about thirty-three million souls.

In Rostov we talked with another high official of the political sections, a brigade commander in the Red Army, with two decorations for valor. He said: "When we first got here the peasants were sullen and apathetic. As one old man put it, 'We are Bezprizorni' (homeless waifs). 'The Government doesn't care whether we live or die.' Our first job was to explain the new decrees, about which the majority had hardly heard, and to mobilize the local Communists and Young Communists, who had gotten terribly slack. Then we tackled the administrations of the collective farms, and I quickly saw what was wrong. In about half of these collectives every crook and loafer had made a beeline for an executive job. In a little collective of a hundred families there were as many as thirty persons on the administration payroll who sat around writing papers or making speeches, but never did a lick of honest work, some of them Communists at that.

"We soon fixed them, I tell you. We kicked out the kulaks and grafters and reduced the administration to a maximum of five and made even them understand they had to do their managing out in the fields, not in warm rooms with a glass of tea and a bottle of vodka beside them. Then things began to move."

My colleague and I were convinced that the "kulak war" was over, and that the Government claims for the excellence of the harvest were justified; but it is significant that at that very time the anti-Soviet news fountains in Riga, Warsaw, Helsingfors and Berlin were spouting "eye-witness stories" about conditions in the Russian grain provinces being worse than the year before. The reason was easy to find: the United States was contemplating recognition of the U. S. S. R., and not for the first nor last time the Soviet's enemies were making an eleventh-hour gas-attack.

It is worthy of note, and perhaps a good augury for the future, that although the United States and Russia have always had utterly different forms of government, the two countries have never been in conflict. Not only has there been no clash of interests between them, but each on occasion has rendered signal service to the other. Thus at a critical period of the American Civil War, when it seemed that England and France were inclined to recognize the Confederacy, the Russians, smarting under their recent defeat by those two powers in the Crimean War, sent naval forces on "courtesy visits" into American waters, a gesture which undoubtedly had its effect in Paris and London. Yet thirty-three years had elapsed before the Government of the Tsars recognized the infant American republic, and there is said to be extant in the Kremlin archives a document recommending recognition of the United States, refused by the Empress Catherine with her written comment that she would have no dealings with a country which believed all men were equal and denied the Divine Right of Kings.

During the Intervention period, shortly after the Bolshevik Revolution, the United States had landed troops at Vladivostok, but as the Bolsheviks were aware, their purpose was rather to keep an eye upon the Japanese than to take action against the Red Army. And it was due to American pressure at the Washington Naval Conference in 1921-22 that the Japanese reluctantly evacuated the Soviet Maritime Provinces, including Vladivostok, in 1922, after four years of occupation. America had contributed lavish and much-needed aid to the Volga famine in 1921-23, despite the fact that anti-Red sentiment was then exceedingly strong in the United States. On more than one occasion in those years renewal of diplomatic relations seemed possible, but American sentiment was outraged by the execution of Monsignor Butchkevich, and President Hoover, who once described the Soviet Union as an economic vacuum, never forgave the Bolsheviks for arresting some Russian employees of his Famine Relief Administration after the Americans had completed their task.

The United States, however, had been favorably impressed by the Russian attitude at the Geneva Disarmament Conference and the preliminary discussions in the years 1930-32, and was furthermore concerned by the Japanese seizure of Manchuria. American hopes of co-operation with the British in this matter had been dashed by the singular, and to this day unexplained, behavior of the then British Foreign Minister, Sir John Simon, who unexpectedly declined to proceed with a jointly concerted course of action. Washington certainly viewed with dismay the prospect of a Japanese stroke against Soviet Siberia, to occupy not merely the coastal areas but the whole region east of Lake Baikal.

Prior to assuming office, Mr. Roosevelt, then President-elect, had intimated his intention of "reviewing the Russian situation" in a sense favorable to recognition. The U. S. S. R. had warmly adhered to the Briand-Kellogg pact in 1928 for outlawing war as a means of national policy, and had further demonstrated its pacifism by signing pacts of non-aggression and friendship with many of its neighboring states. The Soviet Foreign Commissar, Maxim Litvinov, attended the London Economic Conference in mid-summer, 1933, where he gave further evidence of Russia's good intentions by organizing a series of "Definition of Aggression" conventions, as pendant to the Kellogg pact, between the Soviet Union and its neighbors and Czechoslovakia and Yugoslavia. In London the Foreign Commissar had conversations with President Roosevelt's personal representatives, William C. Bullitt and Raymond Moley, then Assistant Secretary of State. The avowed purpose of their discussions was economic, concerning Soviet purchases of cotton and other American products, but it was generally believed that recognition was also mentioned and would not be long delayed.

The ground for a Russo-American agreement was doubtless prepared in London, but the agreement itself may have been hastened by a curious incident which occurred about that time near Vladivostok. One fine summer day a powerful Japanese fleet, which may or may not have been accompanied by transports—on this point accounts vary—appeared in the waters between Japan and the Russian mainland about a hundred miles from Vladivostok, for which apparently it was headed at full speed. The Japanese ignored Russian radio messages, whereupon the Soviet military and naval authorities took prompt action. As the Japanese armada neared Vladivostok it was greeted by a fleet of Soviet planes, bombers and fighters, hastily summoned from air fields along the coast. No shot was fired, no signals were exchanged; but the Japanese flotilla changed its course, swung left, and steamed southeastwards. Russian planes followed it until they saw that the Japanese were making for one of their southern naval bases. No publicity was given to this mysterious affair, nor any explanation offered by the Japanese except a vague assertion that their fleet had been engaged in maneuvers. The Russians did not press the matter, but they were convinced that the Japanese had some ulterior purpose, if it was only, as seemed probable, to test the defenses of Vladivostok.

There is reason to believe that Washington was at least aware of this incident when, on October 10th, President Roosevelt sent a letter to Kalinin, President of the U. S. S. R., indicating his wish to discuss the renewal of diplomatic relations between the two countries. Accordingly on November 7th, by a happy coincidence Russia's national holiday, the anniversary of the Revolution, Foreign Commissar Litvinov arrived in Washington, where he was given a cordial reception. Perhaps unwisely, he had committed himself to the statement that outstanding questions between the U. S. A. and the U. S. S. R. could be settled in half an hour's talk. Litvinov may have been right, but he was to find that democracies do not settle important international affairs so quickly as dictatorships, and it was not until November 17th that agreement was announced.

The Americans were chiefly interested in two points, the debt to the United States contracted by the Provisional Government of Russia during the period between the fall of the Tsar and the Bolshevik Revolution, and the much-vexed question of Communist propaganda in the United States. The Russians were ready to give satisfaction on both issues, but for their part were mainly concerned with American credits to aid their industrial program, the Second Five-Year Plan. Both sides proffered more, in a sort of honeymoon glow, than could easily be delivered. The Soviet Government had always insisted too strongly upon the fact that it was only a *primus inter pares* member of the Comintern, without supreme authority over that organization, for Litvinov's pledge to be anything more than a "gentlemen's agreement." The Soviet stand on foreign debts was equally positive and well-known; therefore on this point too, as Washington was aware, no concession could be outright. It was no less clear that the President could not pledge the United States to grant Russia unlimited credit. In view of what happened later, it was unfortunate that Litvinov hurried back to Europe, eager to capitalize there Russia's greatest diplomatic success, without waiting to work out the interwoven question of debts and credits. It was just as unfortunate that a number of prominent but unauthorized Americans spoke wildly of global credits to Russia ranging from five hundred million to a billion dollars. Such statements were recorded in the leading newspapers of the United States, and aroused false hopes in the Kremlin, which never to this day has been able to realize that even the most important American newspapers and news agencies are not the mouthpiece of Washington, as *Pravda* and *Izvestia* are indeed the voice of Moscow.

In December, 1933, however, those hurdles were still to be jumped, and the Kremlin might well congratulate itself upon a most successful year. On the home front it had brought the peasants to Socialism, thus winning the battle which Lenin said mattered most. Abroad, it had joined hands in friendship with the United States to offset threats from Japan, the covert enmity of Britain, and the overt hostility of Hitler. The nation's food supply was fully assured, and American credits would surely smooth the progress of the Second Five-Year Plan, whose stress upon war preparedness against Japan or Germany was not unwelcome to Washington, as Litvinov must have learned.

In consequence the Seventeenth Congress of the Communist Party, held in January with two thousand delegates representing almost three million members and candidates, was an all-round triumph for Stalin. With the exception of Trotsky, impotent in exile, all the old Oppositionists had now returned to the Party fold, and to make the occasion complete, the later Opposition *Troika*—Bukharin, Rykov and Tomsky—ate humble pie once more in the most abject terms. The Congress was informed that the gap between the First and Second Plans had been bridged, and that it was now proposed to make a capital investment of 133 billion roubles—as compared with 60 billion for the First Plan—in the Second Five-Year program. Small wonder that the Moscow press called this the "Congress of Victors" and proudly proclaimed that the Soviet ship of state had come at last to fair water after many perils and storms.

As far as human judgment could decide, this jubilation was justified, and the Kremlin hastened to meet the brightened future in an appropriately liberal manner. In foreign affairs the Soviet Government made known its willingness to join the League of Nations in order to co-operate more effectively with the forces of international pacifism and good-will. True, the sudden pact of friendship between Poland and Nazi Germany in January, 1934, was an ugly fly in the international good-will ointment, but that did not prevent the Soviet Government from joining the League in September, despite last-minute opposition by the Poles. Internally, too, there developed a new policy of conciliation with ex-Oppositionists and even with former class enemies, based on a theory that bygones should be bygones, that henceforth all Russians might unite in support of the Soviet Government, now firmly and successfully established at home and abroad.

The most eminent champion of conciliation was Sergey Kirov, Secretary—that is Party Boss—of the Leningrad Communist Party. Kirov, although younger than Stalin, was one of his closest friends and was regarded by many as his eventual successor. Of unimpeachable proletarian origin, he was considered a hard man, which made his support of the conciliation policy—the first open plea for unity of all Russians that had been made since the Bolshevik Revolution—all the more significant. After its revolution, in 1789, France had been unified by the unceasing pressure of foreign war; but Russia—at peace since the war with Poland in 1920—had been torn by a succession of internal conflicts and schisms. Now, in the hour of triumph, Kirov advocated the burying of all hatchets, the coalition of all forces—former enemies as well as friends—to work together without prejudice or ill-feeling, for their country's sake. It was a liberal idea which accorded well with Russia's entry into the League of Nations, but it was doomed to perish stillborn when Kirov was assassinated in Leningrad on December 1, 1934.

Chapter 19

THE TREASON TRIALS

By a tragic coincidence another notable assassination had occurred less than two months before, when the Serbian King Alexander was killed by a Macedonian terrorist at Marseilles. At first sight the King's murder seemed to be only a link in the chain of blood and revenge that so long had bound the stormy Balkans, but its consequences proved scarcely less fatal to the chances of joint European action against threatened aggression than the effects of Kirov's murder upon unity and conciliation in Russia. Because the French Foreign Minister, Jean Louis Barthou, was wounded, perhaps accidentally, by Alexander's assassin, and died on the way to hospital.

Barthou's position in Europe had been one of vital importance. Almost alone among the French elder statesmen he had gauged the future possibilities of the Nazi danger and had realized that Hitler's "blood purge" in the previous June had strengthened and consolidated the Nazi Party instead of being, as was generally believed, a sign of its impending dissolution. As a former War Minister, Barthou had great authority and influence in the French Army, which had far more confidence in him than in most of his fellow-politicians. He was also admired and trusted in England. Some weeks before his death, Barthou visited London and held a number of conferences with English military and political leaders. His stubborn logic compelled them to accept, albeit reluctantly, three cardinal principles upon which he said Anglo-French policy must henceforth be based. First, that Hitler and his Nazis were bold and clever men, firmly in Germany's saddle, determined to avenge the defeat of 1918.

Second, that they must be checked now before they grew too strong, and that they could only be thus checked by resolute united action. Third, that such action should be taken not only by Britain and France, but must include the U. S. S. R.

Barthou had no light task to convince the British leaders, and no other Frenchman could have done it. As I hinted earlier, their attitude in regard to the Japanese invasion of Manchuria and Japanese ambitions generally had been sufficiently equivocal to cause doubts in the United States and the utmost suspicion in the U. S. S. R. Also it was by no means certain that some of them at least had not welcomed the rise of Hitler as a counterpoise to French military power on the continent of Europe. But Barthou was not content with having his way in London. Almost singlehanded he won the consent of his colleagues in the French Cabinet to his program of close co-operation with the Soviet Government, of which he had earlier been an uncompromising opponent. He drummed into their heads the fact that Hitler was master of Germany since Hindenburg's death, that the Nazis were stronger instead of weaker after the June blood purge, and that the interests of Russia, now eager to join the League of Nations, were so dependent upon peace that the U. S. S. R. would be certain to support a united front against Hitler.

Barthou worked tirelessly to pave the way for Russia's entry into the League and to lay solid foundations for what was later known as "Collective Security" against Hitler. His task was facilitated by Germany's withdrawal from the League, which was really due to Hitler's fury over the failure of the Nazi coup in Vienna which involved the murder of the Austrian Chancellor Dollfuss. Even so, when the League Assembly in September adopted a resolution inviting the U. S. S. R. to join the League, seven countries abstained from voting and three—Switzerland, Holland and Poland—voted against the proposal. Undismayed, Barthou prepared a Franco-Soviet pact of friendship and collaboration which would compensate, as he told his colleagues, for the defection of Poland, which had signed a similar pact with Germany in the previous spring. The Franco-Soviet pact was almost ready for signature, but Barthou wished to complete it by engaging Yugoslavia and Czechoslovakia. That would have set the crown upon his activities during the spring and summer. That was the chief purpose of King Alexander's visit to France; but Fate intervened to strike down the one European statesman of the period who combined foresight with energy. As I said, Barthou's killing was probably accidental; he was only wounded in the arm, and bled to death because of a misplaced tourniquet.

The murder of Kirov also appeared at the outset devoid of political significance. He was shot by a young man named Nikolayev, husband of Kirov's personal secretary, who was said to have been on intimate terms with her chief. Apparently Nikolayev's action was not prompted by jealousy as such, but by rancor. He had been a member of the Communist Youth Party, but had been suspended for misconduct and apparently counted upon Kirov to reinstate him and find him a satisfactory job. More than once he had appealed to Kirov to fulfil his alleged promise in this matter, but Kirov had brushed him aside. That was the story on the surface, but inquiries conducted by Stalin in person soon raised more sinister possibilities. Nikolayev had attempted suicide after the shooting, but his wound was not mortal and his confession and diary showed that he had intended to kill Kirov earlier and had only been prevented by an accident. It then appeared that the local OGPU authorities had known about this and had been lax, to say the least, in Kirov's protection. The suspicion grew that they, without direct complicity in the murder, had been willing to allow it to be attempted if not accomplished. If the conciliation policy which Kirov was advocating had been put into effect, the OGPU, which had grown extremely big and powerful during the last few years of trouble and conflict, would obviously have played a much less prominent rôle. It was not impossible, therefore, that the local OGPU authorities had decided to allow an attempt on Kirov's life, or even his actual murder, in order to block the policy of conciliation, or at least to show that their services could not yet be dispensed with. This may sound incredible to Western ears, but it is significant that the OGPU chief in Leningrad was executed on a charge of culpable negligence, and that his superior, the OGPU president, Yagoda, was later (in 1938) shot as a traitor.

Whether or not Yagoda was then trying to sow seeds of suspicion in Stalin's mind, the fact remains that Stalin was deeply affected by Kirov's death. He had fought his political opponents without mercy or compunction, but had repeatedly shown himself willing to accept their flimsy promises to mend their ways. On one occasion he had reminded Zinoviev and Kamenev that expulsion from the Party was worse than death for a Communist. When, after long forbearance, he had applied this extreme measure to them and others, he had rescinded it at their request. Kirov, perhaps his closest friend, had encouraged Stalin's generosity, which made the murder of Kirov all the harder to forgive. Henceforth Stalin must have felt, as he began to learn the possible ramifications of Kirov's murder, that no mercy could be shown, and that every sign of treason or conspiracy must be sifted and probed to its uttermost depths.

Stalin's life as an underground revolutionary in the decade 1906-16 had conditioned him and his fellow-conspirators to the highest degree of doubt and wariness, even about their relatives and friends, because their lives might depend upon it. As ruler of Russia in the winter of 1934-35, his suspicions evoked by the murder of Kirov were intensified by ominous portents in the international sky. Barthou's proposal of a British-French-Russian coalition had been wrecked by his death, and his successor, Pierre Laval, seemed as unwilling to sign the pact of friendship with Russia as he was unable to retain the confidence of Britain in a tripartite agreement. In March Hitler practically denounced the Treaty of Versailles by re-establishing military conscription in Germany, without raising more than a perfunctory protest from Germany's former enemies. Russo-American relations had not fulfilled their initial promise; the expected American credits were not forthcoming, and a series of misunderstandings had replaced the first flush of warmth and enthusiasm. In May, it is true, Laval was induced to sign the Franco-Soviet pact, but with such reluctance and reservations as to make it little more than a gesture. The British still held aloof, and it was evident that Barthou's work had been in vain.

In June Zinoviev, Kamenev and other members of the old Leningrad Opposition were tried secretly for complicity in the murder of Kirov. There seems to have been a somewhat tenuous link between them and persons with whom the assassin Nikolayev was acquainted, and there were also ugly suggestions of extraneous, that is non-Russian, influences at work. Be that as it may, the accused were all acquitted but not released from custody, and the inquiry continued in an atmosphere of growing darkness and disquiet from abroad. The latter point is important because, by accident or fate or evil hostile design, there was now an interplay between the effects of the Kirov and Barthou assassinations.

On the face of things, the two murders had no connection and both were more or less accidental as far as political inferences could be drawn. Or were they? That was the question which became more pertinent as Italy, now set on Abyssinian conquest, swung away from France and Britain towards Germany, and the end of the Russo-American "honeymoon" was marked by a curt protest by the American State Department against Russia's failure to abandon Comintern activities in the United States. Italy's Abyssinian campaign and Geneva's futile attempt at sanctions are a matter of record. They helped to weaken Soviet confidence in the League, which had never been very great, and to strengthen Russian doubts of French and British sincerity. Meanwhile Yagoda and his OGPU, honestly or to serve his own devious ends, rebuilt the case against Zinoviev, Kamenev and their associates in Leningrad, with the new suggestion, made openly for the first time, that foreign enemies had supported their conspiracy to murder not only Kirov but other Soviet leaders, including Stalin himself. Once that suggestion was accepted, each fresh event in Western Europe helped to reinforce it and to establish the connection between Nazi-Fascist moves on the European chessboard and the anti-Kremlin activities of their tools or dupes in Soviet Russia.

The matter can best be explained in the form of logical syllogisms, each of two premises and a conclusion, as follows:

Syl. I.

First premise: That Hitler's aims were not merely to break the Versailles Treaty and to restore German equality with France and Britain, but to avenge the last war and obtain the domination of Europe.

Second premise: That this goal could not be achieved and retained without the possession of the Soviet Ukraine and North Caucasus, whose geographical position had a strategic value only equalled by the economic value of their natural resources—oil, grain, livestock, manganese and cotton.

Conclusion: That Hitler would attack the Soviet Union.

The justness of this conclusion to the Bolshevik mind was confirmed by the fact that Hitler from the outset posed as the champion of Western Europe against what he termed the "Judaeo-Bolshevik peril." It led inevitably to the second syllogism.

Syl. II.

First premise: That Nazi Germany would attack the Soviet Union.

Second premise: That the Nazis invariably preceded their physical attack by a campaign of boring from within, that is, of what were later called Fifth Column activities, to weaken and demoralize their opponent before the blow was struck. The Bolsheviks had seen this Nazi technique—later employed on a grand scale against Norway, Holland and France, to name only three examples—used with success against the German Communist Party and his other adversaries during Hitler's rise to power.

Conclusion: Germany would develop its Fifth Column activities in Russia to the utmost.

The Bolsheviks have always prided themselves upon their dialectic materialism, that is, upon an unbiased logical interpretation of facts. With no blasphemous intent it may be said that dialectic materialism is one of the sacraments of the Marxist religion, which holds its devotees in a chain of logic no less strong and binding than is the chain of faith to believers in supernatural religions. Their logic told them that Nazi Germany would attack them, and that the preliminary stages of this attack would be an attempt to win the support of every doubtful, disgruntled, subversive and disloyal element in the country. What more fertile soil could be found than the former Opposition, whose members combined personal hostility towards Stalin with the bitterness of defeat and the longing to regain lost power?

All this may sound complicated and far-fetched, but in reality it is simple and true, and what is more, provides the only reasonable explanation of what happened in Russia. The Bolsheviks were caught by their own logic. Once they assumed, as they did assume—rightly, as history showed—that the Nazis would attack them, it followed that there would be a German finger in every treasonable pie, large or small, cooked in Russia. If this wasn't immediately obvious, as in the Kirov case, it must be sought for and found. On that principle they proceeded, and found it because it *was* there. When Stalin and associates believed in 1933-34-35 that Hitler planned to attack them and would use the former Opposition or any other anti-Kremlin forces to further his ends, they were working to some extent on a hypothesis. As time went on this hypothesis, which as I have said was already a logical conviction to them, was confirmed by fact after fact, and it is worth remembering that Zinoviev, Kamenev and company were not brought to public trial on a charge of plotting the murder of Kirov and other Soviet leaders in collusion with foreign enemies until August, 1936, that is after the outbreak of the Spanish Civil War. A month before the trial, the military party in Spain, aided and inspired by Nazi Germany, had launched an armed revolt against the Spanish Government. As Stalin knew well, the revolt had been planned in Berlin by the Spanish General Sanjurjo, who would have led it instead of Franco had he not been killed in an airplane accident. Nazi complicity in the Spanish rebellion was clear in Moscow's eyes, but that was only a remote initial phase of Hitler's ultimate plan, the domination of Europe and the conquest of the Soviet Ukraine and Caucasus. Stalin could not escape the conclusion that Nazi agents were even more active in Russia than they had been in Spain.

The trial of Zinoviev, Kamenev and the so-called "Leningrad Center" in August, 1936, was the first of four sensational treason trials. The second was the trial of Radek, Piatakov, Muralov and fourteen others, in January, 1937; the third of Marshal Tukhachevsky and seven Generals of the Red Army, in June, 1937; and the fourth of Bukharin, Rykov, Yagoda and others, in March, 1938. Altogether some sixty persons were tried, convicted and, with half a dozen exceptions, shot. Save for a handful of secretaries and minor officials, they were all men who had formerly held top rank in the civil or military affairs of Soviet Russia. Their arraignment before the highest Soviet tribunal and their execution shocked and bewildered public opinion abroad and, undoubtedly, in Russia itself. Much of the confusion caused in the minds of foreigners by the procedure, and the conduct of the accused themselves, can never be wholly dispelled; but there are a number of points which throw considerable light upon this sinister chapter in Soviet history:

1. The trials were all conducted by the Supreme *Military* Tribunal of the U. S. S. R., that is, each of them was a court-martial. Even in

Western countries court-martial procedure differs considerably from that of civil cases; but in Russia this difference was accentuated by the Bolshevik feeling that their country was already fighting for its life, although not actually at war. War had not yet been declared, but they felt that it was latent, so to speak, and that treason in such circumstances was as culpable as if enemy forces were already marching to battle.

2. It is the rule in Soviet treason cases that the accused are not brought to trial until they have already confessed their guilt. In other words, treason cases are really decided by the preliminary investigation, which on some occasions lasts for several months, and the public trial is in fact what the Russians call it, a "Demonstration Process," held publicly for the triple purpose of acquainting the whole nation with the details of the case, of determining the exact degree of guilt of each of the accused, and of fixing the penalty.

3. One trial, that of the Generals, was held wholly *in camera*, and in the three others all evidence concerning the relations of the accused with foreign agents was heard behind closed doors. In consequence, this phase of the trials, which was really the most important, all but escaped the notice of foreign observers, and was only given proper attention some years later by the American Ambassador, Joseph Davies, who attended the Bukharin-Yagoda trial, in his book, "Mission to Moscow."

4. The trials followed a definitely ascending scale of accusation in regard to the relations of the accused with foreign agents. This, too, was little noticed at the time, but can now be seen to have corresponded to the development of Hitler's moves in Europe. Thus the first trial brought the accusation of collusion with foreigners in plotting the murder of Stalin and other Bolshevik leaders. In the second the verdict of the court was that the accused had conspired "with the object of expediting an armed attack on the Soviet Union and assisting foreign aggressors to seize its territory." This clearly implies that the Supreme Military Tribunal henceforth took for granted the connection between Soviet conspirators and Nazi plans for invasion. In the third trial Marshal Tukhachevsky and his colleagues were found guilty of planning a military *coup d'état* with foreign assistance, in return for which the foreigners in question were to receive territorial concessions in the Ukraine. The fourth trial summed up the Kremlin's final thesis regarding the four con-

spiracies, that they were all intimately connected and part of the same pattern. As the prosecutor, Vishinsky, declared in his final speech, "This group of accused is only one of the advance detachments of Nazi-Fascist provocators and war-incendiaries. Under the guidance of German, Japanese and other intelligence services, this gang of bandits was working to help the Nazi-Fascist governments to overthrow the Soviet Government."

It is interesting to compare this crescendo with the development of Hitler's plans:

March, 1935. Germany denounced the Versailles Treaty by re-establishing universal military service.

March, 1936. Germany moved troops into the Rhineland, contrary to the provisions of the Versailles Treaty and the Locarno Pact.

July, 1936. Spanish Civil War began.

November, 1936. Germany and Japan signed an anti-Comintern pact, which Italy joined a year later.

January, 1937. Hitler made a speech to the Reichstag, "solemnly repudiating" the Treaty of Versailles.

August, 1937. Japan began war against China.

March, 1938. Hitler occupied Austria.

Although in retrospect it seems easy to check the interplay between the trials and events abroad, foreign observers in Moscow were slow or even loath to perceive it at the time. They did not realize that the trials really represented the Kremlin's effort to stamp out Fifth Column activities in the U. S. S. R., an effort which was only one of several measures, to be described in the following chapter, taken to prepare the country for the expected Nazi attack. As far as foreigners in Moscow were concerned, the issue was obscured by the extraordinary nature of the first trial. The accused behaved in so hysterical a manner, heaping reproaches, accusations and tears upon themselves and upon each other, that foreign diplomats and newspapermen who heard them were led to conclude that there was something fishy about the whole affair, that such abject confession and self-denunciation could not be genuine and must have been produced by some form of pressure. Reports were circulated and given considerable credence in America and Britain, that the accused had been hypnotized or tortured or terrorized by threats against their relatives, even dosed with a mysterious "Tibetan drug" which destroyed their will-power and made them as wax in the hands of the prosecution. All of which really meant that the Anglo-Saxon mentality simply could not understand the masochistic eagerness of the accused not only to admit their guilt, but to paint it in the blackest terms.

In this respect the first trial seems to have been more startling and extravagant than the others, but the odor of doubt and unreality which it created was so unsavory as to taint the other trials also. No one, however, who watched the bearing and heard the statements of such men as Piatakov, former Vice-Commissar of Heavy Industry, and Muralov, who had led the Reds to triumph in Moscow at the time of the Revolution, could think for a moment that they were either terrorized or drugged. Piatakov showed the utmost self-possession throughout, and spoke with the calm clarity and dispassionate logic of a college professor addressing a class of students. He gave no sign of weakness or hesitation, either in tone or appearance, and his whole attitude was that of one who had abandoned hope of life but wished, it might be said, to discharge a load from his conscience, to get the record clear, before the end. It seemed absurd, too, that Muralov, a big two-fisted soldier with a twenty years' career of desperate hazards and hairbreadth escapes as an underground revolutionary, should cringe at the thought of death or yield to any pressure. Even more striking was the conduct of Bukharin, once Lenin's closest friend and the chief exponent of Bolshevik doctrine. Bukharin's "last words," as the final statements of the accused were ominously termed, proved a masterpiece of eloquence. In a clear, unfaltering voice he reviewed the series of ideological errors and divergencies which gradually led him to the evil fullness of treason and conspiracy. Firmly he repudiated the suggestion that his attitude or confession had been influenced in any way by drugs or threats or torture, either physical or moral. He went so far as to disavow another suggestion which had been put forward by foreigners familiar with the works of Dostoyevsky, that there was a peculiar characteristic of the "Russian soul" which inclined Russians to the depths of self-abnegation, a sort of martyr complex, when they knew that all was lost. Like Piatakov, Bukharin gave the impression of a man who had made his peace with the world and wished only to cleanse and satisfy his own conscience by revealing all the motives of his thought and action.

In this connection a plausible explanation was offered in an editorial of the London *Times*. The writer stressed the parallel between the Russian trials and sixteenth-century treason trials in England. He cited the case of the Earl of Essex, who was executed by the orders of Queen Elizabeth in the sixteenth century. His "crime" appeared to consist in having written an indiscreet but far from treasonable letter to Mary, Queen of Scots, who also met death on the scaffold. Nevertheless, in his final speech the Earl declared: "I am the most vilest of men, and had I a hundred lives, they all deserve to be sacrificed as punishment for my crime against God and Her Sovereign Majesty the Queen."

The editorial argued that in Elizabethan England, as apparently in Soviet Russia, men accused of treason were brought to a conviction not only of guilt but of *sin*, and that once this conviction of sin had been established in the mind of a believer, he was psychologically compelled to admit that having sinned in one thing he had sinned in everything. Thus the Russians, especially men of high caliber like Piatakov and Bukharin, had "sinned" against the Party Line and the Kremlin, as the Earl of Essex had sinned against God and "God's anointed," Queen Elizabeth. The parallel indicated by the *Times* between Bolshevism and a fanatical religious movement has been noted by many foreign observers, especially in the early days of the Revolution.

The case of the Generals was different from that of the accused civilians. Not only was it held *in camera*, but the "Court" of a presiding judge and two assistants was reinforced by eight of the highest officers in the Red Army. In addition, more than a hundred high-ranking soldiers from all over the country were summoned as spectators, in order later to give an eye-witness account of proceedings to the troops under their command. It is a matter of record that none of them ever expressed doubts about the genuineness of the charge or the justice of the verdict. In this case at least, there was no possibility that the accused had been "worked on" during a long period of preliminary examination, as they were tried within three days after their arrest, confessed their guilt, were condemned by unanimous verdict, and shot without delay.

All of the Generals were men of the highest standing who had rendered meritorious service to the revolutionary cause, and their execution convulsed the whole Soviet Union with horror and dismay. The charges against them, and the exact nature of their offense, have never been made public officially, but they can be surmised with a reasonable degree of accuracy. The night before Tukhachevsky and the others were arrested, Marshal Gamarnik, Vice-Commissar of War and chief of the Political Department of the Red Army, committed suicide, which gives the key to the puzzle. The Political Department had been originally intended by Lenin as a means of civil control over the Army, but in the course of time it had gradually become a part or appanage of the General Staff, owing allegiance to the Army rather than to the Kremlin. The danger of war, and perhaps doubts provoked by the murder of Kirov and subsequent investigation, led Stalin to decide that a radical change should be made in the status of the Political Department, that it must henceforth revert to its original function as an instrument of civilian control. The Army leaders resented this "interference," and finally decided to prevent it by violent action. During the ten years between the Treaty of Rapallo (1922) and the rise of Hitler, relations between the Russian and German armies had been intimate and friendly. Accordingly, Tukhachevsky, Gamarnik and their colleagues appealed to the German General Staff for support in their projected *coup d'état* or "palace revolution" against Stalin. They hoped to effect the coup through the Kremlin Guard and the students of the military academy in the Kremlin, who, they believed, would obey their orders; but they had the gravest doubts about the mass of the Army and the nation as a whole, which prompted them to seek German aid in return, it is said, for an offer of territory and for economic and political advantages in the Ukraine and North Caucasus.

Shortly after the trial it was asserted that the OGPU was informed by the Czech secret service of treasonable conversations between the German General Staff and Tukhachevsky, who had just visited Prague and Berlin. There are some grounds for this report, because in Prague Tukhachevsky held a meeting with the Czech General Sirovy, Foreign Minister Beneš, and one other Czech leader, to discuss measures for joint defense against Hitler should he attack Czechoslovakia. No secretaries were present at the meeting and no minutes were taken, but the Czech secret service in Berlin, where Tukhachevsky stayed for two days on his way home from Prague, made a startling report to Mr. Beneš. The report stated that high German military circles and the Gestapo were fully informed about the Tukhachevsky-Beneš-Sirovy conversations in Prague. The report gave facts and details which Mr. Beneš recognized as correct, and he was therefore forced to the conclusion that no one but Tukhachevsky could have conveyed this information to the Germans. There is no reason to believe that Mr. Beneš had any knowledge of the conflict between Tukhachevsky and the Kremlin, or of any treasonable discussions between Tukhachevsky and the German General Staff on this account. He was, however, horrified beyond measure to learn that Tukhachevsky had divulged to the Germans the substance of the Prague conference, and promptly transmitted his information on the subject to Moscow. Tukhachevsky's arrest, and that of his fellow-generals, was immediately decided; but Marshal Gamarnik, as head of the Political Department, somehow learned about this beforehand and cheated the firing-squad by suicide.

Chapter 20

THE GREAT PURGE AND NATIONAL DEFENSE

WHATEVER MAY HAVE been the international ramifications of the treason trials, and however authentic or dubious the connection which the Supreme Military Tribunal claimed to have established between the accused and foreign agents, the trials had a positive effect or sequel which did no small harm to the Soviet State. The fact that these men, who had formerly held high office and been closely connected with Lenin, should be traitors, by their own confession and to the Russian public by proof, overwhelmed the country with a flood of demoralization and suspicion. Not only the leaders but the masses were forced to ask: If men like these, the gallant soldiers, the members of Lenin's Politburo, the Commissars and Ambassadors, were thus false to their duty, their country and their cause, where could confidence be placed? The clouds of doubt and anxiety became a storm of frenzy and hysteria, until no man knew whom to trust, and children denounced their parents, brother attacked brother and husband accused wife. The "Great Purge," as it was called, raged for nearly two years, from 1936 to 1938, and caused vast confusion, disorganization and distress at the very time when Stalin was doing his utmost to prepare his country for war.

Stalin's measures for defense were started, one may assume, in 1933 by the revamping of the Second Five-Year Plan to increase greatly the number of armament and munition factories and to locate them as far as possible east of Moscow beyond the zone of enemy attack. In 1934 and 1935 there followed a form of moral preparation for war, the placing of new emphasis upon national patriotism and the duty and privilege of Soviet citizens to defend their country. This was in sharp contrast to the previous stress upon the universal international brotherhood of workers, and the deprecation of national patriotism as narrow-minded chauvinism. The first sign of the change was the reappearance of the old Russian word *"rodina,"* meaning "birthland" or "homeland," instead of the phrase *"Socialistichisky otetchestvo,"* "Socialist fatherland," which had been in use ever since the Revolution. Simultaneously there began a nationwide indoctrination of patriotism by every means at the Kremlin's disposal—press, radio, speeches, theater and motion pictures, books and even music. A picture called "Peter the First" was shown throughout the country because Peter, although a Tsar, had defeated a foreign invader, Charles XII of Sweden, at Poltava in the Ukraine. A similar picture celebrated the exploits of Alexander Nevsky, although a noble and later canonized, who defeated the Teutonic Knights at Novgorod. And copies of Tolstoy's epic, "War and Peace," which related the conquest of Napoleon by Tsar Alexander I, were printed by millions and distributed at a nominal price.

Civilians as well as soldiers were thus fired with patriotic endeavor, but the Kremlin's closest attention was concentrated upon the Army. The Red Army had always been a favored child in the Soviet State. Military service was no longer considered a penalty and burden as in the days of the Tsar, but an honor and path to advancement. Although discipline was maintained, the soldiers were well treated, and better fed, housed and clothed than the average civilian. They were given opportunity to learn a trade or profession, and helped to find better jobs after their service was ended. The new armament plants and the progress of industrialization brought steady improvement in the Army's weapons and its ability to use them. German officers were employed in large numbers during the period of friendship as instructors, and it is even said that on one occasion the Commander-in-Chief of the Reichswehr, General von Hammerstein, conducted Red Army maneuvers near Kiev. Superior officers of the Red Army attended the German War College and Staff School as well as similar establishments in Russia, thus adding a high grade of technical skill to their earlier practical experience in the Civil War and the war with Poland. During the Spanish Civil War many Red officers and soldiers saw service on the Loyalist side in the aviation and tank corps, in transport and on the Staff, and thus learned, no less than their German and Italian adversaries, the methods of the blitzkrieg. Finally, in 1938 and 1939, the Red Army was engaged in border conflicts with Japan on a scale that involved pitched battles with the use of heavy artillery, tanks and large bodies of troops.

From 1936 onwards Soviet military engineers were engaged in building a vast system of defense fortifications around the western borders of the U. S. S. R. Later called the "Stalin Line," it was not a steel and concrete barrier like the Maginot Line, but an arrangement of elastic defense in depth, twenty to thirty miles wide, with prepared artillery positions, tank traps, lines of communication, and depots above and below ground. Its prime purpose was to delay and hamper the blitzkrieg, and more than a million men were employed in its construction for a period of three years. It was supplemented by the removal from frontier areas of "doubtful elements" of the population, former kulaks or persons who were suspected of racial sympathy with a potential invader. Their place on the land was taken by communal farms chiefly formed from reservists after completion of military service, and their families, whose settlements were aided by State funds. Many of the farm buildings were made of reinforced concrete, and were so patterned as to form a loose outer system of blockhouse defense.

Other powerful influences were at work to strengthen the Soviet Union against impending attack, of which the new Constitution of the U. S. S. R., adopted in 1936, was not the least important. Although modelled closely after the Constitution of the United States, it maintained the predominance of the Communist Party, with the result that much of the freedom and democracy which it guaranteed on paper was more theoretical than real. The mass of the nation was still in a state of tutelage or "infancy" with the Communist Party as its guardian; but the Constitution did offer it a means of training in self-government for the future. Far more vital and valuable was the fact that the Constitution gave to everyone in the U. S. S. R. the feeling that they were henceforth free and equal under a common law. Distinctions between Russians, the ruling race, and the former subject races of the Caucasus, Central Asia and elsewhere, were swept away. Irrespective of creed or color, the Uzbeks and Tatars, the Caucasian tribesmen and the Kazak nomads,

the Mongols of the East and the Samoyeds of the North all felt
that they were now citizens of one great country, united not by
the freedom which Americans knew, but by unlimited freedom of
equal opportunity, and by one flag and one country, which protected and nourished them all without infringing their local customs,
language and culture. The centralizing force of the Communist
Party and its junior affiliates was indeed a potent glue to bind
together the disparate races of the U. S. S. R., but their new spirit
of patriotism and unity became in the hour of trial one of those
imponderable factors which decide the fate of nations.

Perhaps inspired by Barthou, but more probably of its own
volition, the Soviet Government left no stone unturned to impart to
the rest of Europe its own awareness of the Nazi peril. Its representatives ran hither and yon offering to all and sundry pacifist
agreements, non-aggression pacts and economic accords. They conducted negotiations not only with nations that might become victims
of Nazi aggression, but with powers unfriendly to Russia, like
Poland and Finland, and, on an economic basis, with Germany itself.
In those years the Russians were like Cassandra, prophesying evil
and striving desperately to avert it, but finding few to heed their
warnings. Even the Comintern was pressed into the campaign for
peace. It instructed foreign Communist Parties to make common
cause wherever possible with Labor and liberal groups and to form
a "United Front against the Nazi-Fascist danger."

The extent, diversity and intensity of the Russian effort helped
to defeat their ends. Foreign Labor and "Left" parties were puzzled
and startled by the sudden bid for friendship and alliance of Communists who but lately had been reviling them as "social Fascists."
Foreign conservatives were even more distrustful, and in some cases
already had made their choice between Hitler and Soviet Russia.
To a degree which the Russians themselves did not realize, their
prestige was diminished by the treason trials and the Great Purge,
which provided ammunition to their Nazi-Fascist enemies and to
the anti-Stalinist anti-Kremlin Communists abroad.

The long, hard fight between Stalin and the intra-Party Opposition in Russia had its natural counterpart outside Russia. As the
struggle developed, foreign Communist Parties followed the lead
of the Comintern Center and expelled their own Oppositionists; but
the latter could not be exiled or muzzled as were their comrades in

Russia. The Supreme Military Tribunal of the U. S. S. R. may have been guilty of exaggeration when it claimed that the exiled Trotsky was hand in glove with the enemies of the U. S. S. R. and leader of a huge conspiracy; but there is no doubt that he and his many sympathizers in foreign Comparties and on their fringes—the so-called "fellow-travellers," "Left intellectuals" and "parlor pinks"—did greatly influence public opinion. They declared that Stalin had betrayed the Revolution and was determined to destroy its earliest and most faithful adherents. They called him traitor and backslider at the very time when the Soviet tribunal was accepting as proved the same accusation against their friends in Russia. Whether the pot or the kettle was black made little difference to Hitler and Nazi Germany and Fascist sympathizers all over the world, to whose propaganda mill all Bolshevik quarrels were grist. Their purpose of weakening, dividing and disintegrating the democratic peoples of the world was much aided by the split in the Bolshevik Party at home and abroad and the effects of the Purge in Russia, which alienated many of Russia's former friends and gave comfort to its enemies.

If the world had thought that Hitler's "blood purge" in June, 1934, presaged Nazi dissolution although the total number of its victims was less than a thousand, it is not surprising that Russia's enemies were encouraged by the "casualty list" of the Great Purge in Russia in the years 1937-38. The death roll ran into thousands, the number of exiles to hundreds of thousands. These figures cannot be controlled, but it is known that from two-thirds to three-quarters of the leading personalities in Soviet Russia were "purged," that is, expelled from the Party and in many cases executed.

It was no longer a purge or cleansing, as the Party had known them before, but a panic madness which struck right and left almost haphazard. The statistics are appalling:

Two-thirds of the Soviet diplomatic corps—ambassadors, ministers, and counselors of embassy or legation—were "liquidated," that is their execution was announced, or they simply disappeared.

Casualties were equally severe in the Army and Navy leadership. It is sufficient to say that of the eight officers of the highest rank who were called as extra judges in the trial of Tukhachevsky and the Generals in June, 1937, only one, Marshal Budenny, survived. The others were liquidated except the Cossack commander, Gorbachev, who died in his bed.

Of the Council of Commissars, numbering twenty-one at the end of 1936, only five were left two years later. One, Orjonikidze, died, and the rest were shot or disappeared.

In the Central Committee of the Communist Party there were seventy-one members elected at the beginning of 1934. At the end of 1938 twenty-one remained active; three died naturally; one, Kirov, was assassinated; thirty-six disappeared; one, Marshal Gamarnik, committed suicide; nine were announced as shot.

In the city of Kiev between August, 1937, and June, 1938, more than half the members of the local Communist Party were officially declared to have been expelled between August, 1937, and June, 1938. No such announcements were made about the other great cities of Russia, but the proportion of expulsions is known to have been about the same.

The Party as a whole had 2,000,000 members and 1,200,000 candidates in 1933, a total of 3,200,000 men and women. In December, 1937, there were less than 1,500,000 members and candidates together. In January, 1937, Stalin referred to "our 2,000,000 army" of Party members and candidates, but in the spring of 1938, after half a million new members and candidates had been admitted, *Pravda* stated that there were no more than 2,000,000 members and candidates.

Nearly all of those thus purged, liquidated, executed, disappeared, exiled, expelled from the Party, were Communists, but that was only a part of the dreadful story. In the downfall of these leaders, rejected as "enemies of the people," were involved countless numbers of their subordinates and appointees, Communist or non-Communist, from heads of department down to office-boy or scrubwoman. They were not arrested or exiled, but they lost their jobs, with the result that every department and directive unit in the country, civil and military, agrarian and industrial, was in a state of turmoil. Efficiency and teamwork disappeared; no one dared to give orders or show initiative; one and all were shaking in their boots. A fantastic and disastrous state of affairs at the time when the Nazis were heaping threats and abuse upon Czechoslovakia, whose Sudetenland was clearly their next object of attack.

Early in August, 1938, Kaganovich, Commissar of Heavy Industry, who had just made a tour of inspection in the Urals, and Voroshilov, Commissar of War, newly returned from a similar tour in the Ukraine, met in Moscow. Both were members of the Politburo and intimate friends of Stalin, who was spending his annual vacation near Matsesta, in his native Georgia. On comparing notes, Voroshilov and Kaganovich decided that the demoralization in the Army and Heavy Industry respectively had reached such a pitch that immediate measures must be taken to restore sanity and order. They flew at once to Stalin's residence in Georgia, and found him in conference with Beria, his fellow-Georgian, now chief of the Caucasian OGPU, and formerly Party Secretary of the Caucasian Federation. One of the younger Bolsheviks, not yet turned forty, Beria, who was devotedly attached to Stalin, had approached the Soviet leader on a mission identical with that of Voroshilov and Kaganovich. The Purge, he said, had almost wrecked the administrative machine of the Caucasus, and for that matter, of other federated states of the U. S. S. R., three-quarters of whose leading personnel had been "purged" or "liquidated," which did not necessarily mean shot, but did involve expulsion from the Party, arrest, and exile or imprisonment. Beria boldly told Stalin that Yezhov, who had succeeded Yagoda the year before as chief of the Commissariat of the Interior (NKVD), in which the OGPU was now incorporated, had passed all bounds of reason and discrimination in his conduct of the Purge; throughout Russia Communists of good standing and unblemished reputation were being arrested and punished as "Enemies of the People" on flimsy and often anonymous denunciations.

It is still a mystery how the Purge, which after all was a regular periodical feature of the Bolshevik Party system, should have fallen into the hands of the NKVD and Yezhov, who appears to have been a lunatic sadist. One can only explain this anomaly by the degree of panic which had engulfed the whole country through the combined effects of war danger and the treason trials. At any rate, Voroshilov and Kaganovich found Stalin more than ready to listen to their tale of woe. Beria was promptly appointed Vice-Commissar of the NKVD (on August 12th), and although Yezhov nominally remained Commissar until December, his power for mischief was henceforth curtailed.

Beria at once set himself to repair the damage as far as he could, and his first official act was to order the execution of five of Yezhov's principal henchmen in the Ukraine for gross malpractice and abuse of power in connection with the Purge. This was the first step in the "purging of the purgers," as it was afterwards termed, which Beria carried out with thoroughness and gusto. On December 8th he was appointed Commissar of the NKVD in place of Yezhov, who disappeared early in 1939 and is said to have shared the fate he inflicted on so many others. Meanwhile Beria instituted a wholesale revision of all cases of expulsion from the Party. Figures published in regard to the key provinces of Moscow and Leningrad showed that more than fifty percent of the expulsions were unwarranted, based upon false, frivolous or groundless accusations. The victims were reinstated, but no reinstatement could bring back the dead to life or atone for what the living had suffered. Immediately the newspapers were full of stories to illustrate the wild extravagance of the Purge, about Party chiefs and OGPU henchmen engaging in "Socialist competition" as to who could purge most people in a given period. Particularly flagrant were reports of men and women Communists with doubtful pasts who had shielded themselves by their excessive zeal in denouncing innocent comrades. Greed, jealousy, rivalry and all manner of personal motives had caused thousands of expulsions; apparently it had been enough to attach the term "Enemy of the People" to anyone for his fate to be sealed.

It speaks wonders for the recuperative power and resilience of the Russian people that the confusion, distress and disorganization caused by the Great Purge were overcome by the middle of 1939, but it is significant that the fatal phrase "Enemy of the People" was henceforth expunged from the Soviet vocabulary, never to be revived in the most arduous days of anxiety and danger ahead. Nevertheless, with all its abuses, sorrows and injury to national morale and industrial production, the Purge had a certain value. It eliminated completely Nazi plans for a Fifth Column in the U. S. S. R., and not only eradicated the "doubtful elements" with whom Nazi agents had tried to co-operate, but destroyed *in toto* their espionage and information services.

Important as it later proved, this gain from the Purge can hardly have offset the loss it caused in Russia, while abroad its ill-effects had no such mitigation. Russia's foreign friends were horrified and stunned into silence by the excesses of the Purge; Russia's enemies used it as a two-edged sword to demonstrate the barbarism and bloody madness of the Bolsheviks against whom Hitler was posing as Europe's champion, and to expose the inner weakness of the U. S. S. R., and its impotence to fulfill its foreign obligations. Nazi propaganda in Paris and London harped incessantly on these two tunes, with such success that Premier Chamberlain, the Bank of England and an influential section of the British Conservative Party were assured that the Nazis were preferable to the Bolsheviks, and the French Foreign Minister, Bonnet, did not hesitate to say in Geneva that Russia could not aid Czechoslovakia against Hitler even if it wished to. In this sense it can truthfully be said that the Purge prepared the way for the Anglo-French surrender at Munich.

Chapter 21

WOMAN'S PLACE

IT IS A singular fact that although the Bolsheviks from the beginning had decreed full legal, political, economic and social equality between men and women in Russia, there were no female defendants in any of the treason trials. By that time, nearly twenty years after the Revolution, women were playing an increasingly prominent rôle in Soviet affairs, both inside and outside the Communist Party, and it was only natural to expect that there would be some women members of the disloyal Opposition. Why there were not can perhaps be explained by the generalization that women as a sex benefited more than men from the Bolshevik Revolution. If it is true that in the final instance Lenin and Stalin won the support of the Russian masses because the masses believed that the two Bolshevik leaders were honestly trying to improve their lot, the same must be still more true about the women of Russia, whose lot—amongst the masses —was worse than that of the men.

Students of national psychology have not failed to remark a peculiar frustration and inner negativeness in the Russian character during the later decades of Tsarism, as depicted by such realistic writers as Dostoyevsky and Turgenev. They ascribed this frustration to the fact that the absolutist, rigid and historically obsolete nature of the Tsarist State prevented men of intelligence and good-will from taking any practical part in the direction of their country's destinies, and drove them into futile opposition or the wilderness of philosophic negation. In the simplest terms, man's function in the modern world can be defined as follows: to protect and provide for his wife and family, to defend and fight for his country, and, last but not least, to have a voice in his country's government. That voice was denied to Russian men by the Tsarist system. Politically they were impotent.

Until the most recent times, the function of women has not been considered political. Even Athens, the cradle of Democracy, did not permit votes for women, although one of Aristophanes' keenest comedies showed the strength of the feminist movement. In Tsarist Russia the function of women was to care for husband and children, and in the ranks of peasants and workers, which formed eighty percent of the population, to share man's physical toil. Among the peasants especially, women worked harder than men, because in addition to their responsibilities for "kids and cooking," as the Germans say, they had to work, and did work, in the fields. In short, from a psychological viewpoint they were performing their natural function, without any major frustration, that is, they were closer to life, and lived a more real life, than their husbands, fathers and brothers.

The American Relief Administration employed in one way or another more than a hundred thousand Russians, men and women, in its two years' fight against the Famine of 1921. The Americans were unanimous in saying that their women employees, whether members of committees to apportion the distribution of food or engaged in physical labor, were vastly superior to the men, from a standpoint of trustworthiness, regularity and general efficiency. This unbiased testimony cannot be disregarded, although there was much disagreement among the Americans about the reasons for it. Some said, "Well, of course, there's a famine, which affects first and most directly women and children and the home. So naturally Russian women feel more strongly about it than their menfolk." Other Americans declared simply that Russian women were more serious and patriotic than Russian men, and much more sober. "Lots of the men," they said, "will drink anything on sight, and if they can't get vodka will try to loot our stores of medicinal alcohol. The women never do that." To this I can add a point from my twenty years' experience of Russia, that I have seen hundreds of intoxicated Russians, including one who lay "dead drunk" in the gutter on a cold and wintry night, and when I came back that way three or four hours later, he was dead and cold forever. In all those years I never saw a Russian woman make of herself a public spectacle through inebriety.

It is impossible and absurd to set an arbitrary distinction between the sexes. Everyone knows that male children are apt to take after their mothers and female children after their fathers, and that thus a balance is preserved by Nature. Nevertheless, the fact remains that if the vast majority of the Russian population was downtrodden and unhappy under the Tsars, the burden fell heaviest upon the women. In consequence, they had intrinsically more to gain from a revolution than men and were, as I said before, more realist and less frustrated than men, when the Revolution confronted them with new problems and opportunities.

Opponents of the Soviet State, or conservative souls who were shocked by equal suffrage of both sexes introduced by the Bolsheviks, complained that women have no political sense, that they are liable to be influenced by the male members of the family, that they are flighty and irresponsible, that more than men they are subject to the superstitions and pressures of the Church, and shouldn't, in fact, be allowed to think for themselves or speak for themselves, much less vote for themselves, without grave danger to the State. This biased view hardly needs refutation, although it is true that the level of feminine education in Russia, especially among the masses, was far below that of the men. Which accounts for the fact that although the Bolsheviks demolished all sex barriers, there were, and are still today, few women in the upper hierarchy of the Communist Party or Soviet Government. There have been such exceptions as the late Madame Krupskaya, wife-secretary and widow of Lenin, who played a prominent rôle in Bolshevik affairs before and after her husband's death, although she never formally held high rank in either Party or Government. And Madame Kollontai, at one time member of the Central Committee of the Communist Party and for many years Ambassador of the U. S. S. R. in Sweden, where she overcame the deep-rooted prejudice, anti-Russian as well as anti-Bolshevik, of a proud and stiff-necked people. Madame Kollontai is a well-educated and intelligent woman, an early leader in the world feminist movement, who has written notable books. Like her diplomatic colleague Litvinov, she eschewed political controversy, although she was one of the "Old Bolsheviks" who opposed Stalin as a group, and thus escaped the fate which overcame so many Soviet ambassadors and foreign envoys. Molotov's wife, Madame Zhemchukina, was for some years head of the Cosmetic Trust of the U. S. S. R., which did a thumping business in Russia and the Middle East and brought in large amounts of much-needed foreign currency. She was a competent woman, well able to rank with her colleague-competitors, Elizabeth Arden and Helena Rubinstein, whom she met on a trip to the United States in 1936 or thereabouts. After establishing the Cosmetic Trust on a sound and successful basis, she was unexpectedly transferred to chairmanship of the Fish Trust, which doubtless smelt less sweet, and then in the Purge years faded somehow from the Soviet picture, for reasons which remain unknown.

Madame Zhemchukina's Cosmetic Trust was able to resist the temptation of cheap synthetic perfumes. It produced them, to be sure, in large and powerful quantities for the masses in Russia, Turkey and the Balkan States, but she was clever enough to investigate personally the age-old production of attar of roses in Bulgaria and Persia, and the ambrosial extracts of natural flower-oils in Grasse and Southern France. On the sun-warmed slopes of the Caucasus and the Crimea, protected from cold winds by mountain chains, there has been developed a natural-perfume industry to rival France or Macedonia. Russian women may work as hard as men, or harder, but they are not indifferent to the charm of scent and powder, rouge and lipstick, skin-beautifying salves, and other aids to beauty, not to mention silk underwear and nylon stockings, if and when they can be bought in the U. S. S. R. It is an old truism that human nature does not change, or changes very slowly. It is perhaps truest about women, who, by and large, represent a conservative element in human life. The young German philosopher, Weininger, who wrote a brilliant book at the age of twenty-two called "Sex and Character" and then committed suicide, made a somewhat arbitrary division of women into two categories, the Mother and the Prostitute, more briefly Eve and Lilith, or the virtuous, frugal lover of home and children, and the naughty spendthrift lover of men. Most women really and physiologically belong in the first category, and this is even true of some who, with or without defiance, have ranged themselves in the second category. But few of them, in either category, are blind to the advantage of artificial allurements, which do not have to be, or be considered, meretricious.

If one wishes, perhaps idly, to stress differences between the sexes, it may be noted that there have been no super-excellent and out-standing women creative artists or philosophers, with the possible exception of Sappho, the Greek poetess, who was ranked by her contemporaries on a level with mighty Homer, and Hypatia, the neo-Platonist philosophic lecturer of ancient Alexandria. Women, it would seem, are more realist and practical than men, less prone to chase will-o'-wisps. More than men they desire security, order, and temperate happiness, and as Horace said long ago, "Wars are detested by mothers," though a road to adventure and glory for their sons. Women more than men are loyal to time-honored folkways, to belief in God, the supreme resort of human weakness and human sorrow, and to a steadfast insistence upon such old and simple things as Marriage, Family and Home.

Lenin, the philosophic atheist and destroyer of old things, was neither mad nor evil when he attacked the wealth and corruption of the Orthodox Church of Russia, its servile support of Tsarism and its superstitious hold upon peasant ignorance. Lenin's motives were altruistic when he decreed that children would fare better if taken from squalid peasant hut or city tenement, where their hard-worked mother could give them no proper care, and placed in orphan asylums. He was altruistic when he decreed that marriage and divorce had been too expensive and remote for the downtrodden masses of Russia, and must now be free to all, without any cost in money. He wished to liberate his people from the chains of money and superstition, to make, if you please, every Soviet citizen a cog in a great machine, but—such was the paradox—a free cog, with self-respect. Even the bearing of children was, he said, a matter of individual choice, for woman alone to decide, and he legalized abortion.

Lenin's motives, I repeat, were undoubtedly altruistic, but his well-meant reforms did not suit the women of Russia. The old cliché, "Be it ever so humble there's no place like home," was stronger than Lenin's theories; they wanted their kids at home, no matter how squalid it was. The women of Russia were women; they didn't like abortion, nor the free-love system of marriage and divorce, which was only the scratch of a pen, costing a dime or less, to regulate the most profound, important and permanent of human relationships. And so the laws were changed. Abortion was abolished, and the system of marriage and divorce was set back upon a basis far more liberal than of old, but far more solid than the first Bolshevik pro-gram of free-love short-term contract and unlimited promiscuity.

Women's influence in Russia must also have had its part in the wartime "Recognition" and "Pact of Friendship" between the Soviet Government and the Church. It need not be said that women are more superstitious than men, but no one can deny that most of them sit at home when their sons and husbands and brothers go forth to fight a war. They sit at home and wait, in anxious dread. The words "In the time of our trouble we called upon the Lord" are never so true as in wartime. When her man may be killed tomorrow, what can a woman do for hope and consolation? I know there are good political reasons for rapprochement between State and Church in Russia. The Church is a force of unity, and the Orthodox Church of Russia can have vast influence over its allied communities in Bulgaria, Serbia, Greece and Rumania; but, as with marriage-divorce laws and the status of home and family, so too with the Church in Russia: the swing back from Bolshevik theory to ancient habit and practice has been made for the women of Russia.

If it be true, as of course it was, that the victory of Bolshevism depended upon and was decided by the winning of the peasants to a Socialist regime, the support of the women in the villages was unquestionably one of the prime factors in Stalin's successful effort to socialize agriculture. The woman farm-worker today presents her book of work-hours on full equality with men, she shares with them the advantages of opportunity through education, and perhaps sur-passes them in patriotism. Nevertheless, women do not stand fully equal with men in the U. S. S. R. In office, professional and indus-trial work their wages are still somewhat lower than those of men in equivalent positions, and efforts made to correct this inequality have not yet been wholly successful.

I suppose this is true the whole world over, but that does not detract from the value of feminine support of the Stalinist regime. Without wishing to challenge the Marxist economic interpretation of history, one can find cases where economics are not the determin-ing factor. As for instance the case of women, whose economic position has hitherto been, in general, inferior to that of men. If Freud, however, is right, that a man's character is formed and dominated by the first seven years of his life, it obviously follows that his unconscious mind—which the Freudians declare is his *real* mind—will have conditioned him to submit to feminine influence and to obey feminine orders. The mother, grandmother, nurse or governess has almost invariably and almost entirely control over the masculine infant during those early and (according to Freud) decisive years. Which would seem to make the importance of women, and their potential influence upon men, far greater than any disability they might be supposed to suffer from economic inferiority. This has always been true everywhere in every age, and it may almost be said that men have had to invent religion and priests, statecraft and war and soldiers, in order to maintain their equality with women.

It cannot be wholly denied that there has been in the U. S. S. R. an atavistic prejudice against feminine equality in capacity, politics and wage rates. On the other hand, equality and freedom of Opportunity through education have produced a great number of successful and competent women in the middle ranks of Soviet life, in every phase of endeavor. It is still too soon, considering the handicap under which they had started, for women to have reached the highest points; but the very fact of that handicap has made them most devoted to the Soviet regime which removed it. To take a simple instance, but one which applies to nearly three-fourths of the women, that is the peasant women, in Soviet Russia today, the collective farm system has made a vast difference in their lives and pursuit of happiness. In the old days Russian peasant women worked like men in the fields and had in addition to look after their husbands and children, prepare food, wash clothes, and clean house. Even the youngest babies were set out alone in the grain fields in order that their cries of hunger and distress might scare off marauding crows. Hundreds of Russian women have told me that the period from spring to autumn in their villages was one long grind of overwhelming work, gave them no time to rest, and left them too exhausted almost for sleep. "Today," they said, "that's all gone. Now the farm work is done by brigades; each group in the whole Collective has its allotted task. Some do the cooking, some look after the children, some take care of the poultry and the pigs, and others work in the fields. But for all of us there's a seven-hour shift, with time for meals, and overpay during the harvest if we work longer than that. We have the same rights as the men, the same book of 'labor-days' by which

our share in the harvest is apportioned. Can't you see why we stand
firm for Lenin and for Stalin, who have brought about this change,
who have made us human beings instead of hopeless drudges?"

I make bold to say that the support and adherence, the courage
and self-devotion of the women of Russia has been the greatest
factor in the progress of the nation from its depths of degradation
and defeat in 1917 to its victorious resistance in 1943, for the best
and most excellent of reasons. First, that Russian women as a sex
benefited proportionately more than men from the Bolshevik Revolution; second, that being less frustrated than men and therefore
more closely attuned to the realities of life, they were able to see
more clearly what Bolshevism had done for them and their children,
to give them something to fight for, dearer than life itself.

As I said earlier, women in Russia have not yet, for the most part,
reached high office or positions of dominant importance, although
the middle ranks of scholarship, science, business, and even industrial
management, show a large and growing number of feminine executives. For obvious reasons they have not, either, played a prominent
role in warfare. The "Women's Death Battalion" of the grotesque
Kerensky period has no place in Soviet realism. Theoretically,
women are admitted to the armed services on the same level as men,
and I personally have known women members—in one case a commander—of bombing and fighting airplane squadrons. I have met a
woman cavalry captain, no less competent and respected than her
masculine fellow-officers. There have been women sharpshooters in
the Regular Army, and women leaders of guerrilla bands. But
speaking generally, women in the Red Army have the same auxiliary
function as the WACs and other feminine branches of the American
armed services.

During the war Russian women have undertaken men's functions
in agriculture and industry to a far greater extent than has been the
case in the United States, for the obvious reason that the war has
been fought on Russian soil, with a terrific drain on manpower. This
cannot fail to have a corresponding effect upon the position of
women in Russia. It will jump them from actual and economic inferiority to the full legal equality established by Soviet law. Most
significantly, this change will accord with the movement of the
U. S. S. R. towards conservatism. It will not lead to matriarchy as

such, but it cannot fail to contribute to a more genuine companionship and equality between the sexes, and offer an example which may be of no small value to the Western world.

It is, however, interesting to remark that the stress of war—with its attendant problem of homeless refugee children—has produced a surprising change in the Soviet system of education. This educational system had already one important change when it was decided, in the middle thirties, that the study of history, Russian and foreign, of law and of the "humanities," should replace the original Bolshevik concept that history began with the Revolution of 1917, and that everything must depend upon the rigid doctrine of Marxian economic determinism. This second, war-time, change involves a difference of education between girls and boys of what would be called in America high-school age. Instead of following, as heretofore, an identical curriculum, the education of high-school boys is now directed along specifically masculine lines, that is pre-military training and technical or professional courses in agriculture, industry and so forth. Girls, however, are now directed towards such feminine vocations as housekeeping, cooking, sewing, and the care of children. Ostensibly, this is a war measure, but it may well represent a definite and interesting recognition of the fundamental difference between the natural and basic functions of men and women.

Chapter 22

MOSCOW AND MUNICH

By the end of August, 1938, no doubt could remain that Hitler was prepared to use force to "reunite to the Fatherland" the Germans of the Sudeten area of Czechoslovakia. The Soviet Foreign Commissar, Litvinov, multiplied his efforts to open Europe's eyes to the danger and to prove that now or never Collective Security must be made a reality. In vain; the smaller powers were too terrified to act, and France and Britain refused to take the lead. Litvinov's vehement declaration at Geneva that the U. S. S. R. was ready to fight for Czechoslovakia, to protect whose independence France was pledged by treaty and England morally bound, was received with open skepticism. Nazi propaganda in Paris and London had done its work too well, and the Russians were forced to conclude that the French and British governments were playing Hitler's game. Their conclusion was vindicated by events. True, there was a moment when British public opinion seemed to stiffen its government's backbone, when the British Fleet was mobilized and Chamberlain declared that Britain, France *and Russia* would defend the Czechs. Instead, the British Premier flew to Germany to confer amicably with Hitler, and a few days later the Munich agreement announced that Czechoslovakia had been sacrificed.

The Russians had no part in the Anglo-French negotiations with the Nazis. At Munich they were neither admitted nor even consulted, and to the ugly fact of their resounding diplomatic defeat was added the humiliation of having been ignored and treated as if they didn't matter or almost didn't exist. With profound chagrin and fury they believed that their worst fears had been confirmed, that not only Czechoslovakia but the U. S. S. R. had been offered to Hitler as a victim by the Franco-British appeasers. The Bolsheviks saw with dismay that their old nightmare of attack from the West was becoming the horrid truth, and accepted as an article of faith the theory, which may or may not have been correct, that Messrs. Daladier and Chamberlain had given Hitler *carte blanche* to execute his designs against the Soviet Ukraine and North Caucasus. It mattered little whether the long-feared invasion would be made by Germany alone or by a coalition; the Russians knew themselves friendless in a hostile world.

Moscow's reaction to Munich was one of wounded pride and savage anger, but hardly of dismay, despite the Kremlin's certainty of what Munich presaged. It was as if the Bolsheviks were like a man who has dreaded for years a dire event and done his best to avert it, but finds his efforts vain, and says, almost with relief: "All right, now I know where I stand. If I have to fight, I'll fight, and depend on myself alone." In March, 1939, a congress of the Communist Party was held in Moscow for the first time in five years, and Stalin rose to the occasion with a report to his fellow-Communists which may have lacked the fire and magic phrases of Winston Churchill's wartime speeches, but which faced the facts clearly and squarely. He wasted no time on recriminations or regret for the past, dismissing treason at home and treachery abroad in a few harsh sentences. The U. S. S. R., he said, had rid itself of traitors and enemy agents, and still adhered to the stand it had taken in foreign affairs, to strive for peace, to assist where possible the victims of aggression, but above all to resist aggression against its own borders without fear or hesitation. It mattered little that the efforts of the U. S. S. R. to maintain peace had not been supported—he did not say "betrayed"—by other powers. The U. S. S. R. was alone, but it would continue to strive for peace and refuse to let itself be used as a cat's-paw by anyone.

These last words were both cryptic and prophetic. Stalin meant them as a warning to France and Britain that he saw through their schemes of embroiling Nazi Germany with the U. S. S. R. That was all that he said about the international situation, and he devoted most of his long address to a detailed report of Russian progress in industry and agriculture, in education and health, and in unity and cohesion, since the preceding Congress. He said in substance that as far as internal affairs were concerned, the past five years had witnessed three great achievements: the U. S. S. R. had become an industrial state; its agriculture had been modernized and mechanized by the Collective Farm system; the new Constitution of 1936, which assured freedom and equality to all Soviet peoples, had found triumphant expression in the elections of December 12, 1937. By a secret ballot 96.8 percent of 94,000,000 electors had approved the delegates to the Supreme Soviet of the U. S. S. R. (corresponding to the Congress of the United States) whose candidacy had been supported by the Bolshevik Party. This proved the complete triumph of Socialism in Russia, and proved also that the nation as a whole was satisfied with the Bolshevik regime and could face the future undismayed.

The significance of Stalin's speech was hardly noted abroad. Most of it was dismissed as bombast and rodomontade. In Western Europe especially, and in the United States, public opinion, still obsessed by the Trials and the Purge, did not realize two points of cardinal importance in Stalin's favor. First, that the Kremlin had been strengthened and Russia unified by the Trials and the Purge and the fight for collectivization, as Hitler had been strengthened by his blood purge in 1934. Terrible as had been the cost in Russia, the essential fact was true that the opponents of collectivization and of the regime itself were dead or exiled, anyway "liquidated" and impotent for good or ill. They were gone like the Tsar or Kerensky, and their place had been taken by people who approved collectivization and benefited by it, who believed in the genuineness of the treason trials and were loyal to the Stalinist regime. Secondly, that the diverse races of Russia now thought of themselves as members of one great family, citizens of one great country, for whose defense they were ready to die. Foreigners did not know that the Bolsheviks had succeeded in making the land of the Ukraine "his own country" to the Central Asian Uzbek or the Buryat Mongol, so that the whole vast conglomerate was equally patriotic and determined for the defense of Tashkent or Tiflis, Kiev or Rostov, Leningrad or Vladivostok.

By a curious paradox the cause of Russia's weakness, or at least friendlessness, abroad, was the source of its strength at home. Foreigners, potential friends and potential foes alike, believed that the

U. S. S. R. had been reduced to negligible weakness by the Trials and the Purge, which had indeed involved the liquidation of seventy-five percent of its military and civil leaders, with the all-important exception, however, of Stalin and his small group of stern and devoted associates. At this time the acme of misunderstanding between Soviet Russia and the rest of the world was attained. Perhaps the simplest explanation is that foreigners could not keep up with the swift movements and changes on the Russian chessboard. In the middle of 1938 Russia *was* disorganized, and it *was* true that military discipline and industrial coherence had sunk to a dangerous ebb. But things moved fast in Russia, and by the end of the year—still more by the opening of the Eighteenth Party Congress in March—Stalin and Beria had actually redressed the ill-effects of the Purge and were able to reap its benefits. It became a source of strength in that treason had been suppressed, doubt had been dispelled and unity restored. The methods were ruthless and drastic, but the result was there. If proof were needed, it can be found in the savage conflict with the Japanese at Changkufeng, on the Russo-Manchurian border, in the summer of 1938, which began as a trifling frontier skirmish.

Between the frontier of Japanese-controlled Korea and the Soviet area south of Vladivostok, there was a sort of No Man's Land whose exact limits had never been clearly determined. In June, 1938, the Japanese learned that the Russians were planning to establish a new submarine and air base on Possiet Bay, at the extreme southern limit of Soviet territory. Whereupon they seized a hill called Changkufeng, situated in the No Man's Land about twenty miles from the sea, which gave artillery control over Possiet Bay. The Russian Frontier Guard expelled the Japanese patrol which had seized the hill. The Japanese came back in force and annihilated the Russian Frontier Guard. The Russians countered in turn, and within ten days two large armies, seventy or eighty thousand men on either side, with planes, tanks and heavy guns, were fighting for the mastery of the narrow ridge. The battle was won by Soviet dive-bombers whose pilots had learned about "blitzkrieg" in Spain. They blew the top off the mile-long ridge, incidentally inflicting losses on their own front-line troops, and the Russian infantry drove the Japanese into the valley below. Although this battle received small attention from the rest of the world, it was one of the strangest and perhaps not least important conflicts in history. Each antagonist apparently thought that the other was bluffing, and reinforced his own strength in order to build up the bluff, until the fight rivalled Gettysburg in numbers of troops engaged, and surpassed it in duration. Then, suddenly, both sides seem to have realized that the bluff had gone too far, and called the whole fight off. They reached an "amicable" settlement, by which, however, the Japanese for the first time in Russo-Japanese history abandoned a field of battle. They recognized that the ridge was Russian territory, and withdrew discomfited to the valley five miles southwest. This astonishing episode may throw light upon subsequent Russo-Japanese relations. At any rate, it gave the Kremlin the comforting assurance that its Red Army in Siberia was neither impotent nor demoralized. The following year the Japanese tried again, on the even vaguer border line between Inner Mongolia, which they controlled, and Outer Mongolia, controlled by Russia, at a place called Nomanhan. In this struggle the brunt was borne by native levies on both sides, although regular Japanese and Russian troops, planes, tanks and artillery were engaged. In a "war" which lasted six weeks, the Japanese were again defeated, and again withdrew from the battlefield.

The Changkufeng affair confirmed the Kremlin's belief that it had been strengthened, not weakened, by the Trials and the Purge. The Party Congress of March, 1939, unanimously approved Stalin's policies and thus put him in a much stronger position than anyone abroad could imagine. He knew, if foreigners didn't, that his battle at home had been won, and that his Red Army in the East could deal with the Japanese. In consequence, at the very moment when the West—friends and enemies alike—was discounting Soviet Russia, Stalin still had strong cards in his hand.

For his subtle Georgian mind, sharpened to razor-edge by twenty years of underground conspiracy, the situation was unique. The British and French had betrayed him, had thrown Russia, with the Czechs at Munich, as a mewling babe to glut the Nazi wolf, but Stalin knew that Russia was neither mewling nor a babe, and that it stood strong behind him. And now for the first time his hands were entirely free from foreign entanglements, to play his own and Russia's game. That, in history's perspective, was the real effect of Munich, that Stalin had a free hand. This became apparent in the spring of 1939 when Hitler coolly moved into Prague and occupied

Memel in Lithuania and put Rumania at the pistol-point of an economic agreement which was equivalent to German suzerainty over the whole Danube Basin, and the French and British governments appealed to Stalin for aid.

Where now was Chamberlain's boast of achieving "peace in our time"? Where now were the "fruits of appeasement," of the sacrifice of Czechoslovakia and the scurvy treatment of the U. S. S. R.? Chamberlain's policy was bankrupt, and the babes he had thrown to the Nazi wolf had only whetted its appetite for further conquest. In hurried anxiety the British Government guaranteed the integrity of Poland and announced that it would protect Rumania also. Neither promise in the circumstances could have any possible meaning without the support of the Soviet Union. The Soviet position was one of some delicacy, between the devil and the deep sea—that is, between a dangerous potential enemy and friends it did not trust. Stalin's first instinct was to gain time, and secondly to play both ends against the middle. Despite Munich, he seems to have still been willing to deal with the Franco-British if at the eleventh hour an arrangement could be made with them to oppose Hitler resolutely.

At any rate, on March 18th the U. S. S. R. addressed a strong protest to Germany against the Nazi seizure of Prague, only three days after it occurred; but Stalin evidently felt the need of trying to pin down the French and British governments and get them to declare themselves openly. He may have ascribed Machiavellian subtlety to Chamberlain's diplomacy, because in answer to the Franco-British appeal for Russian support against Hitler in regard to Poland and Rumania, the Soviet Government proposed an immediate six-power conference of the U. S. S. R., Britain, France, Rumania, Poland, and Turkey. Chamberlain declined to commit himself, and the proposal was allowed to drop; but on March 22nd the British Minister of Overseas Trade, Mr. H. F. Hudson, reached Moscow, ostensibly to negotiate an extension of trade relations between Britain and the U. S. S. R. After a week's visit, Mr. Hudson departed, announcing that his mission had been successful and that he had laid the foundations for a new trade agreement. Simultaneously the Russians issued a communiqué stating that Mr. Hudson had had a long conversation with the Soviet Premier, Molotov, and that *matters of international importance* had been discussed as well as commercial affairs. No reference was made to this point in the communiqué issued by the British Embassy, a point noted by the Russians as further evidence of British duplicity. The British for their part subsequently charged the Russians with having used Mr. Hudson as a "come-on" to spur similar discussions with Germany, which at the time were also labelled "commercial negotiations."

The belief that the Kremlin was "playing a double game" at this time and for the next two years has been so firmly anchored in public opinion that it requires some explanation, because the phrase has a strongly invidious sense. It would be fairer and more correct that the Russians were maneuvering as dexterously as possible to achieve two main objects: first, to gain time at all costs; second, to avoid being exposed to or drawn into war with Germany.

In this difficult game Stalin had two trumps whose importance the other players hardly realized: first, that the U. S. S. R. was more united and loyal behind him, better prepared for war, both morally and materially, than the world at large believed; second, that none of the economic deals, revolving credits and so forth, made with Germany at any time in the past ten years, had been abrogated by the Hitler regime. It is moreover a fact that Mr. Hudson's visit to Moscow forestalled by a few days a similar visit projected by one of the German economic leaders. The German visit was cancelled, but it was announced that the "commercial discussions" would be held later in Berlin.

At the beginning of May Moscow produced a *coup de théâtre* in the shape of the sudden removal of Litvinov from the post of Commissar of Foreign Affairs and his replacement by Molotov. Litvinov's position as the Soviet representative at Geneva and champion of Collective Security, even more than his Jewish origin, lent color to the belief that the Kremlin was contemplating a change of policy in the German direction. At the same time Litvinov's removal was a sharp hint to the Franco-British that if they really did want Russia's support they had better take prompt action.

Mr. Chamberlain, whose policy seems to have been one of fumbling bewilderment rather than the astuteness with which the Russians were disposed to credit him, responded by a proposal to send a special diplomatic mission to Moscow, which the Russians accepted. They hoped, and it is said, requested, that the mission should be headed by a prominent figure in English public life, for instance the Foreign Minister, Lord Halifax. Instead, its chief was a comparatively minor Foreign Office official, Mr. William Strang, former Counsellor of Embassy in Moscow, where he had not been on the best of terms with the Soviet Foreign Office. On the other hand, the object of negotiations was simple and might, one would think, have been easily attained, that the three Powers, Britain, France and the U. S. S. R., should sign a declaration informing Hitler that they would jointly oppose any further act of aggression on his part. Russia would thus be involved in the Franco-British guarantee to Poland and Rumania, but it was hoped that the tripartite gesture of solidarity, with which the United States was known to be in sympathy, might cause Hitler to pause at the last moment.

For a time it seemed that an agreement might be reached. The Russians, however, still suspected that the Franco-British were trying to wave them like a red rag under Hitler's nose, or, in Stalin's phrase at the March Congress, to "make the U. S. S. R. a cat's-paw" for their own ends. The British feared that the Russians were using the Moscow parley to bring pressure upon Germany, with which trade negotiations were now proceeding in Berlin. In this atmosphere of mutual distrust no agreement was possible, and Mr. Strang returned to London empty-handed.

The Russians considered the whole affair a further proof of British insincerity, but they did not take sufficiently into account the fact that the public opinion of Britain, and perhaps the private opinion of Mr. Chamberlain himself, had changed greatly since the days of Munich as a result of Nazi aggression in Czechoslovakia, Memel and Rumania. At any rate, in the middle of the summer a second attempt was made by the Franco-British to enlist the U. S. S. R. against Hitler's designs upon Poland, which was clearly destined to be his next victim. On this occasion an Anglo-French military mission was sent to discuss measures for the coordination of joint aid to Poland against Hitler. Once more the personnel was insignificant from the Russian viewpoint, and Russian misgivings were heightened by the fact that their French and British guests preferred a leisurely six-day voyage by sea to a plane trip of twelve hours.

The Russians stated their case bluntly. They demanded "territorial guarantees" in Finland and the Baltic States, by which they meant that their own military and naval forces should occupy strategic points and some of the islands, notably Hango, in the Gulf of Finland. Furthermore they proposed that two Russian armies should enter Poland in the north and south, which would be independent of the Polish General Staff although acting in co-operation with it. The Russians did not hide their belief that Poland could not withstand a Nazi invasion nor their anxiety lest they themselves might be forced to carry a beaten Poland on their shoulders, or in other words be dragged into war against Hitler in the most unfavorable circumstances. The French and British representatives declared that the Russian conditions were impossible, that they involved the infringement of the sovereign rights of independence of the Baltic States and Finland and Poland. The Russians refused to budge, and the only result of the talks was to confirm the Russian belief that their "friends" were trying to embroil them in war with Germany.

At this point there occurred a striking historical parallel between the present and the past. Such parallels are proverbially dangerous, but this one is so remarkable that it cannot be ignored. In the early part of the nineteenth century, Tsar Alexander I of Russia had fought side by side with the Austrians and Prussians against Napoleon. Later he came to distrust his allies, and startled his own people and the world by signing a pact of friendship with the new self-appointed French Emperor, for the same two identical reasons as led Stalin on August 23, 1939, to sign a pact with Hitler—to gain time for Russia, and from distrust of Russia's allies. Like Alexander, Stalin knew who was his real enemy. Like Stalin, Alexander had lost faith in his so-called friends.

The Russo-German pact struck London and Paris like a thunderbolt. Whatever else it might mean, it was clearly a triumph for Hitler, and left Poland as a morsel for him to devour at will. Within a week his armies crossed the Polish frontier without warning, and despite the heroic resistance of Warsaw, the Polish armies were easily defeated in a brief three weeks' campaign. Any hope the Poles might have had of prolonging the struggle in their eastern marshes was shattered by the Russians, who had climaxed their deal with Hitler by a cynical agreement to partition Poland between Russia and Germany—the third such agreement to be made in two hundred years. The French and British governments left Poland to its fate. It is true that with ill-disguised reluctance and under pressure of public opinion they both declared war on Germany, a war for which they were so unprepared that not a plane nor a man nor a gun was sent to aid the Poles, and no hostile action was undertaken against Germany in the West except some greatly over-advertised skirmishing in Western Alsace, where the French tried to save face by occupying a few German towns and a narrow strip of territory in what was soon widely known as the "sitzkrieg" or "phony war." Strange as it may seem, the British air force in this period was employed in dropping over Western Germany nothing more dangerous than pamphlets telling the population how naughty Hitler was.

The Franco-British declaration of war reassured Stalin but slightly. He had won his first objective of gaining time for Russia by keeping it out of war, but he still was far from sure that Hitler might not at any moment come to terms with the French and British and move eastwards against the U. S. S. R. Nearly a century before, Lord Palmerston, then Premier of England, had said: "The policy of England must invariably be dictated in the final instance by England's interests." Stalin thought the same; without regard for public opinion abroad, he pursued his own devious path with no guide or compass save the interests of his country. He took advantage of his agreement with Germany to seize not only the eastern areas of Poland, but to introduce Red Army garrisons into strategic points of the Baltic States, where, it was admitted, they behaved circumspectly. To the West, of course, to Britain and America, this was further evidence that Stalin and Hitler were working hand in glove. This impression was confirmed by the terms of the Russo-German economic arrangement, by which the U. S. S. R. supplied Germany with more than a million tons annually of oil and grain and large quantities of manganese, cotton and other raw materials, in return for German machinery. The West did not pause to reflect that more than half of all the machines and machine-tools imported by the U. S. S. R. during the Five-Year Plans came from Germany; that their replacement could only be provided by Germany, and that neither the United States nor Britain was prepared or able to sell such equipment to Russia. Thus Russia gained by its agreement with Hitler not only time but territory, an outer "glacis" beyond its depth-defense line, not only territory but the machines and tools which its war plants urgently needed.

On September 17th the Russians moved forward into Eastern

Poland, avowedly to occupy the Polish territory allotted to them by their partition agreement with Germany. The Poles declared—and still declare—that this was the final "stab in the back" which ruined their hopes of continuing to resist the German invasion, even by guerrilla warfare, in their eastern marshes. This was partially true, because the Russian advance did complete the debacle of the Polish armies, which the Russians disarmed and interned without any serious combat. On the other hand, the Polish Government had fled two weeks before to Rumania, and the Russians had no wish nor reason to rescue the debris of Poland's brave but defeated troops. Their immediate purpose was to occupy as quickly as possible the Polish area whose possession they had wrung from Germany as part of the price for their pact of friendship and their supplies of oil and grain and manganese and cotton. That they did this with no regard for Polish or Anglo-American public opinion is neither to their detriment nor their credit; it simply showed that Stalin, fully alive to the danger of Nazi invasion, was determined to put as much space as possible between his prepared defense zone and the coming blitzkrieg.

The truth of the matter was that, like Tsar Alexander before him, Stalin was building his strength against an attack he foresaw, and trying to reinforce his bulwarks of defense. One of Russia's weakest points against a German attack was the exposed position of its second city, Leningrad, the former capital, which was located less than thirty miles—that is, within cannon-range—from the Finnish border. The Russians accordingly proposed in the autumn of 1939 that the Finns should lease to them for a term of years the island of Hango, one of the strategic points in the Gulf of Finland, and cede several hundred square miles of territory south of Viborg in the narrow isthmus between Lake Ladoga and the Baltic. In return the Russians offered to Finland a larger belt of territory in Soviet Karelia north of Lake Ladoga, where the population was largely of Finnish origin. The Finns, with the help of foreign military engineers, had built a powerful defense system called "The Mannerheim Line," after their leading soldier, Field-Marshal Mannerheim, an inveterate enemy of the Russians, across the middle of the Viborg isthmus. They had built it for defense, but from the Russian viewpoint Finland was no longer a small, weak power which might need defense against Russian aggression, but a *place d'armes* from which

German aggression against Russia might be prepared behind the shelter of the Mannerheim Line. Unfortunately for hopes of agreement, there was an age-old antagonism between Russia and Finland hardly less bitter than between Russia and Poland. The Finns perhaps were unaware of Hitler's intention to use their country as a base for invasion; or perhaps they hoped he would do so. In any event they refused the exchange of territory, and in November Russia attacked them.

Once more the West hailed this as a fresh proof of Soviet infamy, and openly rejoiced when the Finns successfully repulsed the first Red Army onslaughts. The Russians had undoubtedly underestimated the courage and patriotism of the Finnish nation, and had thought to bring Finland quickly to its knees. They were rudely undeceived, and the first ten weeks of the war proved disastrous to Soviet plans and Soviet prestige. Military experts all over the world said gleefully that the Russians were now paying for the execution of Tukhachevsky and his Generals, and for the confusion of powers which must fatally result from the Kremlin's attempt to establish civil control through the Political Department and political commissars over its military machine. They accepted so readily the idea of the Red Army as a giant with feet of clay that they failed to notice how easily and swiftly the Mannerheim Line was stormed at the end of February, when General Stern brought four panzer divisions and two mechanized divisions from the Far East to blast it with a Russian-type blitzkrieg, heavy tanks and dive-bombers, parachutists and massed artillery. Finland's strongest positions were overwhelmed in seventeen days; but the Western world, including the Germans, took little account of the real weight behind the Bear's paw, and ascribed the Russian victory to the exhaustion and numerical inferiority of the Finns.

On March 12th Russia and Finland made peace on Russia's terms. The isthmus was occupied up to Viborg, and Hango and other key islands in the Finnish Gulf admitted Soviet garrisons. The war had been only an interlude on the fringe of the central drama whose action was still undetermined. Despite foreign skepticism about the Red Army's strength, and despite certain weaknesses in its training and organization which the war revealed, Stalin could draw from it two encouraging assurances. The Red Army was fundamentally a strong and efficient machine, as the final drive had shown, well-equipped and disciplined, lacking neither dash nor loyalty. Still more important had been the attitude of the Russian people, which proved that the long campaign to inculcate patriotism had borne good fruit. Although losses had been severe and disappointments many during the first three months of the war, there had been no sign of faltering or discouragement. The country had followed the Kremlin's lead without question or grumbling, even in face of the fact that no mention of the true reason behind Russia's move against Finland, that is the fear that Germany would use Finland as one of the bases for its attack upon the U. S. S. R., was ever made by the press, radio, or public speakers. It was evident that the treason trials and the Purge had strengthened rather than weakened the cause of Russian unity: the nation had shown it was ready for the supreme test before it.

Chapter 23

BORROWED TIME

DURING THE WINTER of 1939-40 the Russians were inclined to believe that the British and French governments still hoped to avert a "real" war with Germany, still hoped, perhaps, that Hitler would attack the U. S. S. R. without molesting them. After Chamberlain's first boasts of "peace in our time" at Munich had proved vain, he had fallen back upon the defense that he had won a year for France and Britain to prepare themselves. This was equally fallacious; in reality German strength against France and Britain, which had been in the ratio of ten to six in the autumn of 1938, had become fully twenty to seven by the end of 1939. In other words, it was the Germans, not the French and British, who had taken advantage of the breathing-space and the "phony war." To mention a single instance, French airplane production in 1939 dropped so low as to be incapable of replacing the monthly losses of training, dropping pamphlets over Germany, and engaging in perfunctory conflicts with German pilots in Alsace. British production of planes and tanks was little better, at the time when German factories were working night and day.

The Russians were aware that their fate hung poised in the balance, that Hitler must be tempted to swing his weight against them, to seize the Ukraine and the Caucasus, then turn and say to the pusillanimous leaders of France and Britain: "All right, I've got what I want. I will spare you, on condition that you acknowledge my mastery and restore the former German colonies in Africa and the Pacific." Why Hitler did not act thus in the spring of 1940,

with at least the tacit approval of the French and British govern-,
ments, is a mystery. If he had, there is little reason to suppose that
they would have done anything except hope piously that he might
be lost or frozen in the boundless steppes of Russia. Hitler's book,
"Mein Kampf," and his subsequent speeches had made it clear
enough that the Ukraine and the Caucasus *were* his ultimate objective, and the Russians had long been expecting his onslaught. On
that account they had braved ill-repute in Western Europe and in
the United States to partition Poland, to garrison the Baltic States,
and drive the Finnish frontier further back from Leningrad. They
had done what they could to prepare for the wrath to come; but
now they went further still to avert, if possible, the danger. They
signed a new agreement with Germany, increasing their deliveries
of oil and grain, and waited, breathless.

The four weeks from March 12th, when Russia signed peace with
Finland, to April 9th, when Hitler struck at Denmark and Norway,
must have caused in the Kremlin a state of tension only equalled
by the dreadful days of 1932, when the Ukraine and North
Caucasus were stripped of gasoline, food and seed-grain to strengthen
the Red Army against a Japanese drive towards Lake Baikal. Now
again, it seemed to the Russians that the issue hung in the balance,
as a decade earlier they had waited to see would Japan move north
or south. Hostile critics of the U. S. S. R. have declared that this
period, the early spring of 1940, marked the depths of Soviet
ignominy. The Russians, these critics averred, made a disgraceful
pact with Germany; they raped East Poland and the Baltic States
and Southern Finland. They instructed the foreign Communist
parties all over the world to protest against the Franco-British
"imperialist" war; they increased their supplies of raw material to
Germany, and grovelled at Hitler's feet.

In Tolstoy's "War and Peace" there is a passage where a hot-
headed young Russian officer makes the same accusations against the
policy of Tsar Alexander I about his pact with Napoleon. In both
cases the answer is the same, that Russia, under Stalin and Alexander,
put its own interests first and cared little for foreign opinion. On
April 9th Hitler struck at Denmark and Norway, and Stalin knew
that the obloquy he had incurred abroad mattered nothing in comparison with what he had gained by Germany's move to the west
instead of the east. What a relief that was, what a crown of success

to his policy! What a final negative to Chamberlain's hopes of winning immunity for Britain and France and embroiling Germany and Russia!

Throughout those winter months, from the defeat of Poland at the end of September until the Nazi attack on Norway in April, the Bolsheviks had known the weakness of the French and British governments—had known it, indeed, since Munich—and had more than suspected their hope that Hitler would drive east instead of west. They must have wondered, as future historians will wonder, at the choice which Hitler made. They must have known that London and Paris were still wholly ungeared for war, that they were waiting for Hitler to find "appeasement" in the rich grain lands of the Ukraine and the oil fields of the Caucasus. Why did not Hitler do so?

To this deep and cardinal question there are three possible answers. First, that Hitler overestimated the strength and energy of the French and British governments. After all, his representatives, Abetz and Ribbentrop, had told him that neither France nor Britain would go to war for Poland. But they *had* gone to war for Poland in a burst of popular sentiment. So Hitler could not be sure that the British and the French might not again surprise him should he strike at Russia. Second, he may have underestimated the Soviet power of resistance, may have shared the belief of military experts everywhere that the Finnish War had exposed the Red Army as a giant with feet of clay, and thus been led to regard the U. S. S. R. as a fruit that was ripening for him to grasp at ease in his own good time.

Those are practical reasons, but there may have been another psychological reason spurring Hitler to action in the West. I mean a fanatical conception of himself as the chosen leader to avenge Germany's defeat in 1918 by its ancient enemy, France, an uncontrollable desire whetted by his own sufferings on the Western Front in the war, to pay France back for his own and Germany's pain. And perhaps in the final instance a reluctance, almost a fear, which runs from Clausewitz and before him, to Bismarck, the German fear of Russia. Bismarck expressed that reluctance when he said that Germany should try to make friends with Russia, and must always avoid conflict with it. Bismarck was a Prussian, and in the Prussian heart there has been a strange atavistic dread of the dark outer forces in the East, of the huge Slavic mass which seemed to loom like a thunder cloud over Europe. If one accepts the view that Hitler, although an Austrian, really has owed his ascendancy to the fact that he expressed most truly the heart and soul of the German people in its bitterness of defeat, it is not unreasonable to suppose that his horror and hatred of Bolshevism was also an expression of the German dread of Russia. From a viewpoint of cold logic, from an unbiased comparison of German and Russian strength, Hitler must have thought, after the apparent weakness shown by the Red Army in Finland, that it would not be hard for him to seize the Ukraine and the Caucasus and drive the Russians back towards the East. A factor little noticed by contemporary writers may have influenced his decision. He knew that in the West, in Denmark and Norway, in Belgium and Holland, in France and in England itself, his Fifth Columns were firmly entrenched, whereas in Russia they and his Information Service had been destroyed by the Purge.

What followed was Hitler's justification. Denmark fell without a blow, and the Norwegian "Quislings" made easy the Nazi victory over Britain's bewildered efforts to rescue a lost cause. Then Hitler turned on Belgium. Emboldened by easy victory, reassured by Fifth Column support, Hitler swung his blitzkrieg into Holland and Belgium and France. It is not my part in this book to apportion the pros and cons, to say whether France was defeated by brilliant German strategy or by its inner corruption, that is, by the Fifth Column tactics which had overwhelmed Belgium and in combination with the dive-bomber destruction of Rotterdam paralyzed Dutch resistance. It may be true that the maneuver by which the Franco-British armies were drawn northward into Belgium while the German panzer spearhead cut swiftly at Sedan, and through Sedan across Northern France to Abbeville on the coast, was the cause of France's defeat. But the "Fifth Column" in France was also the reason why France could not rally from the blow.

The Nazi victory in France put a new problem before Stalin. This success, whose suddenness and completeness had been unsuspected by the Germans themselves, seemed to show that Germany had won the war, that England would sue for peace and that within a few weeks or months Hitler could turn around and demand from Russia the possession of the Ukraine and the Caucasus, which would ensure German predominance. Stalin was not blind to the danger, but it is curious to reflect that he, who had shared with Lenin hatred of British intervention in the Russian Civil War, who had felt the ignominy of Munich, nevertheless is reported to have said in June, 1940: "The Nazis have not beaten England. The English under Churchill have changed and are determined to resist. Unless Hitler can cross the Channel, his war in the West is not won, and when he understands that he will be forced to reverse his direction and to strike at us."

Unfortunately, I have only second or third-hand authority for this statement, although I believe that Stalin made it and that it did correspond to the facts of the situation. In any case Stalin hardened his heart and sat there watching and waiting to see what Hitler would do, whether he'd risk the Channel, or whether, like Napoleon in a similar impasse, he would turn around and go East.

Stalin perhaps foresaw that the Germans would try to blast England from the air, in the summer of 1940. He may have thought they would succeed, he may have thought they would fail; but without regard for that he enacted a decree which was equivalent to the wholesale mobilization of Russia's industrial and agricultural manpower. This decree, in July, 1940, fixed to their jobs all Russian industrial and agrarian workers, high or low, from office-boys to bosses, from milkers of cows to directors of collective farms. None of them could leave or change their jobs without permission. In effect, this was a mobilization of the civil manpower and woman-power of the whole country. Its purpose might have been accomplished by a decree of mobilization, but Stalin was too shrewd for that. A mobilization decree would in the circumstances have been a challenge to Germany, and Stalin still wished to gain every day, every week, every month of time for his preparation. He said in effect to the Russian workers and peasants, "You are mobilized, which means that you have to redouble your efforts and work overtime against the Nazi danger. But I don't want to let the Nazis know that you are being mobilized, so you must choose whether you will accept this decree as something that drives you forward to new efforts and allows you to get extra pay for overtime and so forth, or whether I shall have to declare the mobilization which will put you on a level of army wages and give an evident hint to our enemies."

The Russian people accepted, on both counts, but many foreign observers misunderstood the purport and effect of the decree. Instead of seeing that it was meant to avoid precipitate action by Germany and to give the Russian masses better wages and living conditions than they would have had under a total mobilization, these observers thought that this was another and heavier straw upon the back of the Russian camel. They considered it a proof that Stalin was afraid both of Germany and of his own people, whereas all that he wanted was to stimulate Russian production of food and war material. Russian factories and collective farms worked furiously in the fall and winter of 1940-41, aware that the breathing-space which Stalin's agreement with Hitler had won for them in 1939 was nearly at an end. At this critical moment the Soviet State gained strength from its arbitrary system of centralization. It was able to drive its workers and peasants to the limit of their effort because the idea of greater reward for greater service had been adopted, because they had the incentive of personal profit in addition to the no less powerful incentive of patriotic service. By this time they all knew, the whole Soviet Union knew, that Germany was their enemy and that a clash with Germany could not long be averted. The workers were paid for overtime, the peasants won rich returns from their plentiful crops, but all of them now knew that they were living on borrowed time, that today or next week or next month the Nazis would attack them.

In the winter of 1940-41 there was another period of anxiety. The Nazi air attack upon England was being checked, yet Hitler had full mastery over Western Europe save Britain. Would he turn against Russia now? To Stalin that seemed unlikely, because of Russia's oldest and best of allies, General Winter. Sure enough, the Nazis swung southwards in the spring into Yugoslavia and Greece, with an evident threat against Turkey. "Another scrap of borrowed time," said the Russians. "Another month or two to strengthen our preparations and increase our war production."

This was the turning-point in Russo-German relations, when Stalin could feel at last that the time he had gained was paying dividends. Now at long last Russia began, cautiously, to express its dissatisfaction about Germany's advance to the Black Sea by the absorption of Rumania and Bulgaria. Earlier the U. S. S. R. had taken advantage of German pressure upon Rumania to occupy Bessarabia, as formerly it had taken advantage of the Nazi invasion

of Poland to occupy Poland's eastern provinces. Now, in the spring
of 1941, when Yugoslavia suddenly decided to defy Germany and
fight instead of yielding, the U. S. S. R. made the strong anti-
German gesture of recognizing the new Yugoslav Government and
supporting, morally at least, the Yugoslavian action. This could
only mean that the Kremlin was watching with care the international situation, that it was coming to know that Hitler had not yet
won, that England was unconquered, and that behind England, distant but potentially unlimited in its strength, was the United States.

If one accepts the thesis that Stalin had long ago decided that
Nazi Germany was his enemy, that he was willing to accept all
manner of disrepute to maintain peace with Germany while he built
up his strength, that in the autumn of 1940 he perceived that Germany could no longer win a quick and easy war in the West and
must therefore turn against Russia—a turn which he could no longer
avert—his policy in 1941 can be understood without difficulty. He
saw that he was the next object of German attack, and from that it
followed logically that Britain, and behind Britain America, were
henceforth his potential allies, no matter what might have happened
before in the days of Munich and Chamberlain. Clear-sighted as
he was, Stalin knew that Yugoslavia and Greece could offer small
resistance to the Germans; yet nevertheless he ventured to offer
Germany virtual defiance in Yugoslavia's behalf, and almost simultaneously began moving Soviet troops westward from Siberia.

By a fortunate coincidence for the U. S. S. R., the Japanese
Foreign Minister, Matsuoka, came to Moscow about this time,
ostensibly on a trip to Western Europe, to Berlin and Rome, to
solidify the tripartite alliance of Germany, Japan and Italy, which
had initially been called the Anti-Comintern Pact. Despite that
ugly—in Soviet eyes—nomenclature, Matsuoka paused in Moscow
to suggest a pact of friendship between Japan and the U. S. S. R.
For the past five or six years the Russians, aware of the German
danger, had shown a willingness to settle their frontier and other
disputes with Japan, by the signature of some such pact. The
Japanese had always replied with a demand, which the Russians
declined to accept, that each and all of the causes of dispute should
be settled before any general agreement could be reached. The
Russians took a different view, that first of all, as a proof of mutual
good-will, a pact of mutual friendship, a pact of non-aggression,

should be signed between the U. S. S. R. and Japan, which would, the Russians said, facilitate the later settlement of all these difficult questions. Both sides stuck to their guns, and the answer was a deadlock, until Matsuoka made his journey to Moscow, Berlin and Rome in the spring of 1941, ostensibly to consult Japan's German and Italian friends, but really to open fresh negotiations with the U. S. S. R.

In April, 1941, Matsuoka returned from Rome and Berlin and paused again in Moscow, where somewhat unexpectedly he accepted the Soviet viewpoint, that the U. S. S. R. and Japan should sign a pact of friendship and non-aggression and leave settlement of disputed issues to a later date. Considered dispassionately as a move in the diplomatic chess game, this was a victory for the U. S. S. R., which had carried its point of putting the signature of the pact before the settlement of details. On a wider international scale both sides could consider the pact a victory and advantage. For the Russians it diminished the danger of a Japanese move against their eastern borders, a matter of vital importance at the time when they believed a Nazi attack on their western borders was only a matter of weeks. For Japan the pact gave a similar assurance of Russian passivity at a time when Japan was contemplating a program of expansion elsewhere. There was no real friendship on either side, and to many foreign observers the treaty seemed no more than a scrap of paper to be torn up at any moment. Actually it was a salient instance of two countries following a policy dictated by their interests, and the pact was not only observed scrupulously for more than three years, but led to the satisfactory settlement of such vexed questions as the frontiers between Manchukuo-Korea and of the border between Inner and Outer Mongolia, which had never been determined before, as well as the fishing rights in Soviet waters, which had been a perennial cause of friction.

Berlin gave the pact its official blessing, and Goebbels used it as a propaganda reminder to the world that four great powers were now in full and irresistible alignment; but Moscow showed its satisfaction in so unusual and studied a manner as to baffle foreign observers. Stalin came personally with Premier Molotov and War Commissar Voroshilov to see Matsuoka off at the station and bade him farewell with the utmost warmth, in the presence of a large delegation from the German Embassy, with whose members he also chatted cordially. This incident may be said to have marked the lowest point of Soviet unpopularity in the United States and Britain, where the impression was solidly created—to last long and be hardly dispelled—that the U. S. S. R. had indeed thrown in its lot with the forces of aggression. American opinion in particular was outraged by the attitude of the Communist Party of America, which opposed every step towards aid for Britain, or even America's own preparedness for war, as noisily as two years before it had howled against the Nazi danger. The American Communists were doubtless obeying Moscow's directives, and surely must have shared Moscow's knowledge of Hitler's real intentions; but all they accomplished was to make Moscow's cause more loathsome and distasteful in the mouths of decent men.

There was, however, one dissenting voice in the chorus of Anglo-American abuse. The British Ambassador in Moscow, Sir Stafford Cripps, in a rare flash of prescience told the American and British newspaper correspondents there at the end of February that he was certain Hitler would attack the U. S. S. R. before the end of June. He based his opinion on three grounds. First, that Hitler was now aware that England could not be defeated by a lightning war, nor forced to accept an "equitable" peace, that the struggle would be long and arduous, and whether the United States participated or not as an active combatant, the weight and effect of America's material aid to Britain would grow greater and more dangerous with every week that passed. Hitler therefore could no longer be satisfied by an agreement with Russia which provided him with oil, grain, manganese and cotton upon purely trading terms, but must assure for himself the outright possession of the sources of these supplies. Second, that Hitler no longer dared to wait, because he knew that Soviet industry and mechanized agriculture was now advancing by leaps and bounds instead of at a tortoise crawl. Finally, said Sir Stafford, Hitler underestimated the strength of the Red Army as a result of its initial fiasco in Finland and the patriotism, preparedness and will to fight of the Soviet peoples. The Ambassador's hearers were startled and incredulous, but he maintained his position with the logic and vigor which had made him an outstanding figure in the British law courts, and his foresight was justified almost to a week.

On June 22, 1941, the Nazi armies invaded Soviet territory, without ultimatum, warning or any intimation of grievance. It has been often stated that Germany was dissatisfied by the time-lags and poor quality of Russian raw material deliveries. This is incorrect, although it is true that the U. S. S. R. had indirectly expressed its disapproval of Nazi absorption of Rumania and Bulgaria, and had made the significant gesture at the end of March of recognizing the new Yugoslav Government which dared to offer resistance to Hitler. Nevertheless, it is a fact that only two days before Hitler invaded Russia the German Ambassador, Graf von der Schulenburg, attended a ceremonial dinner with Molotov, the Soviet Premier and Foreign Commissar. The atmosphere at this party was friendly; cordial toasts were exchanged, and none of those present remarked any sign of friction or ill-will.

Chapter 24

THE TITANIC STRUGGLE

To MOST OF the world, the Nazi invasion of Russia was unexpected, and foreign opinion was equally at sea about Soviet capacity for resistance. With almost complete unanimity, foreign "experts" announced that Russia would be beaten in three weeks, if indeed it ever tried seriously to fight. This was especially true of the military experts, who had failed to realize the true lessons of the Finnish campaign, or that the execution of disloyal generals four years earlier did not necessarily destroy the power and spirit of the Red Army. Many people in the United States, and perhaps in Britain also, were surprised by the speech of Winston Churchill on the evening after the attack, when he declared that the British Government henceforth would regard the U. S. S. R. as an ally against Hitler, and expressed his confidence in Russia's strength and courage. An "off the record" story illustrates Churchill's attitude. One of his friends said, "Winston, how can you support the Bolsheviks, you who led British intervention against Lenin and once admitted that you had spent a hundred million British pounds to aid the 'White' armies of Kolchak and Denikin?"

The Premier replied curtly, "If seven devils rose from hell to fight against that man Hitler, I'd shake them all by the hand and give each a bottle of brandy and a box of my best cigars."

Churchill went further. In a passage of his speech which has never been fully explained (for to my mind the Hess story, later divulged, does not fully cover this point), he said that His Majesty's Government had foreknowledge of the Nazi invasion of Russia and had warned Moscow about it. At all events, Churchill's stand and that of Britain was clear in the new conflict, and his words had no small effect in the United States. A comic note was added by the American Communist Party, which on June 21st had been picketing the White House with banners, "America, stay out" and "Down with Roosevelt's attempts to drag us into the War." Two days later it reversed itself and called on its faithful to "Join the battle for world liberation from the Nazi-Fascist Tyrants."

It is a moot point to what extent the U. S. S. R. and the Red Army were surprised by Hitler's sudden attack. Powerful Red forces had undoubtedly been concentrated in the western regions of the U. S. S. R., along a vast arc from the Black Sea to Lake Ladoga, north of Leningrad, and for some months there had been a steady westward flow of troops and military supplies from Siberia into European Russia. The Soviet's initial plan of campaign, moreover, seemed to indicate a high state of awareness; perhaps unwisely, as the events showed, the Red High Command elected to meet the German shock in its outer marches, where much precious material was lost and too many lives were sacrificed. German superiority in transportation, which had always been the weakest link in the Russian chain of defense, produced the paradoxical situation that although the Russians were superior in numbers along the whole front, the enemy's rapid concentrations constantly enabled them to outnumber the Russians at given points of attack. The invaders held the advantage of initiative and broke through the defense by greater weight of manpower and material. Their advance was rapid, especially across the open plains of the Southern Ukraine, but never from the outset was there any rout or debacle of the Russians, such as had occurred in Poland or France.

Most remarkable of all, there was no panic flight of the civilian population to block the roads and demoralize the defending forces. Now when the shock came, the collective farm system and the preparations made long beforehand in urban centers proved their value. Collective and communal farms, especially in the western provinces of the U. S. S. R., had been trained to meet invasion. Their method of division of labor by shifts or "brigades," as they were called—one brigade to look after children, another to prepare food, another to care for poultry and pigs, another for cattle and horses, others for work in the fields—helped them enormously.

Automatically the brigade units undertook new functions, like actors well rehearsed. One brigade conducted the evacuation of children and older people, another of animals, machinery and supplies. A third destroyed everything which could not be removed, according to the "scorched earth" program adopted earlier by China. Others, young men and women trained to the use of arms, sought shelter in woods and marshes where depots of ammunition had been stored for guerrilla warfare. All of them knew what to do, and did it according to plan.

The scheme of evacuation had been carefully prepared, not only of people, animals and foodstuffs from the countryside, but of machines, even whole factories, from the towns and cities. At Christmas, 1941, the Germans boasted that they had occupied the territory in which one-half of the heavy industry of the U. S. S. R. was situated. On paper their claims were not unjustified, although fully seventy-five percent of Russia's newest war factories were located east of Moscow, in the Urals and in Siberia beyond. But Goebbels omitted to state how much machinery and tools were moved eastwards from the factories of the Donets Basin, the Ukraine, White Russia and Leningrad by the workers who had handled them, and how much more which could not be moved was deliberately demolished, like the great Dnieper dam and power stations, by the men and women who had built them.

Foreign observers in Moscow have described with amazement the interminable convoys of trucks and freight-cars moving eastwards with evacuated machinery and supplies. I was told by one of the attachés of the British Embassy how he saw young men and women workers clustered like swarming bees along a train of flat-cars carrying machinery from the Donets through the October snow to Sverdlovsk in the Urals. In default of tarpaulins and passenger cars in which to ride, they protected the machines from damp with their bodies, as they made their own way eastwards. Not easily could the Nazis cope with such devotion. That indeed was the factor which astounded even the harshest critics of the U. S. S. R., the self-sacrificing patriotism of the Russian people, and the smoothness, order and extent of its planned evacuation. There was confusion in the ranks of the so-called "experts" who had prophesied Russia's collapse, had even declared that a Mobilization Order could not be carried out lest the peasant masses should use their arms against their rulers who had forced collectivization upon them. How different was the reality, how strong Russia's will to resist, how increasingly deadly to the invaders the action of guerrillas, boys and girls of the Comyouth organization, and their non-Party fellows behind the German lines!

Yet Russian losses were heavy and German gains were great in the first summer campaign, which, by a coincidence that might have seemed ominous to anyone with Hitler's regard for dates and anniversaries, began in the same week as Napoleon's ill-starred adventure. Odessa was conquered and Kiev and most of the Ukraine. White Russia was overrun, and the Baltic States. Leningrad was beleaguered, and by mid-autumn the Nazis were striking so hard at Moscow that the Soviet Foreign Office and most of the Commissariats, as well as foreign embassies and legations, were removed to Kuibyshev (formerly Samara) on the Volga. Stalin, who for twenty years had held no important office in his country's government, became Premier and, with the title of Marshal, Commander-in-Chief of the Red Armies. He and his closest associates, Molotov, Voroshilov, Kaganovich, Beria and Mikoyan (Commissar of Trade), remained in Moscow; but Stalin soon made his military headquarters, with Voroshilov, in an armored train. For a moment it seemed that Leningrad was doomed, and Moscow's fate was uncertain. Then the Russians rallied and broke the double German threat against the capital from north and south, from Klin to Orel. In the south the Germans were checked, and Klin was retaken by the Red Army, which drove forward on a wide front. Moscow was saved, and had not suffered much from German air attacks. A bitter winter came to Russia's aid, and the German tide was rolled back, although the Russian winter offensive did not succeed in taking any important objectives save the city of Rostov, gateway to the Caucasus, which the Red Army was forced to relinquish later.

In the late autumn of 1941 Hitler had boasted that the Soviet armies were annihilated, and that nothing was left for the Germans but a mopping-up campaign to complete their victory. Nevertheless, Leningrad still held out, sorely pressed but indomitable; Moscow was disengaged; and Rostov had been recovered. The Red armies had won a breathing-space, and their morale was still high, their matériel renewed from the factories of the Volga, the Urals and Siberia, when Hitler launched his second great offensive in the spring of 1942. The Crimea fell after an epic defense of Sevastopol, Rostov was retaken, and the Nazi forces plunged deep into the North Caucasus, through the Don grain land to Maikop's oil fields, with Baku on the Caspian, center of Russian oil production, as their goal. In the North, Leningrad was almost encircled by a ring of steel, but Moscow seemed outside of the Nazi line of attack, which developed principally towards Stalingrad, on the Lower Volga, with the obvious intention of cutting the Volga artery along which supplies of oil, grain, meat, cotton, copper and manganese now flowed from the Caucasus to the North and East. Once firmly established upon the Volga, with its supply lines cut, the enemy could swing north against Moscow and south to Baku at his leisure.

The battle for Stalingrad was the culminating and decisive struggle of the Russo-German War, comparable to Gettysburg or, in more recent times, to the Battle of Verdun in the first World War. It is interesting to note what General Ludendorff, Germany's greatest commander in World War I, said about the Battle of Verdun, where he, as commander of the Eastern (Russian) Front, took no part in inception or execution of the long-drawn struggle. Ludendorff wrote that "When a battle of attack becomes a battle of attrition, that is when the objectives aimed at by the initial attack can no longer be rapidly won, and the combat develops into a see-saw struggle, the attack should be abandoned." He believed that German insistence upon the conquest of Verdun, which Germany never achieved, was a prime factor in Germany's loss of the war. The same might be said about Stalingrad, where the profits of victory were obvious, but where a similar insistence robbed the Germans of other objectives more easily to be gained, as for instance Baku and its oil, and finally involved them in a great disaster.

Like Verdun, Stalingrad became a symbol of victory or defeat. Its former name, Tsaritsin, had been changed to commemorate its defense against the "Whites" in the fall of 1918 by Stalin himself. By 1942 it had become a great industrial city, with huge war factories and one of the largest tractor-tank plants in the U. S. S. R. It was the key to the Volga, Stalin's city, Russia's Verdun. Here the Red Army exhibited the ultimate desperation of resistance. It simply refused to yield, to acknowledge it was beaten, like its ancestors in the dreadful battle of the Moskva immortalized by Tolstoy in "War and Peace." Now as then, the Russians would not accept defeat. Under a terrific concentration of air and land bombardment, the Red Guards died where they stood and others took their place with equal courage and self-sacrifice. The Germans held the city; their victory was won, but the Russians wouldn't admit it. They fought on in holes and cellars, devoted and indomitable, pinning the Nazis to a murderous slugging-match while autumn froze into winter and German transport was clogged as new Russian forces gathered to relieve the shattered city.

What prompted German insistence upon the fight for Stalingrad even when the Soviet counter-attack was already outlined clearly, has never been fully known. It has been suggested that Japan had promised to attack Soviet Siberia if and when the Battle of Stalingrad should be won by the Nazi arms. Another theory is that Hitler, too conscious of symbolic values, overruled his Generals and forced them to go on fighting when prudence dictated retreat. This view may be correct, because Hitler boldly declared, "My army is in Stalingrad and will never leave it." His words for once were true. As the Russian counter-attack developed, the German forces, perhaps a quarter of a million strong, were encircled and their westward retreat cut off. For the first time since Jena, more than a hundred and thirty years before, a German Field-Marshal, von Paulus, surrendered on the battlefield, with what was left of his army, gaunt, half-frozen and starving, a symbolic battle indeed, a turning-point of war.

This titanic and perhaps decisive struggle had violent political repercussions. With their backs to the wall, the Russians appealed loudly to the rest of Hitler's enemies, in whose ranks the United States was now enrolled, for a great action to divert some of Germany's strength. Anglo-American leaders had indeed promised such a diversion, a "Second Front," as it was called, as early as June, 1942; but their efforts were still confined to fighting in North Africa, where only a small number of German divisions were engaged, and to air attacks upon Germany itself, increasing steadily in severity but hardly to be described as a Second Front. True, the American and British forces in the Pacific undertook a somewhat hazardous diversion at Guadalcanal in the Solomon Islands, and in New Guinea, which may have aided the U. S. S. R. indirectly by preventing Japan at a most critical moment from opening *its* second front against the Soviet provinces of Siberia. This, however, is only conjecture, and the mass of the Russian people, if not its leaders, undoubtedly felt that it was bearing most of the brunt of the war.

The visit of Winston Churchill to Moscow in the late summer of 1942 did not fully assuage Russian anxiety that they were being left to fight alone. The British Premier and Marshal Stalin had difficulty in reconciling the amount of Anglo-American material aid to Russia—tanks, planes, guns, explosives and other military supplies—loaded upon convoys sent to the Russian ports of Murmansk and Archangel, with the amounts which the Russians actually received. The quantity of such supplies received in Russia in the critical summer of 1942, when the U-boat danger was at its greatest in the North Atlantic and Anglo-American flotillas were further subjected to the most savage of air attacks from bases in North Finland during the twenty-four hours of daylight in the northern latitudes, was often less than half of what had been loaded and sent. In addition, Stalin complained that Anglo-American attempts at diversion of German strength were inadequate, and mentioned specifically that on one occasion modern American fighter planes destined for Russia had been unloaded in British waters and sent to another destination. Churchill did his best to reassure the Soviet Generalissimo. He explained the difficulties of maritime transport in waters infested by U-boats, and of a mass attack upon the northern shores of Germany's "Fortress Europa" without overwhelming superiority in the air and on the sea. He admitted that the American planes consigned to Russia had been transferred to another theatre of operations, and may have told Stalin—as was later indicated by an exchange of messages between the two Premiers—that the Anglo-Americans were preparing an invasion of Morocco and Algeria.

It was unquestionably an awkward moment in relations between the U. S. S. R. and the two great powers of the West, but it had no dire effects and the misunderstanding, if any, was mitigated by the victory of Stalingrad, by the Anglo-American conquest of North Africa, and by the great improvement in shipment of supplies to Russia, not only across the Atlantic where the U-boats were progressively overcome, but through Persia by a successful development of road and rail transport from the Persian Gulf to the Caspian Sea. From the autumn of 1942 onwards, at least four-fifths of foreign supplies for Russia reached their destination intact.

Russia's winter offensive in 1942 partially raised the siege of

Leningrad, recovered certain strong points in the German north-western defense system, like Veliki Luki, recaptured the great Ukrainian city of Kharkov, and for a moment seemed to threaten the whole German line in the Southern Ukraine. The Germans counter-attacked, and Kharkov again was lost; but it was already evident that the opposing forces were growing more equal. The Nazis still had greater mobility and were able to concentrate their forces more rapidly, but they had lost the advantage of initiative, while the number and quality of Russian planes, tanks and artillery had been enhanced by their own increase in production and by supplies from the United States and Britain.

Once more, in the summer of 1943, the Germans attempted an offensive; but it never looked dangerous and was speedily checked. This time the Russian riposte was immediate and effective. All along the front Soviet troops swept forward, taking one strong point after another. They recaptured Kharkov and pressed on across the Donets Basin to the River Dnieper, where the Germans had declared they would make a definite stand. For a time, in September, it seemed that the German boasts were justified and that the Russians had shot their bolt. Nazi propaganda worked overtime through its channels in Sweden, Switzerland and Spain to convince American and British opinion that the Russians could go no farther, or that they did not wish to press home their attacks and might even be on the verge of concluding a separate peace. Quite accidentally, color was lent to these rumors by a renewal in the Soviet press of agitation for the "Second Front." Goebbels redoubled his efforts, and the cables from Stockholm and Berne hummed with reports "from reliable sources" that the U. S. S. R. would make peace with Germany unless there was an immediate Anglo-American invasion of North-western Europe.

Meanwhile the Anglo-American armies had conquered Sicily and invaded the Italian mainland, simultaneously subjecting the industrial cities of Germany to a day-and-night bombardment whose violence and volume far surpassed the air blitz against England in the winter of 1940-41. The destruction of Hamburg in particular and of metallurgic centers in the Ruhr Valley was terrific, and the Germans were forced to weaken their Russian front by the withdrawal of aircraft and anti-aircraft artillery to meet the growing menace from the sky. The walls of Fortress Europa still were strong, but the fortress lacked a roof. At this time, too, the Russians began to note that although the number of German divisions on their front—some two hundred and ten, they estimated, two-thirds of the whole German Army—had not been lowered by Allied attacks in the West, the numerical strength of these divisions was diminishing. In other words, the same phenomenon was apparent as had occurred in the final phase of World War I. German divisional strength, originally 14,000 to 15,000 men, had dropped to 9,000 or 10,000, although for convenience of manipulation and maneuver the divisional staff and framework remained intact. This was most important, because the Russians had been strenuously pleading for Allied action to withdraw at least fifty divisions, out of 210, from Germany's Eastern armies. A reduction in German divisional strength of one-third would have an even greater effect as far as the total forces on the Eastern Front were concerned.

There was, too, a startling difference in the nature of Russian new demands for a Second Front in the West. During the Battle of Stalingrad it was almost a cry of despair, "Aid us or we perish," but now the Russians were saying, "If you others will strike a blow, if you will dare to take a chance, however risky it seems, we may win the war right quick, and thus save countless lives." No longer a diversion, but a final drive to victory, was the burden of Russia's song. And as if to confound the enemy mischief-makers who were staking everything upon their sole remaining card, the hope of causing bad blood between their three major opponents, the United States, Britain and Russia, the Red Army suddenly leapt the Dnieper barrier and streamed westwards across the flatlands of the Southern Ukraine. They paid no heed to Nazi suggestions from Sweden and Switzerland that the Anglo-Americans deliberately stood aloof to watch Russ and Teuton bleed each other to death. Curiously enough, the counterpart of such reports, in the form that the U. S. S. R. might still make a separate peace when its territory was cleared of invaders, or alternatively, would rush on to Bolshevize all of Europe, found some credence in the United States. As did another story, that the U. S. S. R. for its part would never make war with Japan but watch with folded hands while Japan and the United States bled each other to death.

The Red Army had its answer to Nazi propagandists. It had seen its Russian dead in the reconquered areas, and seen, too, how they had died. Great trenches and ravines filled with bodies of men and women whose mouths were choked with earth to show they were buried alive. Mass graves where bodies of wounded soldiers were heaped pell-mell, charred beyond recognition, to show they were burned to death; and cruelest of all, the crowded corpses of children, slain by machine-gun bullets. That the Red Army saw as it advanced, and heard the shocking tales of maddened and mutilated survivors. Would they make peace with the Nazis who had done such things to their folk? Not Stalin nor any dictator, not one who rose from the dead, could have held the Russians back, after what they had seen, or check their thirst for vengeance, their resolve to pay blood with blood. If any doubt could subsist about Russia's fury to avenge its dead, the publicity given to Nazi atrocities from one end of the Soviet Union to the other must inevitably have dispelled it. Each detail of horror was piled on horror's head through the length and breadth of the U. S. S. R. by press and radio, by photographs and word of mouth. For more than six weeks after the offensive was resumed in mid-September there was no mention in any Soviet communiqué of prisoners having been taken. "So many Germans killed," ran the reports, so many Nazis slaughtered, but of prisoners never a word. No good augury this, for the separate-peace rumors spread to alarm the United States and whet its suspicions of Russia and Russian motives.

As the Anglo-American forces forged doggedly northwards through the Italian mountains and, whenever weather permitted, rained bombs on the German cities, Nazi propaganda grew more frantic in its attempts to capitalize every possible source of conflict in the United Nations camp. The Russians paid little attention to this subversive nonsense, but it found some echo in the United States, where many people were still distrustful of Soviet intentions and bewildered by Soviet policy. They did not understand, for instance, that the U. S. S. R. had bitter memories of Munich and was determined to be treated henceforth and forever as a great power, on full terms of equality with the United States and Britain. The Russians made little secret of their resentment that the two Western powers took upon themselves the task of settling affairs in North Africa, Sicily and North Italy without consulting Russia, and that the British Foreign Office and American State Department went so far as to prevent the visit of a Soviet representative to North

Africa, by an ancient process known as "passing the buck." The Russians indicated plainly that they were not pleased by these maneuvers and meant their voice to be heard in the present and future settlement of Africa and Italy, of the Balkans and later of France and all the rest of Europe. Once more "reliable sources" in Berne and Stockholm worked overtime to foment discord and foster misunderstanding, but in the second half of October there was held a meeting of the Foreign Ministers of the United States, Great Britain and the U. S. S. R. Significantly, the conference met in Moscow, and in addition to their daily meetings with Molotov, Soviet Commissar of Foreign Affairs, the American Secretary of State, Mr. Cordell Hull, and the British Foreign Minister, Sir Anthony Eden, had long private conversations with Stalin, who followed proceedings most attentively throughout. The conference concluded with a joint statement that the three powers concerned would fight the war to a finish together and would do their best to co-operate in framing the peace and in post-war reconstruction. This must have sounded a death knell to Nazi hopes of disunion.

_____ *Chapter 25* _____

A PROMISE FOR THE FUTURE

ON THE DAY before the conference opened, *Izvestia*, the official mouthpiece of the Soviet Government, published an illuminating editorial whose optimistic tone contrasted with the guarded and hope-for-the-best attitude of American and British sentiment. The writer significantly based his expectations that the conference would be a success on the fact that the U. S. S. R. had *now* been admitted on equal terms to Anglo-American politico-military commissions in North Africa and Italy, and that Stalin as well as President Roosevelt and Premier Churchill had signed the joint declaration approving Italy's entry into the war on the side of the United Nations. In short, Russia's principal demand, for full parity with the U. S. A. and Great Britain, had already been granted.

Unquestionably this was a diplomatic victory for the U. S. S. R., but in return for it the Russians pledged themselves to a degree of collaboration, present and future, military and political, which had hitherto been lacking. The thread of Russian admission to full equality runs through the whole text of the communiqué about the conference, issued simultaneously in Moscow, Washington and London.[1] The subsequent meeting of President Roosevelt, Premier Churchill and Marshal Stalin confirmed and reiterated the principles of equality and co-operation established at Moscow, and set, one might almost say, a seal upon the progress and evolution of the U. S. S. R. from 1917 to 1943. A long and arduous stage from the

[1] See appendix.

275

status of outlaw nation—"Red enemies of God and man"—to Russia's
new position as one of the three great powers in a world whose
purpose henceforth would be unity and friendship instead of rivalry
and war.

In a bare quarter-century the U. S. S. R. has accomplished ages
of growth. The most ignorant and backward of all white nations
has moved into the forefront of social, economic and political consciousness. Its obsolete agricultural system has been modernized and
mechanized; its small and artificial industry has become gigantic
and self-supporting; its illiterate masses have been educated and
disciplined to appreciate and enjoy the benefits of collective effort.
Americans, and the Western world in general, have misunderstood
or ignored the true course of Soviet history. We have failed to
realize that the Bolshevik Revolution, that Bolshevism itself, was not
fixed but fluid, not a state but a process. We saw the initial acts of
the Soviet Government, its peace with Germany which released
a million German troops to break the Western Front in March,
1918, and almost lose us the War, and its attacks upon the three
fundamental principles that underlie our civilization, Home and the
Family, Religion and the Church, Money and the Rights of Property. Inevitably and naturally we opposed the Bolsheviks on these
counts, and were further outraged by their impudent pretension to
make us follow their line. Without questioning Bolshevik sincerity,
it was absurd and pretentious for them to think that the Western
world, which had won self-government and freedom by a thousand
years of struggle, should accept the new-fangled dogmas of a handful of fanatics whose nation was less than a hundred years from
semi-slavery and had never known self-government in any form.
Less than a hundred years ago Russian peasants—four-fifths of the
population—were sold like animals on the land. They were little
better than slaves, and right up until the Bolshevik Revolution they,
and for that matter their masters, had had no voice in the government of their country.

When once the Bolshevik Revolution broke the ancient ice dam,
when it shattered the iron band around the Russian tree, it was
only natural that the Bolsheviks who had broken the dam and the
band should wish to share their victory and spread their revolutionary doctrine across the whole world. Great as Lenin was, he confused the restrictions upon Russian growth and the political slavery

of the Russian masses with the apparent subservience of Western democratic nations to a land-owning and financial oligarchy. He did not realize that the Western peoples had curbed the powers of kings and oligarchs, landed or financial barons, and that in the final instance the vote of the people, the "government of the people, by the people, for the people" was real and imperishable.

But we, too, fail to understand that Sovietism, Bolshevism—call it what you will—was impermanent and subject to change. Lenin had understood that the masses, however ignorant, must always somehow be right, that, obscurely, they knew what they wanted, and that if he lost touch with them his cause was doomed. Slowly and gradually Lenin and his followers came to see that the three great fundamentals—Home and the Family, Religion and the Church, Money and Property—were not the obscure creation of some capitalist Demon, but the development, through hundreds and thousands of years, of human habit and practice, of human hope and desire, of human aspiration, of human need. The history of the Soviet Union has been a steady swing away from the early ideas of extreme or "militant" Communism to more practical and reasonable methods, and inevitable compromise. Stalin was bitterly attacked by Trotsky and the "Old Bolsheviks" as a backslider from initial ideals. But he won and they lost because he *was* practical and dared to reconcile the present possible goal with the ultimate hoped-for goal.

To put it simply, the Bolsheviks swung way, way off to the "Left," and believed with fanatic enthusiasm that they could make a new "Left" Heaven upon Earth. Some of them, the Old Bolsheviks and Trotsky, continued to believe it, but Stalin realized that a compromise was necessary. He declined to allow the growing Russian tree to be bound anew by the iron band of Marxist dogma. He allowed a free development on Russian rather than dogmatic Marxist lines.

Whatever may be said, history *does* repeat itself, and the development of the Soviet Revolution follows that of the other greatest social upheaval of modern times, the French Revolution, with as close a parallel as that between the policy of Stalin in 1939, who made a deal with Hitler because he distrusted his potential allies (Britain and France) and wished to gain time, and Alexander I, who distrusted his allies Austria and Prussia and wished to gain time to prepare for Napoleon's attack. The French Revolution swung away

from the Church and religion and worshipped the Goddess of Reason in the Elysian Fields. The French Revolution killed a king, as
the Russians killed their Tsar, and called all men *"citoyen,"* as the
Russians called them *"tovarisch."* The French Revolution killed
kings and nobles and broke everything down to flat equality, and
went from there to the Empire of Napoleon.

In Russia, too, the wheel turned. The bottom became the top
and the top became the bottom. But the forces of merit and energy
released by the Revolution found their natural expression in authority and strength. Unlike the French, the Russians had, from 1920 to
1941, no foreign enemies to cement their unity and hasten their
process of evolution. They fought among themselves, and from
their conflict was established the power of Stalin, little less great—
or greater—than that of Napoleon, Emperor of the French.

It was a process of change, so imperceptible as to be scarcely
noticed by the rest of the world, but no less important and no less
changeful for that. The old distinctions of class had vanished, but
there came new distinctions of rank, a new ruling class whose
strength was measured by performance and success, to take the
place of the obsolete hereditary rulers. Slowly but surely the Bolsheviks abandoned their first wild attacks upon the Home, upon
the Church, and upon wages. They modified their marriage-divorce
laws, they ceased pressure against the Church, and they introduced
the principle of "greater reward for greater service." They put the
principle of nationalism, of national defense against the threatened
German invasion, above their former ideas of international brotherhood of workers throughout the world. They became nationalists
instead of internationalists.

The War has emphasized a hundredfold the move towards nationalism in Russia. It has done—this national war with Germany—for
Russia what war did for Revolutionary France in the later years of
the eighteenth century. It has established national unity and hastened
the change from a proletarian, international workers-of-the-world-
unite revolution to that of a national struggle against a foreign
enemy.

In France, as in Russia today, this process was accompanied by a
whole gamut of nationalist phenomena. The French and the Soviet
Revolution tore epaulettes off officers, tried to reduce military ranks
to a flat equality, called everyone *"citoyen"* or *"tovarisch."* They

swung the pendulum to the "Left," but the pendulum swung back. In Russia today, as in the France of Napoleon, the titles of General and Marshal, the right to wear epaulettes and decorations, have been introduced. In other words, there has been recognition of service and rank, as opposed to the impractical idea of universal equality.

This is only one phase of Soviet evolution. Henceforth Soviet ambassadors will wear a diplomatic uniform resplendent with gold lace. Soviet Marshals wear golden stars with diamond trimmings. There has been established a Soviet school of officers, named after Suvarov, the General of Catherine the Empress, and a Suvarov decoration, and another decoration named for Kutusov, the General of Tsar Alexander I against Napoleon. And a new Order of Victory, made of platinum and jewels, worth fifteen thousand dollars, to correspond to the Congressional Medal or the English Victoria Cross, as an emblem of valor. That shows how the pendulum swings. In addition there has been a definite rapprochement, a pact of friendship and recognition, between the Soviet atheist State and the Orthodox Church of Russia. When Stalin received in the Kremlin the Church leaders and allowed them to assemble the Holy Synod to elect a Patriarch of the Orthodox Church of Russia, that was a most significant act. It did not mean that the Bolshevik Kremlin admitted the authority of the Orthodox Church of Russia, but it *did* mean that Stalin recognized the value of the Orthodox Church of Russia as a foreign political force—in Bulgaria, Serbia, Rumania and Greece—and as a unifying factor in the U. S. S. R. itself.

The wheel turns, and what was zero can come again to the top. Russia today is a Great Power, and now demands equality with the other two Great Powers of the world, the United States of America and the British Commonwealth, after Germany and Japan are beaten. The Russians, I think, have abandoned their first fanatical impulse to impose their ideas and their methods upon the Western Powers. They have before them a tremendous and most difficult task of national reconstruction. Their richest areas, industrial and agricultural, have been devastated by the German invaders. Their task of reconstruction is terrific and requires our help.

There is the key to Soviet Russian policy in making the Peace and in the future world. Immediately, they will need foreign help for reconstruction. But above all they will need peace. They will know that the United States will be the strongest force in the world in production of steel and ships, tanks and airplanes, even of man-power. It will be to their interest to co-operate with the United States, because—if for no other reason—they and the United States want peace for development of their own resources.

The promise of the Moscow conference may fail, perhaps, of achievement. Difficulties may arise, and the friendship which it beckons between the U. S. S. R. and the U. S. A. may be spoilt. There is still a wide deep gap between the individualist system of the United States and the collectivist system of the U. S. S. R. Nevertheless, there are no causes of fundamental conflict between the two countries, and every word of the Moscow protocol should be carefully studied, from the resolute clarity of its earlier passages to the biblical solemnity of its final call for vengeance. Well might the American Secretaries of War and of the Navy describe it as a United Nations victory more notable than any battle.

In addition to the basic statement of the Moscow protocol, that the three great powers involved would fight the war together to a finish and stand together in framing Peace and post-war recon-struction, a statement which confounded the hopes of enemies and answered the doubts of friends, it specifically recognized the claims of China and by implication, as Chinese spokesmen promptly noted, threw light upon Russia's future attitude towards Japan. But above all—and here lies its prime historic significance—it involved the rec-ognition by the United States and Britain of Russia's passage from the larval state of revolutionary pariah, through an indeterminate cocoon period of half-friend, half-foe, to full acceptance as an ally and great power.

Appendix

The conference of Foreign Secretaries of the United States of America, Mr. Cordell Hull; of the United Kingdom, Mr. Anthony Eden; and of the Soviet Union, Mr. V. M. Molotov, took place at Moscow from the nineteenth to the thirtieth of October, 1943. There were twelve meetings. In addition to the Foreign Secretaries, the following took part in the conference:

For the United States of America: Mr. W. Averell Harriman, Ambassador of the United States; Maj. Gen. John R. Deane, United States Army; Mr. H. Hackworth, Mr. James C. Dunn and experts.

For the United Kingdom: Sir Archibald Clark Kerr, Ambassador; Mr. William Strang, Lieut. Gen. Sir Hastings Ismay and experts.

For the Soviet Union: Marshal K. E. Voroshilov, Marshal of the Soviet Union; Mr. A. Y. Vyshinski and Mr. M. Litvinov, Deputy People's Commissars for Foreign Affairs; Mr. V. A. Sergeyev, Deputy People's Commissar for Foreign Trade; Maj. Gen. A. A. Gryzlov of the General Staff, Mr. G. F. Saksin, senior official for People's Commissariat for Foreign Affairs, and experts.

The agenda included all questions submitted for discussion by the three Governments. Some of the questions called for final decisions, and these were taken. On other questions, after discussion, decisions of principle were taken. These questions were referred for detailed consideration to commissions specially set up for the purpose, or reserved for treatment through diplomatic channels. Other questions again were disposed of by an exchange of views. The Governments of the United States, the United Kingdom and the Soviet Union have been in close co-operation in all matters concerning the common war effort, but this is the first time that the Foreign Secretaries of the three Governments have been able to meet together in conference.

In the first place there were frank and exhaustive discussions of the measures to be taken to shorten the war against Germany and her satellites in Europe. Advantage was taken of the presence of military advisers representing the respective Chiefs of Staff in order to discuss definite military operations with regard to which decisions had been taken and which are already being prepared in order to create a basis for the closest military co-operation in the future between the three countries.

Second only to the importance of hastening the end of the war was the recognition by the three Governments that it was essential in their own national interests and in the interests of all peace-loving nations to continue the present close collaboration and co-operation in the conduct of the war into the period following the end of hostilities, and that only in this way could peace be maintained and the political, economic and social welfare of their peoples fully promoted.

This conviction is expressed in a declaration in which the Chinese Government joined during the conference and which was signed by the three Foreign Secretaries and the Chinese Ambassador at Moscow on behalf of their Governments. This declaration published today provides for even closer collaboration in the prosecution of the war and in all matters pertaining to the surrender and disarmament of the enemies with which the four countries are, respectively, at war. It set forth the principles upon which the four Governments agree that a broad system of international co-operation and security should be based. Provision is made for the inclusion of all other peace-loving nations, great and small, in this system.

The conference agreed to set up machinery for ensuring the closest co-operation between the three Governments in the examination of European questions arising as the war develops. For this purpose the conference decided to establish in London a European advisory commission to study these questions and to make joint recommendations to the three Governments.

Provision was made for continuing, when necessary, the tripartite consultations of representatives of the three Governments in the respective capitals through the existing diplomatic channels.

The conference also agreed to establish an advisory council for matters relating to Italy, to be composed in the first instance of representatives of their three Governments and of the French Committee of National Liberation. Provision is made for addition to this council of representatives of Greece and Yugoslavia in view of their special interests arising out of aggressions of Fascist Italy upon their territory during the present war. This council will deal with day-to-day questions other than military preparations and will make recommendations designed to co-ordinate Allied policy with regard to Italy.

The three Foreign Secretaries considered it appropriate to re-affirm, by a declaration published today, the attitude of the Allied Governments in favor of the restoration of democracy in Italy.

The three Foreign Secretaries declared it to be the purpose of their Governments to restore the independence of Austria. At the same time they reminded Austria that in the final settlement account will be taken of efforts that Austria may make toward its own liberation. The declaration on Austria is published today.

The Foreign Secretaries issued at the conference a declaration by President Roosevelt, Prime Minister Churchill and Premier Stalin containing a solemn warning that at the time of granting any armistice to any German Government, those German officers and men and members of the Nazi party who have had any connection with atrocities and executions in countries overrun by German forces will be taken back to the countries in which their abominable crimes were committed to be charged and punished according to the laws of those countries.

In an atmosphere of mutual confidence and understanding which characterized all the work of the conference, consideration was also given to other important questions. These included not only questions of a current nature but also questions concerning treatment of Hitlerite Germany and its satellites, economic co-operation and assurances of general peace.

Joint Four-Nation Declaration

The Governments of the United States of America, the United Kingdom, the Soviet Union and China:

United in their determination, in accordance with the declaration by the United Nations of January 1, 1942, and subsequent declarations, to continue hostilities against those Axis powers with which they respectively are at war until such powers have laid down their arms on the basis of unconditional surrender;

Conscious of their responsibility to secure the liberation of themselves and the peoples allied with them from the menace of aggression;

Recognizing the necessity of ensuring a rapid and orderly transition from war to peace and of establishing and maintaining international peace and security with the least diversion of the world's human and economic resources for armaments;

Jointly declare:

1—That their united action, pledged for the prosecution of the war against their respective enemies, will be continued for the organization and maintenance of peace and security.

2—That those of them at war with a common enemy will act together in all matters relating to the surrender and disarmament of that enemy.

3—That they will take all measures deemed by them to be necessary to provide against any violation of the terms imposed upon the enemy.

4—That they recognize the necessity of establishing at the earliest practicable date a general international organization, based on the principle of the sovereign equality of all peace-loving States, and open to membership by all such States, large and small, for the maintenance of international peace and security.

5—That for the purpose of maintaining international peace and security pending the re-establishment of law and order and the inauguration of a system of general security, they will consult with one another and as occasion requires with other members of the United Nations with a view to joint action on behalf of the community of nations.

6—That after the termination of hostilities they will not employ their military forces within the territories of other States except for the purposes envisaged in this declaration and after joint consultation.

7—That they will confer and co-operate with one another and with other members of the United Nations to bring about a practicable general agreement with respect to the regulation of armaments in the post-war period.

Declaration Regarding Italy

The Foreign Secretaries of the United States, the United Kingdom and the Soviet Union have established that their three Governments are in complete agreement that Allied policy toward Italy must be based upon the fundamental principle that Fascism and all its evil influence and configuration shall be completely destroyed and that the Italian people shall be given every opportunity to establish governmental and other institutions based upon democratic principles.

The Foreign Secretaries of the United States and United Kingdom declare that the action of their Governments from inception of the invasion of Italian territory, in so far as paramount military requirements have permitted, has been based upon this policy.

In furtherance of this policy in the future the Foreign Secretaries of the three Governments are agreed that the following measures are important and should be put into effect:

1—It is essential that the Italian Government should be made more democratic by inclusion of representatives of those sections of the Italian people who have always opposed Fascism.

2—Freedom of speech, of religious worship, of political belief, of press and of public meeting shall be restored in full measure to the Italian people, who shall also be entitled to form anti-Fascist political groups.

3—All institutions and organizations created by the Fascist regime shall be suppressed.

4—All Fascist or pro-Fascist elements shall be removed from the administration and from institutions and organizations of a public character.

5—All political prisoners of the Fascist regime shall be released and accorded full amnesty.

6—Democratic organs of local government shall be created.

7—Fascist chiefs and army generals known or suspected to be war criminals shall be arrested and handed over to justice.

In making this declaration the three Foreign Secretaries recognize that so long as active military operations continue in Italy the time at which it is possible to give full effect to the principles stated above will be determined by the Commander-in-Chief on the basis of instructions received through the combined Chiefs of Staff.

The three Governments, parties to this declaration, will, at the request of any one of them, consult on this matter. It is further understood that nothing in this resolution is to operate against the right of the Italian people ultimately to choose their own form of government.

Declaration Regarding Austria

The Governments of the United Kingdom, the Soviet Union and the United States of America are agreed that Austria, the first free country to fall a victim to Hitlerite aggression, shall be liberated from German domination.

They regard the annexation imposed on Austria by Germany on March 15, 1938, as null and void. They consider themselves as in no way bound by any changes effected in Austria since that date. They declare that they wish to see re-established a free and independent Austria and thereby to open the way for the Austrian people themselves, as well as those neighboring States which will be faced with similar problems, to find that political and economic security which is the only basis for lasting peace.

Austria is reminded, however, that she has a responsibility, which she cannot evade, for participation in the war at the side of Hitlerite Germany, and that in the final settlement account will inevitably be taken of her own contribution to her liberation.

Statement on Atrocities

Signed by President Roosevelt, Prime Minister Churchill and Premier Stalin.

The United Kingdom, the United States and the Soviet Union have received from many quarters evidence of atrocities, massacres and cold-blooded mass executions which are being perpetrated by Hitlerite forces in many of the countries they have overrun and from which they are now being steadily expelled. The brutalities of Nazi domination are no new thing, and all peoples or territories in their grip have suffered from the worst form of government by terror. What is new is that many of these territories are now being redeemed by the advancing armies of the liberating powers and that in their desperation the recoiling Hitlerites and Huns are redoubling their ruthless cruelties. This is now evidenced with particular clearness by monstrous crimes on the territory of the Soviet Union which is being liberated from Hitlerites and on French and Italian territory.

Accordingly, the aforesaid three Allied powers, speaking in the interests of the thirty-two United Nations, hereby solemnly declare and give full warning of their declaration as follows:

At the time of granting of any armistice to any government which may be set up in Germany, those German officers and men and members of the Nazi party who have been responsible for or have taken a consenting part in the above atrocities, massacres and executions will be sent back to the countries in which their abominable deeds were done in order that they may be judged and punished according to the laws of these liberated countries and of the free governments which will be erected therein. Lists will be compiled in all possible detail from all these countries, having regard especially to invaded parts of the Soviet Union, to Poland and Czechoslovakia, to Yugoslavia and Greece, including Crete and other islands; to Norway, Denmark, the Netherlands, Belgium, Luxembourg, France and Italy.

Thus, Germans who take part in wholesale shooting of Polish officers or in the execution of French, Dutch, Belgian or Norwegian hostages or of Cretan peasants, or who have shared in slaughters inflicted on the people of Poland or in territories of the Soviet Union which are now being swept clear of the enemy, will know that they will be brought back to the scene of their crimes and judged on the spot by the peoples whom they have outraged. Let those who have hitherto not imbued their hands with innocent blood beware lest they join the ranks of the guilty, for most assuredly the three Allied powers will pursue them to the uttermost ends of the earth and will deliver them to their accusers in order that justice may be done.

The above declaration is without prejudice to the case of German criminals whose offenses have no particular geographical localization and who will be punished by joint decision of the governments of the Allies.

Index

INDEX

INDEX

INDEX

INDEX